+LDVIVR99

L'ART DE VIVRE

DECORATIVE ARTS AND DESIGN IN FRANCE

1789-1989

L'ART DE VIVRE

DECORATIVE ARTS AND DESIGN IN FRANCE

1789-1989

Catherine Arminjon
Yvonne Brunhammer
Madeleine Deschamps
France Grand
Raymond Guidot
François Mathey
David R. McFadden
Evelyne Possémé
Suzanne Tise

THE VENDOME PRESS
COOPER-HEWITT MUSEUM
THE SMITHSONIAN INSTITUTION'S NATIONAL MUSEUM OF DESIGN

Cover:
Wallpaper border, 1800-15
Xavier Mader, designer
Joseph Dufour, manufacturer
Block-printed paper (12 colors)
Bibliothèque Forney, Paris

Frontispiece:
"The Tennis Players," wallpaper, 1925
Lina de Andrada, designer
Paul Dumas, manufacturer
Printed paper (13 colors)
Bibliothèque Forney, Paris

Published by The Vendome Press
515 Madison Avenue
New York City 10022

Distributed in the United States and Canada
by Rizzoli International Publications
597 Fifth Avenue,
New York City 10022

Cooper-Hewitt Museum
2 East 91st Street
New York City 10128

Editor Nancy Aakre
Editorial Assistant Cynthia Plaut
Translators
Randall Cherry — "Forty Years of French Design"
M.E.D. Laing — "The Art of Dining"
Maxwell R.D. Vos — The Preface, "National, International, and Universal Expositions and the French Decorative Arts,"
"French Taste in Fashion: Myth and Reality," and "Bijouterie and Joaillerie"

Arbook International, Paris
Art Director Marc Walter
Designer Thomas Gravemaker

Photoengraving by Arbook International

Typesetting by Eurocompo, Paris

Printing by Artes Graficas, Toledo, Spain D. L. TO: 367 -1989

Library of Congress Cataloging-in-Publication Data

L'Art de vivre: decorative arts and design in France, 1789-1989 / David Revere McFadden... [et al.].
p. cm.
Bibliography: p.
ISBN 0-86565-976-1
1. Decorative arts-France-Themes, motives. 2. Design-France-Themes, motives. I. McFadden, David Revere. II. Cooper-Hewitt Museum.
NK947.A7128 1989
745.4'4944 — dc 19   88-63278 CIP

Unless otherwise indicated in a caption, manufacturers are located in Paris.

CONTENTS

FOREWORD

Cooper-Hewitt Museum, the Smithsonian Institution's National Museum of Design, is proud to participate in the international celebrations surrounding the bicentennial of the French Revolution through the presentation of *L'Art de Vivre: Decorative Arts and Design in France 1789-1989*.

For nearly one hundred years, our Museum has been devoted solely to decorative arts and design, serving professional designers, architects, historians, and educators, as well as a large and diverse general public. Our debt to France in the formation of our own collections is twofold: not surprisingly, an impressive number of our finest textiles, ceramics, drawings, prints, wallpapers, and other decorative arts are French in origin, indicating the reputation of quality that is a part of our perception of French design and decorative arts. Secondly, and of special importance for Cooper-Hewitt, is the fact that our founders—the Hewitt sisters—were inspired by the Musée des Arts Décoratifs in Paris and built their collections, the beginnings of what are now the national collections of decorative arts and design, along similar lines and according to a similar philosophy. It was their intention to create a tangible "library" of inspiration and ideas for designers and to facilitate links between individual artists and industry.

L'Art de Vivre: Decorative Arts and Design in France 1789-1989 surveys two hundred years of French design, highlighting important one-of-a-kind objects and also a wide range of manufactured pieces, produced and promoted by a growing number of industries that emerged in France after the Revolution of 1789.

The impact of French design traditions during the past two hundred years has been considerable, as even a passing glance reveals. The complex interrelationships that comprise the social, cultural, and economic context of nineteenth-century decorative arts, for example, are only now beginning to be fully understood and appreciated, and the same is certainly true for our own century. Americans may be familiar with styles popularly referred to as Art Nouveau and Art Deco, both of which have generated attention in exhibitions and the marketplace. Few of us, however, have had the opportunity to examine these styles within a broader context and to appreciate the stylistic affinities and continuities that exist between different periods in French design history. This opportunity is provided by *L'Art de Vivre*, one of the most ambitious surveys of French decorative arts ever organized in the United States.

In fact, there is a single theme that weaves throughout the entire span of this exhibition, as well as throughout this book which it inspired. It is the continuity provided by French tradition and its complex relationship with the spirit of innovation and change. Like language, French design has been inspired by a perennial dialogue between the past and the present; the grammar of French design revealed in this exhibition and publication also serves to indicate trends that may be realized in the future.

An ambitious project like *L'Art de Vivre* would not have been possible without the dedication and determination of many contributors to the exhibition and publication. Special thanks are extended to colleagues at the Musée des Arts Décoratifs in Paris, without whose expertise and cooperation the project could not have been successfully completed. Yvonne Brunhammer, Conservateur en chef, deserves special praise for her unflagging enthusiasm and generosity; we also wish to thank conservateurs Marie-Noël de Gary, Nadine Gasc, Marie-Noëlle de Grandry, Daniel Marchesseau, Odile Nouvel, Jean-Luc Olivie, and Evelyne Possémé for their roles in the project. Colleagues at other institutions, museums, and collections in France and the United States are too numerous to mention individually, but we wish to express our profound gratitude for their help as well.

The project was facilitated in untold ways by an international advisory committee, created in the early stages, consisting of Madame Michel David-Weill; Gérard Gaveau; Olivier Le Fuel; Robert Bordaz, Président of the Union des Arts Décoratifs; Jean Coural, Directeur of the Mobilier National; and Antoinette Hallé, conservateur of the Musée National de Céramique.

To Mr. Joe M. Rodgers, United States Ambassador to France, and to the Honorable Emmanuel de Margerie, French Ambassador to the United States, as well as to embassy staffs in Paris, Washington, and New York, we offer sincere thanks for their continued interest, support, and encouragement.

Many colleagues at the Smithsonian Institution have contributed to the success of this bicentennial project. Among those deserving special acknowledgment is Sir Valentine Abdy, European Representative of the Smithsonian Institution, who has been a source of advice and assistance in the many negotiations surrounding this project. We also wish to thank Alexis Gregory of Vendome Press for the production of this handsome volume.

It would have been impossible for the Cooper-Hewitt Museum to be a participant in the international celebrations of the French bicentennial without the financial support so generously offered to us by the Comité Colbert. *L'Art de Vivre: Decorative Arts and Design in France 1789-1989* has become a reality owing to the dedicated efforts of the Comité Colbert; throughout the many months of preparation, the individuals who comprise the Comité have gone out of their way to assure the success of the project. The Cooper-Hewitt Museum shares with the Comité Colbert our pride in the final product, and we offer them a special salute on this important anniversary. To Jean-Louis Dumas-Hermès, Président, to Remi Krug, Chairman of the Cultural Committee, to Hervé Aaron, the Comité's representative in the United States, and especially to Christian Blanckaert, Président Délégué, a profound and sincere thank you.

I wish especially to acknowledge the support and participation of Air France. From the period of initial research to the transportation of precious works to and from New York, Air France has remained a generous friend of this Museum. We also acknowledge additional contributions from V.I.A., from André Chenue & Fils SA for the transport of works, and from Gras Savoye SA for insurance assistance.

This mammoth undertaking has been developed, nurtured, and presented with intelligence and visual acumen by David R. McFadden, Curator of Decorative Arts at Cooper-Hewitt Museum. Without his tireless energy, and that of his staff, this glorious exhibition and publication would not have been possible. My thanks to him for his perceptive eye and dedication.

Just over a decade ago, the United States celebrated its own bicentennial as a republic. How appropriate it is to lend our voice to the celebrations in 1989 surrounding France's own birthday. It is hoped that *L'Art de Vivre: Decorative Arts and Design in France 1789-1989* will foster understanding and appreciation of French decorative arts and design in America and will underline the close cultural friendship that has existed between our countries over the past two hundred years. The quality of our lives is determined and affected each day by design; it is hoped that this exploration of the "art of living" in France will remind us of the significance and meaning of the decorative arts—past, present, and future.

Dianne H. Pilgrim
Director

ACKNOWLEDGMENTS

Accomplishing a project as ambitious in scope as *L'Art de Vivre: Decorative Arts and Design in France 1789-1989* required the goodwill and hard work of an impressive cast of colleagues, experts, officials, and friends.

The Comité Colbert deserves special thanks for being model sponsors—providing the wherewithal to accomplish the project, along with a daily infusion of enthusiasm and bonhomie that made the work a pleasure. To Président Jean-Louis Dumas-Hermès our profound gratitude, and likewise to Christian Blanckaert, Président Délégué, who believed that this project was a worthwhile and important endeavor for the Comité Colbert to undertake. Mr. Blanckaert, who possesses a keen and perceptive mind and eye, tempered with wisdom and good humor, responded with admirable efficiency and kindness to a barrage of comments, questions, and requests.

At the Comité Colbert, we were assisted by a memorable constellation of professionals who proved that competence and graciousness are happy partners: Valérie Hermann-Le Pors and Constance de Margerie deserve special thanks, but my gratitude is extended to every member of the staff.

A very special thank you is in order for Catherine Vial, who served as liaison between New York and Paris. Catherine has represented the project and Cooper-Hewitt Museum in Paris with consummate skill and diplomacy.

A very special acknowledgment must be given to individuals who have played key roles in the organization of this exhibition and preparation of this catalogue. They include Jean-Claude Baumgarten of Air France, whose generous help and cooperation was vital to the success of this project; Mr. Patrick Talbot, Cultural Counsellor to the French Embassy, New York; Hervé Aaron, who has been an unfailing source of support and a warm and loyal friend of Cooper-Hewitt Museum; and Jacques Scandelari of Synergetic Communications for his work on the video aspects of the project.

We also wish to acknowledge the important role of V.I.A. (Valorisation de l'Innovation dans l'Ameublement), created in 1979 with the aim of enhancing the public image of French furniture design throughout the world. V.I.A.'s commitment to international design was made manifest in this exhibition by providing a substantial number of V.I.A.-sponsored pieces, many of which are now a proud part of the permanent design collections at Cooper-Hewitt. Jean-Claude Maugirard and Aline Fouquet of V.I.A. deserve thanks from our entire museum.

I also thank my colleagues at the Musée des Arts Décoratifs in Paris: Jean-Luc Olivie, Evelyne Possémé, Véronique de Bruignac, Odile Nouvel, Nadine Gasc, Marie-Noël de Gary, Marie-Noëlle de Grandry, Daniel Marchesseau, Gérard Mabille, and also Sonia Edard of the Photographic Service. A most heartfelt and sincere thank you is reserved, however, for Yvonne Brunhammer, who served as Primary Consultant to this project. Her exceptional intelligence and knowledge of French decorative arts and design are admired by her many friends and colleagues, and I salute her fondly through this publication.

It has taken many years of discussion to bring about this project, and many individuals have played exceptionally significant roles in the history of the project. It is only fitting to thank Jean Bergeron, former Président Délégué of the Comité Colbert, under whose administration the groundwork was established to permit this exceptional international event to take place. We are also grateful to our Smithsonian colleague, Sir Valentine Abdy, who, since the very beginning, has served as guide and advisor in Paris. He has given much time and effort to *L'Art de Vivre*, and any success that we enjoy is shared willingly with him.

Other individuals from both France and the United States whose assistance has been deeply appreciated include: Sheila Machlis Alexander, Garance Aufaure, Clotilde Bacri, Emmeline Bauer, Philippe Bessis, Chantal Bizot, Robert Bizot, Reggie Blaszcyk, Edith Boislandon, Michel Bour, Katell le Bourhis, Frederick R. Brandt, Mme M. Braun, Yves Brayer, Claude Bromet, Mel Byars, François Canavy, Jean-Louis Capitaine, Gisèle Chalaye, Jacqueline Chambord, Carla Chammas, Dominique Clemenceau, Andrew Connors, Alexis Contant, Chantal Gastinel-Coural, Rachel Crespin, Ralph Culpepper, François Curiel, Emile Decker, Elaine Evans Dee, Anne de Fayet, Henri Delbard, Madeleine Deschamps, Jean Drusedow, Alastair Duncan, Agnès Duplessis, Anne Fabien, Suzanne Frantz, Olivier Gaube de Gers, Hamlin M. Gilbert, Jr., Thomas Gravemaker, Marie-Catherine Grichois, Debra Healy, Paul Hollister, Colta Ives, Phillip M. Johnston, David W. Kiehl, Harold Koda, Angus Lajeunesse, Dwight P. Lanmon, Clare Le Corbeiller, Anne Lech, Anne-Claude Lelieur, Paul Lerner, Phyllis Magidson, Françoise Maison, Ketty Maisonrouge, Nancy McClelland, Matilda McQuaid, Yolaine Medelice, Guy Sarrauste de Menthière, Chantal Meslin-Perrier, R. Craig Miller, Christopher Monkhouse, Bernard de Montgolfier, Jacques Mouclier, Florence Müller, Jeffrey Munger, Véronique Nansenet, Sylvie Nissen, Jo Anne Olian, James Parker, Jacqueline du Pasquier, Claudine Pinelli, Béatrice de Plinval, Anne L. Poulet, Tamara Préaud, Priscilla Price, Penny Proddow, Dr. Olga Raggio, Margot Raissac, Philippe Renaud, Roxane de Saule, Rex W. Scouten, Carlene Stephens, Suzanne Tise, Ann Van Devanter Townsend, Jean Vallier, Anthony Victoria, Roberta Waddell, Marc Walter, Deborah Dependahl Waters, James C. Welch, John Sampson White, Stephanie Wilsker, Gillian Wilson, Barbara Woytowicz, and Ghenete Zelleke.

Members of the Comité Colbert were among the most generous and cooperative of lenders to the exhibition and they, along with others in France and the United States, made this exhibition a reality. We thank each listed below. To any inadvertently overlooked, or associated with this project after this volume was at press, our apologies along with our thanks.

FRANCE

ABC (Atelier de Bijoux Contemporains), Academy, Air France, Algorithme, Aluminor Luminaires, Bibliothèque Forney, Paris, Christian Blanckaert, CMB, Cartier, Centre de Recherches sur les Monuments Historiques, Ministère de la Culture et de la Communication, Clen/Manade, Le Creuset, Denize Arcens Associés, Gilles Derain, Christian Duc, Rena Dumas, Geneviève Dupeux, En Attendant les Barbares, Enfi Design, Fenêtre sur Cour, Fermob, Fond National d'Art Contemporain, Galerie Adrien Maeght, Paris, Caroline Imbert, Roger Imbert, Jean Couzon, Claude Lalanne, Didier La Mache, Olivier Le Fuel, Lumen Center, Manufacture Nationale de Sèvres Archives, Migeon et Migeon, Mobilier National, Moulinex, Musée d'Art Moderne de la Ville de Paris, Musée de la Mode et du Costume, Falais Galliera, Paris, Musée des Arts Décoratifs, Bordeaux, Musée des Arts Décoratifs, Paris, Musée Carnavalet, Paris, Musée Marmottan, Paris, Musée National de Céramique, Sèvres, Musée National Adrien-Dubouché, Limoges, Musée National du Château de Pau, Musée National des Techniques du Conservatoire National des Arts et Métiers, Paris, Musée Picasso, Paris, Musée de la Publicité, Paris, Musée de Sarreguemines, Nemo Studio, Néotù, Odiot, Private Collection, Quartz Diffusion, Paris, Roset, Valentine Schlegel, Société Nouvelle de Chaumet, Philippe Starck, Tebong, Didier Tritz, Union Française des Arts du Costume, Musée des Arts de la Mode, Paris, V.I.A. (Valorisation de l'Innovation dans l'Ameublement), Vitrac Design, Jean-Michel Wilmotte, Zuber & Cie, Rixheim.

UNITED STATES

Barry Friedman Ltd., New York, The Carnegie Museum of Art, Pittsburgh, Cooper-Hewitt Museum, The Smithsonian Institution's National Museum of Design, The Corning Museum of Glass, Corning, New York, Dalva Brothers, Inc., New York, Fashion Institute of Technology, New York, Foreign Intrigue, New York, French Institute/Alliance Française, New York, Audrey Friedman and Haim Manishevitz, The J. Paul Getty Museum, Malibu, California, J.G. Furniture Systems, Jacques Jugeat, Ltd., Christie and Edwin Lefkowith, Miles and Lyn Lourie, Marisa del Re Gallery, Inc., New York, The Metropolitan Museum of Art, New York, Museum of Art, Rhode Island School of Design, Providence, Museum of the City of New York, Museum of Fine Arts, Boston, The Museum of Modern Art, New York, National Museum of American Art, Smithsonian Institution, National Museum of American History, Smithsonian Institution, National Museum of Natural History, Smithsonian Institution, The New York Historical Society, The New York Public Library, Philadelphia Museum of Art, Primavera Gallery, New York, Private Collection, Mr. and Mrs. Stewart Resnick, Lisa Taylor, The Time Museum, Rockford, Illinois, Glenn and Mary Lou Utt Collection, Vecta, Virginia Museum of Fine Arts, Richmond, The Walters Art Gallery, Baltimore, The White House, Washington, D.C.

At Cooper-Hewitt Museum, staff members in every department have responded to the heavy responsibilities of this project with unfailing enthusiasm; even when unnamed individually, the debt of gratitude owed them is happily acknowledged. Our Director, Dianne H. Pilgrim, has been a source of strength to me during an unusually demanding time. Her vision of the Cooper-Hewitt's role as an international laboratory of design research and documentation has underlined the timeliness of this project. Special thanks are due Cordelia Rose, Steven Langehough, and Lisa Roth of the Registrar's office for undertaking the complicated negotiations to bring this exhibition safely to and from Cooper-Hewitt Museum, and to perform this miracle with such grace and patience. Dorothy Globus, Curator of Exhibitions, and Todd Zwigard, guest architect, are to be saluted for accomplishing their own special miracles in our galleries. Nancy Aakre, Editor, and Cynthia Plaut have seen this publication from outline to finished product with consummate skill; the final appearance of this volume is due to their loving care at all stages.

The Department of Decorative Arts could not have succeeded in the project without the able and generous assistance of a very special group of volunteers, interns, and others who worked long hours under less than ideal conditions. A special thank you to Rosemary Corroon, Julia Haiblen, Barbara Hatcher, Nadine Keller, Ingrid Kummer, Charmine Kwo Chen, Camille Landau, Ann Leibowitz, Doris Schnelling, Betty Ann Schoenfeld, Solveig Wilmering, and, in particular, Louise Mitchell for her work on fashion.

Departmental staff members Piera Watkins and Andrew J.N. Gary deserve special acknowledgment for their contributions. By far the two most significant staff members in this entire project were Deborah Sampson Shinn and Lucy A. Fellowes. Their intelligence and expertise, as well as their impressive resources of energy, have been essential to L'Art de Vivre. Their vision of the exhibition and publication, along with their knowledge of the field of French decorative arts and cultural history, have guided and inspired us all, and they deserve the profound respect I have for them.

I wish to end these acknowledgments on a more personal note. L'Art de Vivre: Decorative Arts and Design in France 1789-1989 would not have existed as an idea without the brilliant inspiration of someone who has loved France and French decorative arts in a special and personal way. From the initial stages of the discussions that eventually culminated in this exhibition and publication, her spirit, intelligence, and warmth have continued to guide and inspire us. The art of living has meant something very special to us because of Lisa Taylor, and it is to her that this book is warmly dedicated.

David McFadden
Curator of Decorative Arts

COMITÉ COLBERT MEMBERS

Baccarat
Bernardaud
Champagne Bollinger
Boucheron
Breguet
Bussière Arts Graphiques
Caron
Chanel
Parfums Chanel
Charles
Château Cheval Blanc
Château Lafite-Rothschild
Château d'Yquem
Christian Dior
Parfums Christian Dior
Christofle
Coquet
Courvoisier
D. Porthault
Daum
Delisle
Didier Aaron
Orfèvrerie d'Ercuis
Faïenceries de Gien
Givenchy
Parfums Givenchy

Guerlain
Guy Laroche Couture
Hédiard
Hermès
Parfums Hermès
Hôtel de Crillon
Hôtel George V
Hôtel Le Bristol
Hôtel Plaza Athénée
Hôtel Royal Evian
Jean Patou
Parfums Jean Patou
Jeanne Lanvin
Champagne Krug
La Chemise Lacoste
Lalique
Parfums Lanvin
Champagne Laurent-Perrier
Lenôtre
Léonard
Champagne Louis Roederer
Louis Vuitton
Manuel Canovas
Mauboussin
Mellerio dits Meller
Restaurant Hôtellerie Michel Guérard

Nina Ricci
Parfums Nina Ricci
Oustau de Baumanière
Pierre Balmain
Pierre Frey
Puiforcat
Rémy Martin
Revillon
Parfums Revillon
Robert Haviland & C. Parlon
Rochas
Champagne Ruinart
Cristalleries de Saint-Louis
Souleïado
S.T. Dupont
Van Cleef & Arpels
Champagne Veuve Clicquot Ponsardin

ASSOCIATE MEMBERS

Manufacture Nationale de Sèvres
La Monnaie de Paris
Orchestre National de France/Ademma
Théâtre National de l'Opéra de Paris

RENDEZVOUS WITH QUALITY

The only thing that I find more inspiring than France's immensely rich artistic past is the vast potential of her future. This superb exhibition of some of the finest works of applied art to come out of France since 1789 gives us a unique glimpse of both, past and future. It gives us a chance to hone our tastes, to see where they've come from and where they're going. Representing the Revolutionary, Empire, and Restoration periods through Art Nouveau, Art Deco, and more recent styles, these decorative arts remind us of the care and genius with which artists of other eras have given form to their dreams. And each dream explored to the fullest inevitably points to a new challenge: that of keeping tradition alive and forward-looking.

The Comité Colbert was created in 1954 to perpetuate that tradition and to meet that challenge—of dreaming, of innovating, of persisting in the pursuit of quality. Its seventy members—world-renowned French artisans, jewelers and fashion designers, decorators and perfumers, hoteliers and vintners—are proud to sponsor an exhibition that illustrates so perfectly the philosophy of combining "strategy and creativity" first promoted by its seventeenth-century namesake, Jean-Baptiste Colbert.

Our passion is quality. Fortunately, we have been able to build a prospering industry around that commitment. We thank our many American friends for sharing our passion and supporting our industry.

My dream? That French quality will be the stuff of dreams for another two hundred years.

Jean-Louis Dumas-Hermès
Président
Comité Colbert

A STEP FORWARD FOR OUR FUTURE IN AMERICA

With *L'Art de Vivre: Decorative Arts and Design in France 1789-1989*, for the first time the Comité Colbert has proudly assumed the role of a true *mécène*, helping to give birth to a purely cultural event—a major retrospective of two hundred years of the French *art de vivre*.

To expedite the project, the Comité Colbert formed a team with Dianne Pilgrim, Director of the Cooper-Hewitt Museum, and David McFadden, Curator of Decorative Arts. Mr. McFadden's immense talent and impressive knowledge of French decorative arts and history were supported by the Museum's scrupulous organization and by its constant communication with us.

The Comité Colbert in no way influenced or interfered with Mr. McFadden's work. We gave him our constant support and assisted him in reaching every private collection and museum in France, and in approaching any member of the Comité. In no way did we seek to influence the Cooper-Hewitt, believing that the best way to talk to America, is to let America talk about France. Consequently, we are certain that the results of this exhibition will be far-reaching and valuable.

All those involved in the planning of the exhibition and this book worked with great confidence, exchanging strong and useful opinions. Among those who played key roles in New York and Paris were: Hervé Aaron, United States Representative of the Comité Colbert, Ketty Maisonrouge, our United States Coordinator, Harriet Weintraub in Press Relations, Jean-Claude Baumgarten, General Manager of Air France USA, and Alexis Gregory, publisher of The Vendome Press, along with Rémi Krug, President of our Cultural Commission, Valérie Hermann-Le Pors, Project Director at the Comité Colbert, Sir Valentine Abdy, European Representative for the Smithsonian Institution, and Anne de Fayet in Press Relations. In the United States and in Paris, the Comité Colbert presidents initiated and followed the project with constant interest and personal involvement. We were fortunate to have had the chance to form a unique group of diverse and complementary men and women determined to make this exhibition, and all that surrounds it, a great success and a true contribution to the French *art de vivre* and to the industry of French luxury goods represented by the Comité Colbert.

For all of us, the experience of working on this project has been unique, rich, and personally rewarding. The seventy members of the Comité Colbert firmly believe that the Cooper-Hewitt exhibition and this book are a major contribution to the appreciation of France's *art de vivre*, and a step forward for our future in America.

Christian Blanckaert
Président Délégué
Comité Colbert

FRANÇOIS MATHEY

PREFACE

The Art of Living—it is indeed a splendid title, succinct and significant. But real life must be lived, and even survived; only then can we afford to speak of art, if there is such a thing. We can cite the art of makeup, the art of conjuring cards, the arts of writing, dancing, bowing, art on foot, on horseback, at table. With the passage of time, we are tempted to reconstruct from those documents, furnishings, household objects, and paintings that have come down through the years a way of life in which everything was rare and exquisite, admirably harmonious and impeccably executed, affectionately intended, justly conceived, nobly proportioned, and finely detailed. It is a nostalgic view of the past, as though we could never again aspire to a world so steeped in art. Yet we are at the same time ready to believe that beauty continues through the ages to be the moving cause of design, and in this belief we find cause for inward rejoicing. The Frenchman of today sees himself as heir-apparent to his forebears, who flourished when France was the greatest power in Europe and shone brightly among the nations.

The only problem is: which forebears are we talking about? What society are we looking at? What are the criteria and the methods whereby, without doing violence to the truth, we can conjure up an "Art of Living" from such disparate fragments? To be sure, we have learned to focus only on the finest that has come down to us. Since the French Revolution confirmed us in our title to the inheritance of the nation, we see ourselves as beholden for our patrimony to Hugues Capet, Henri IV, Louis XV, and even his mistresses and lights-of-love, rather more often than to Voltaire and Rousseau, and much more often than to the working people of town and country. These last have bequeathed to us nothing more material than an inexhaustible fund of patience, good sense, and the manual skills that Nature teaches those who converse with her every day. When heed must unremittingly be paid to times and seasons, when everything must be duly foreseen, weighed, negotiated with the master, moderation becomes the immemorial birthright of the countryman who must weather the passing years; the French national character derives from the historic predominance of the farmer in France. Now that we no longer till the soil, can that character be preserved?

In any case, fighting their way out of, almost endemic poverty, the common people began to prosper after the Revolution; since the lessening of material constraints tends also to relax those on the mind, they soon learned so to apply their new freedom in the pursuit of advancement that it became almost an art form itself. We, then, are the posterity of the landed gentry, of the *noblesse de robe*, perhaps even of the clergy—but also of the Third Estate, that composite of townspeople, manual workers, and peasants that came into being when the Revolution overthrew the old order. But the objects that have been handed down through all the hazards of war, fire, and waste as mute witnesses of everyday life have come to rest in museums, where they reflect only a limited part of this broadly inclusive heredity.

The truth can be approached only through the disciplines of anthropology; we must rummage through the trash cans of history, unriddle inventories, chronicles, and marriage contracts. This is not how museums work; they make arbitrary selections according to criteria that at any given moment (for in museology, too, there are trends) best seem to illustrate their high notion of our forebears. Their choice of objects deemed typical of the most refined and cultured circles of the period illustrates what we have come to call "taste"—that is, the taste of the ruling or possessing class. Before the Revolution this class lived and worked in Paris, where the power was; it comprised no more than a few hundred people, revolving in a rigid hierarchy around the sovereign—great officers of state, lawyers, and financiers. At the time the population of France was 26 million, 23 million of them country folk who had only the vaguest idea of what was going on in Paris. Paris set the tone for everything—art, fashion, literature, and politics—and the ripples spread through the provinces. Paris was the meeting place for the best minds and the largest numbers. The capital acted as a stimulant on the body politic; its imagination caught fire; its curiosity anticipated and even outstripped the bounds of reason. Our present-day ideas of art are so intimately linked to tradition and education that they cannot be framed independently of them, or of the background they take for granted. Moreover, we are not speaking solely of art; the very idea of beauty is, so to speak, common to an entire culture, particularly in those pre-Revolutionary times, when working people and the middle classes took their cue from the great. Only when economic classes begin to draw apart can they formulate a taste peculiar to themselves.

True, fashions changed before the Revolution, but the slow wisdom of succeeding generations would accept only those trends enthroned by the Academy, rather than the seasonal fluctuations of our own time. Taste, defined as the sense of pleasure engendered by a work of art, evolved, but retained certain standards of reference in its concern for proportion, decoration, and balance, whether in architecture, furniture, or any other area of design. Taste may have been determined by the royal mistresses, but it was accepted by everybody. There was a stylistic development from a reasoned baroque to the most rational classicism, but in a curious way such diversity was the outgrowth of an underlying unity, embodying a constant hierarchy of values. The community of craftsmen was intelligent enough (not to say truculent enough) to present the designs demanded of it, without calling this underlying unity in question. The break would come with the suppression of the guilds under the Revolution, but as early as 1762 the Academy established an unhapppy distinction between "artists" and "craftsmen." Nevertheless, Academy and guilds could enact what rules, aesthetic or ethical, they chose; the artist capable of choosing freedom in the name of art was never constrained by them. Clearly, creative talent is exceptional, and those possessed of it will always be few. Famous painters or cabinetmakers may differ widely, indeed diametrically, in temperament, origin, or style; we do not confuse them one with another, yet all are intimately linked to the time and place in which they worked. Time smooths out individual differences, imposing a common denominator of contemporaneity. It is easy to forget that in the mid-eighteenth century there were almost 3,500 craftsmen (nowadays we would call them artists) living in Paris. A few of their names—not more than a score at most—figure repeatedly on museum labels, as though their owners had appropriated to themselves the entire favor of posterity. Yet, except in a few crafts, they are very much alike: they all have skill, which is imparted by an apprenticeship; they are all thorough masters of their trades. The trades may tend to flatten out individuality, but they do impose a uniform level of taste. Art histories and museums abound in "School of" and "Attributed to," which differ only in the minutest particulars from the authenticated productions of the master referred to, yet it is in the admirable work of all these anonymous craftsmen that the taste of a society is disclosed. True, this particular agreeable society lived in happy ignorance of impending doom; but when it became conscious of its dreadful destiny, it took pride in perishing amid its art. It was a time of terrible testing, in which the old order gave triumphant proof that it did, indeed, understand the art of living.

One social class disappeared, to be replaced by another with the same outfit of illusions, of accumulated good intentions and ill-founded convictions. Where once the gavotte was danced, there rang out the raucous strains of the revolutionary song. Now art was to inform every aspect of life. David was at the height of his powers; the splendor of classical antiquity would be reaffirmed. However, while the Declaration of the Rights of Man could proclaim liberty, its promulgation of equality among men was an illusion. The guilds were suppressed, but the worker was not thereby emancipated; he remained at the mercy of his employer, while the arcana of craftsmanship were forgotten. Unions were not legalized until 1884, and even then they were concerned to ensure the individual freedom of the worker, not the quality of his output. In evoking certain latent aspects of national unity, the Revolution threatened that wonderful harmony of taste and inspiration, emanating from Paris, that had set the tone for all Europe. Art could have foundered in mere technical facility, but the memory of a great tradition prevailed. Fine craftsmanship is a duality: it requires an executant, but also a source of inspiration and control, sometimes an artist, and always a customer. The latter need not be a great lord; power had changed hands. In the wake of revolutions and wars there were new fortunes, but Fortune is not wholly capricious—she singles out only those who can grasp and retain her.

The new wealthy had the prudence of bankers—they were not so foolish as to squander the inheritance on which they had laid their hands. The national wealth consisted not only in great estates, but in furniture and works of art that now adorned the life of the new middle class and bore witness to its triumph. Society was protected by a new code of civil law. The safety of property was assured, and within a generation the new possessors had deftly insinuated themselves into the old tradition, and were now its defenders. Alas, the orchestra had no great conductor. Neither David nor Percier nor Fontaine survived the Empire. The Jacob family quickly grasped that art was no longer the preserve of a small privileged class, and that many a bottom yearned to plant itself in a mahogany armchair. There was eager demand from all levels of society. Small manufacturers —of glass, furniture, fabrics, and ceramics—sprang up everywhere. Advances in technology replaced the handmade, one-of-a-kind article with small runs of machine-made products, and with the growth of industrial corporations; these, in turn, gave way to true mass production.

It was a buyer's market; what art lost in elegance and originality it gained in mass-produced sentimentality. Art no longer boasted canons, except for those of the Salon, catering to a few lonely believers in the errant values of the Academy; the sole criterion was to please. While art thus prettified itself decoration abounded. Everybody, everywhere, had tasseled curtain pelmets, squat, overstuffed armchairs, birds on the mantelpiece, and pictures eclipsed by their frames. France grew rich, kitsch was king, Madame Bovary was bored, and Nana had a good time. Art for all came to mean trash for all. Looking back, we can see charm in it, and we are, as always, indulgent to the errors of the young (especially when the young happen to be our grandparents).

But art at the close of the nineteenth century— domesticated, cloying, edifying, and picturesque—with its varnished, competent, pretentious paintings, its auction-sale credenzas, its silvered cruet stands, was the antithesis of real design. Taste had gone astray; by a malign sociological irony it was eventually to be vindicated (imperfectly) on museum walls. Art was even more malign: it went into hiding and denied itself except to those worthy of it. Thus there arose a living art, on the fringes of a mass production that dared not speak its name. Impressionism, Nabis, Art Nouveau, Cubism, Purism, Surrealism, Pop Art succeeded one another, each school claiming closer allegiance than its predecessor to all kinds of contemporary plastic artists.

After more than half a century of petit bourgeois aberrations, the principles of imagination, of truth, of enjoyment, even of morality, reasserted themselves. Every participant made a serious, good-humored contribution. Granted, the average Frenchman couldn't understand what was going on, but no matter. Anything can happen in Paris, because in that city you are allowed to laugh unaffectedly at art. The artists and craftsmen of Paris rediscovered the joys of work well done. The collectors of Paris knew what they wanted, and got it because they were demanding, and because art loves to surmount the restrictions imposed on it. There was reason to fear that everything produced in Paris would be hallmarked "B.C.B.G." Art almost succumbed to the winning ways of the Ecole de Paris; fortunately, Paris grasped the point that a classically conformist unity of style engenders boredom, and that good taste can easily become oppressive.

The past delights both mind and eye and should not be overlooked, but if the quality of life is to be maintained, both mind and eye are in need of constant refreshment. In our own day it has taken great disasters and social revolutions to remind us that we cannot live unless we first strive to be. Life is too precious a gift to be enshrined in mere outward appearance, from which the spirit can take only trivial comfort. We have come late, but we have come to the recognition that the barriers must be surmounted; that art too, deserves its chance. Art is the salvation of life.

DAVID R. McFADDEN

TWO CENTURIES OF
FRENCH STYLE

14

2
Teapot decorated with Revolutionary symbols, about 1795
Manufacture de Sèvres
Porcelain
Division of Ceramics and Glass, National Museum of American History, Smithsonian Institution, Washington, D.C., Alfred Duane Pell Collection

Two centuries of creativity in France are celebrated in *L'Art de Vivre: Decorative Arts and Design in France*. Ranging from interior decoration and fashion to the arts of the table and dining, this publication and the exhibition that inspired it provide insights into aspects of French history and culture that have relevance to our understanding of France's role in the history of the decorative arts and design of the nineteenth and twentieth centuries.

A distinctively French "style" is proposed in the essays that comprise this volume. The authors examine specific fields of creativity such as jewelry and fashion, but also rituals and traditions of the social structure pertinent to our understanding of the context for design in France, most notably in the essays on the arts of the table, on the growth of department stores in Paris, and on France's role in international exhibitions. The ways in which the French interior was conceived and decorated are examined through original documents, and the highly diversified story of contemporary design in France is also reviewed.

What is the French "style" that has made *l'Art de vivre*, or the "art of living," such a vital part of the story of French design? Styles are often characterized in the decorative arts by a constellation of physical attributes—forms, patterns, motifs, structures—shared by a group of objects made in the same period, or for similar purposes. Style, however, has another aspect of meaning that may have relevance to our understanding of French design history. The superficial descriptive elements of objects are only a part of their style—their modes of use, the behavior patterns that they reflect, and their symbolic meaning also contribute to an expanded definition of style. In France, the arts of living cannot be separated from the art of living.

Over the course of the past two centuries, the traditional roles played by the decorative arts in France have been challenged by dramatic political, social, and economic changes in the country. Throughout the two centuries reviewed here, however, a lively dialogue has been maintained between tradition and innovation, in both form and function, that has given French decorative arts their distinctive appearance and unique history.

The complex history of the French Revolution of 1789, which commences this review of design in France, has engaged the attention of historians and critics from that date until the present. For our purposes, it is meaningful to examine the Revolutionary period in terms of its impact on the arts of living. Can parallels be drawn between the political events of 1789 and the progress of the arts during and following the Revolution? What

3
Chandelier, about 1810
Gilt bronze
Didier Aaron & Cie, Paris

4
Design for the Imperial coach, about 1804
Charles Percier (1764-1838) and Pierre-François-Léonard Fontaine (1762-1853)
Watercolor
Collection Hermès, Paris

were the changes that occurred, and what aspects of France's previous history continued to play a role in the development of the French style?

French primacy in the arts was firmly rooted in pre-Revolutionary traditions and can, in fact, be traced back to the cultural policies of Louis XIV. During the seventeenth and eighteenth centuries, France had played a pivotal role in European culture, a fact that was not forgotten in the years surrounding 1789. French artistic superiority, confirmed and defended by Louis XIV and his successors, had a significance beyond the symbolic, in that the economic prosperity of the country as a whole was nurtured by French exports of silks, porcelains, furniture, and silver.

With the political upheavals of the Revolution came a host of other changes that directly affected the decorative arts. The most obvious change was, of course, the disappearance of the aristocratic clients and patrons who had fostered creativity in the country for centuries. Through their direct patronage, the Ancien Régime had supported a cadre of artists and artisans renowned throughout Europe. Royal manufactories, such as Sèvres, supplied the needs of a refined clientele; works by the furniture makers of Paris were sought out by the elite throughout Europe; French silks were legendary, along with carpets and other textiles. With the Revolution, this era came to a close, and the impact on the decorative arts was staggering. Many ateliers—those of silversmiths, cabinetmakers, dressmakers—were closed, with their owners falling victim to poverty or even to the guillotine. Added to this was another major change; the ancient guilds of France— fraternal brotherhoods that had united specific trades —were suppressed.

5
Wallpaper, 1808
Joseph Dufour (active 1805-1836), manufacturer
Block-printed paper (15 colors)
Bibliothèque Forney, Paris

By the late eighteenth century, the guilds had become politically powerful and potentially dangerous to the new republican government. When these guilds were banished, territory was opened

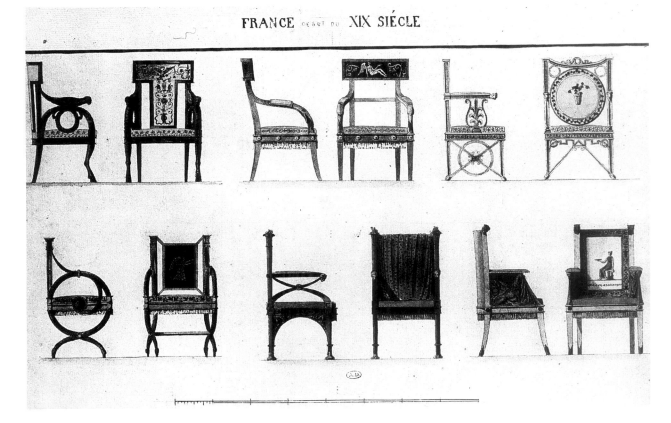

6
Designs for six chairs, early 19th century
Anonymous
Watercolor
Musée des Arts
Décoratifs, Paris

7
Chair, about 1800
Jacob Frères (active 1796-1803)
Mahogany, copper
Musée Marmottan, Paris

up for craftsmen and entrepreneurs because the guilds had also restricted trade and free enterprise by limiting participation in their economic sphere.

By the time that Napoleon came to power as first consul in 1802 and as emperor in 1804, political events had radically altered the history of France. The storming of the Bastille (July 14, 1789), the Declaration of the Rights of Man and Citizen (1791), the execution of King Louis XVI and Queen Marie-Antoinette (1793), and the Reign of Terror under Robespierre had thrust France into the modern era.

The economic importance of the decorative arts to the general health and well-being of France was perceived by Napoleon. He reorganized the foundering porcelain factory at Sèvres to create a *Manufacture Impériale* that could supply luxury porcelains to the imperial court along with prestige for the nation; he patronized the silk weavers of Lyons, recognizing one of the industries that held great economic potential, and, through his patronage, encouraged others to refurbish their houses with silks; and he began massive refurnishing of the imperial residences, bringing together a team of architects and artisans who created the Empire style with their mahogany furniture, gilt bronzes, and painted and papered interiors.

What Napoleon's zealous promotion of French industries accomplished was more than political; by reaffirming the significance of craft-based industries and, at the same time, providing an economic

8
Design for a porcelain table top, 1809
Théodore Brongniart (1739-1813), designer
Manufacture Impériale de Sèvres
Watercolor
Manufacture Nationale de Sèvres, Archives

9
Vase, about 1810-12
Jean Georget (1763-1823), decorator
Manufacture Impériale de Sèvres
Porcelain
French Institute-Alliance Française, New York

10
Armchair, about 1810
Frame attributed to Jacob-Desmalter & Cie
Mahogany, gilt bronze, silk and wool tapestry
The J. Paul Getty Museum, Malibu, California

19

**Clock, made for the
Duc d'Orléans, 1835**
Breguet workshop
Tortoiseshell, gilt
bronze, other metals,
glass
The Time Museum,
Rockford, Illinois

atmosphere that encouraged the founding of new industries, he was launching France into the new century. Traditional values that were inherited from the Ancien Régime—fine workmanship, respect for the best of materials, and refinement of detail and finish—were now integrated into the expanding luxury industries of France. A curious and even ironic situation applied: handcrafted, one-of-a-kind objects were esteemed, even when produced in the industrial sector. Because of this history, design and decorative arts in France have continued to reveal a distinctive profile to the present day: neither "studio craft" nor "industrial design" has ever held the same kind of appeal as the "handmade" object produced in multiples. The full impact of these developments was to be felt in the twentieth century, when true industrial design took on new international importance, culturally and economically.

As patron of French art industries, Napoleon created a climate of economic competition that would serve a modern France. This environment set the stage for the dramatic rise to power of French goods—not only traditional decorative arts such as furniture, glass, porcelain, and textiles, but also a wide range of products that were to be indelibly stamped on the international consciousness as typically French contributions to the "art of living," such as food and wine, haute couture, merchandising and promotion through the *grands magasins*, city planning, and a range of services from grand hotels to domestic servants. From the period of the Empire onward, a dramatic increase in the number and type of decorative arts industries could be noted.

Although many firms closed entirely during the Revolution, those that did survive found ways to accommodate contemporary sentiments in their traditional products. Among the curiosities that can be documented is the use of Revolutionary motifs —Phrygian bonnets, laurel wreaths, tricolor flags, and even armaments—as decorative ornaments on porcelains and other ceramics. The textile printers of Jouy, not inclined to miss an opportunity, introduced patterns depicting the citizens of Paris dancing on the ruins of the Bastille. As the Empire progressed, these prints kept up with the latest fashions, such as the wave of popularity that surrounded Egyptian art and architecture following Napoleon's successful military campaign in that far-flung part of the world. Added to these specific images were more generalized neoclassical motifs that symbolized France's new society.

It was neoclassicism, in fact, that provided one of the clearest and most obvious links between the traditions of the Ancien Régime and the Empire. The delicate and evocative neoclassical style

inspired by the ancient world of Greece and Rome was embraced by the French court and aristocracy during the second half of the eighteenth century. Under Napoleon, the vocabulary of neoclassicism, firmly planted as the most popular style by the 1770s, reiterated republican ideals. When combined with Napoleonic policies of economic improvement, free enterprise, and governmental patronage of industries, neoclassicism witnessed an especially bountiful harvest of designs.

At the same time that Percier and Fontaine were creating suitably impressive salons and chambers for the imperial court, emulation of the Empire style was encouraged among the bourgeoisie. The manufacturers of luxury goods, in particular, exploited the new potential market. The porcelains made at Sèvres, for example, once a royal monopoly, now faced competition from a growing number of privately held firms, such as Dihl and Guerhard, Darte, Nast, and Dagoty, their wares being sold in Paris but also exported abroad.

The histories of other firms during and immediately following the Revolution offer telling evidence of the changing nature of the crafts in nineteenth-century France. The dynasty of furniture artisans founded by Georges Jacob is one example. Born in 1739, Jacob became *maître menuisier* in 1765 and went on to supply furniture to Louis XVI, including a famous set of chairs for Marie-Antoinette's dairy at Rambouillet. Jacob's career, unlike that of many of his contemporaries, did not end with the Revolution, even though his financial losses were substantial. During a period of rupture and change, Jacob allied himself with the younger generation, including among his associates the painter David and the architects Percier and Fontaine. Jacob's success within the sphere of the new government was assured. Before his death in 1814, Jacob turned over his business to his sons François-Honoré-Georges and Georges II, and the firm subsequently became Jacob-Desmalter et Cie. It continued as a family operation until 1847, becoming one of the most prolific "industrial" suppliers of furniture for aristocrats and the bourgeoisie.

The growing success of French industries, particularly the luxury industries, could not be denied. A particularly receptive and eager audience for French goods was found in many foreign countries, including the youthful United States. The taste for French decorative arts was established in the eighteenth century by international figures such as Thomas Jefferson and Benjamin Franklin, but it was given an official sanction under George Washington, who purchased for his own use the furnishings of the French Minister to the United States. This purchase included table porcelains made at various French factories such as Angoulême and Nast (even though all were described as "Sèvres," obviously the best-known firm, even in America). President Monroe continued this tradition of buying French goods for official use, particularly silver from distinguished Paris ateliers such as Fauconnier and Odiot, the latter firm having survived the Revolution through Odiot's service in the republican army and subsequent commissions from the imperial family.

The "French style" so effectively encouraged and promoted under the Empire was already well on its way to international triumph, and from the period of the Restoration of the Monarchy (1815-30) until the establishment of the Second Empire under Napoleon III (1852-70), France achieved a greater and greater reputation as the leader in the field of decorative arts and design. A majority of the firms that set the styles for the century, such as Christofle (1830), Puiforcat (1820), Hermès (1837), Jeanselme (1824; it eventually took over the firm of Jacob-Desmalter in 1847), and Mauboussin (1827), were founded during the first half of the century, followed in the second half of

12
Wallpaper, 1835
Amable Leroy, manufacturer
Block-printed paper
Musée des Arts
Décoratifs, Paris

13
**Interior of the
workshop of
Jean-Baptiste-Claude
Odiot, 1821**
Jean-Baptiste
Desmoulins
Oil on canvas
Collection Odiot
Orfèvre, Paris

14
**The Baccarat
glassworks, 1828**
Baccarat Archives, Paris

15
**Leather workshop at
Hermès, about 1988**
Hermès Archives, Paris

16

"Harcourt" glassware service, first produced 1841
Cristalleries de Baccarat
Glass (modern production illustrated)
Musée Baccarat, Paris

17

Wallpaper, about 1820
Dufour et Leroy, manufacturer
Block-printed paper (4 colors)
Bibliothèque Forney, Paris

18

Vase, about 1840
Cristalleries de Saint-Louis
Opaline glass
Collection Cristalleries de Saint-Louis, Paris

the century by others such as Boucheron (1858) and Ercuis (1867).

Stylistically, classicism continued to exert its powerful influence on the decorative arts during this period of growth and expansion. The lessons of neoclassicism—proportion, order, harmony of parts, and attention to detail and finish—were not forgotten, and their continuing influence in French design can be seen even today. However, in this period France also took part in an international

19
Clock in the Gothic style, about 1830
Maker unknown
Gilt bronze, enamel
Musée des Arts
Décoratifs, Paris

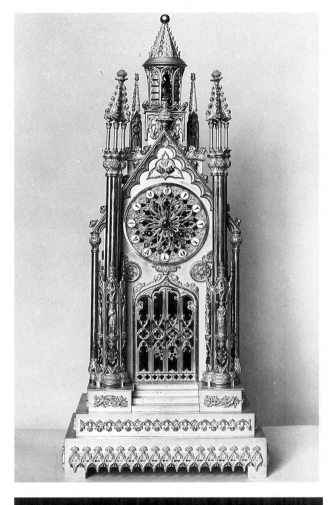

20
Footed vase with Gothic decoration, about 1840
Cristalleries de
Saint-Louis
Pressed glass
Cooper-Hewitt Museum,
New York, Gift of
Cristalleries de
Saint-Louis, 1988-108-1

21
Design for a table, clock, and candelabra in the Gothic style, 1827
Maison Fayolle, aîné
Pen and ink, watercolor
Musée des Arts
Décoratifs, Paris

revival movement that brought history, literature, and geography to bear on style. Most notable in the series of revivals in France during the first half of the nineteenth century that were to become so widespread in Europe and the United States after mid century was that of the "Gothic," sometimes referred to as the "*style troubadour*." The new romanticism was stimulated by literary developments (Victor Hugo's *Hunchback of Notre-Dame* was a sensation in 1834) and promoted in the work of architects such as Viollet-le-Duc. More than a reaction against the pervasive and traditional neoclassicism, medieval romanticism forged a psychological and symbolic link with the foundations of French culture, even though the movement was rapidly popularized to suit the whims of a broad and diverse audience. The Gothic was not the only revival in this period, it must be remembered; a new wave of exoticism emanating primarily from China also influenced the decorative arts, as did the world of nature itself, depicted in the form of lush floral designs in radiant colors in wallpapers, on textiles, on painted porcelains, and in jewelry designs. These vogues of the first half of the nineteenth century, a period that has never received all the attention it deserves from museums and historians, can be seen as the foundation for most of the revival styles so often identified with the Second Empire.

Hand in hand with these stylistic developments were changes in technology that are now more fully appreciated in terms of their impact on the decorative arts. The glass industries in France, for example, introduced many new colors into their repertory, such as a vivid yellow derived from uranium. Technology also began to affect the production methods used at the firms; in the first half of the century, both Baccarat and Saint-Louis introduced press-molded glass at their factories, to provide highly ornamented glassware at greatly reduced prices. Alongside such developments were enhanced avenues of promotion at home and abroad; retail outlets in Paris included boutiques or shops operated by the glass firms, as well as larger and more comprehensive retail shops, such as the Escalier de Cristal in the Palais-Royal, which offered a range of porcelains and glassware from many different factories. It was such outlets that would ultimately serve as prototypes for the department stores that dominated Paris in the second half of the century.

By the period of Napoleon III, France held a proud position as the leader in the world of decorative arts, based on the maintenance of standards of quality in materials and workmanship, made possible through semi-industrialized craft-based production. At various international

Nº 567.

22
Teakettle on stand,
1843-44
Christofle & Cie
Silver plate, ebony
Musée Bouilhet-
Christofle, Paris

exhibitions, the works of French industries were regarded as paradigms; the success of firms such as Christofle is well documented by the number of official and private commissions carried out for table silver and for the newly popularized and much more affordable silver plate. Once again, government intervention supported this new technology; with his choice of less expensive silver plate rather than solid silver, Napoleon III sanctioned popular use of the material, and the success of Christofle's silver-plated wares was assured.

Bourgeois taste was at its zenith in the second half of the century, for better or for worse. The trends set in motion in the earlier decades of the nineteenth century and fostered under the Second Empire continued throughout the Third Republic (1870-1940). However, in these seven decades spanning the nineteenth and the twentieth century, French artists and industry were severely challenged by political revolution, economic setbacks, and the ruptures of war. On the other hand, an international market for decorative arts and design made possible through technological and communication improvements stimulated competition and called into question many traditional beliefs concerning the materials and craftsmanship identified with the French luxury

23
Chair, about 1827
Clément-Louis Bigot,
manufacturer
Maple, amaranth
Collection Roger
Imbert, Paris

24
Teapot, 1827
Leloy, designer
Manufacture Nationale
de Sèvres
Porcelain
Musée National de
Céramique, Sèvres

25
Platter, about 1850
Workshop of
Charles-Jean Avisseau
(1796-1862)
Earthenware
Didier Aaron & Cie,
Paris

industries. From the middle years of the nineteenth century onward, the debate between artists and industry was intensified; independent creators working outside of the industrial sector established themselves as a new force in the creative process in France.

The economic success of the luxury industries in France from the latter decades of the nineteenth century through the first decades of the present century is undeniable. Although often maintaining the "atelier" atmosphere, the firms themselves became generic terms for materials, whether they be silver plate, glass, luggage, or fashion. The individual artisans who worked in these gigantic workshops were submerged within the company image. What then was the role of the creative artist or artisan in France? Did the potential for creativity exist within the bureaucracies of industry, or was it necessary for the true artist to separate creation from the production system?

The answer for a new generation of artists was clear, and many potters, glassmakers, jewelers, and furniture makers staked out new territories for themselves in the realm of one-of-a-kind or limited production. This phenomenon was, of course, an international one, and not restricted to France; the Arts and Crafts movement affected creation and production systems in both Europe and the United

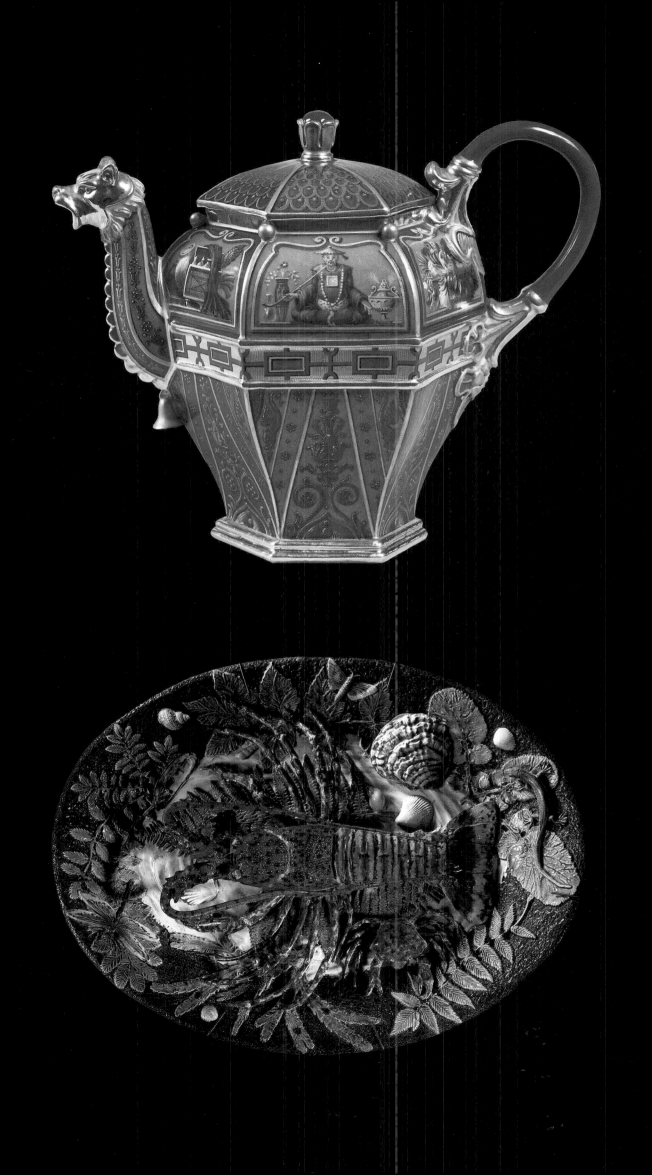

**Ewer and basin,
about 1870**
Faïencerie de Gien
Earthenware
Didier Tritz Collection

States, but in France the movement took hold in a very special way. The skill of the artisan had never ceased to appeal to the French public, and an innovator such as Gallé, Lalique, or Guimard may have been aided, rather than inhibited, by the luxury industries of France. Rather than a "revolution," the Art Nouveau movement was, in many respects, a restatement of the dialogue that had always existed between tradition and innovation and between creation and production, a dialogue that remains a hallmark of French design.

The popularity of revival styles in the second half of the nineteenth century reflected the general interest in the decorative arts, encompassing a broad cross-section of society. Classicism, long favored in France, held a prominent place in the catalogue of styles. Under Napoleon III, a new "Renaissance" occurred, producing a range of decorative arts from the brilliantly crafted jewels of Mellerio, Boucheron, and Falize to opulent tablewares in the classical manner produced at Sèvres, Baccarat, and Christofle, along with wares made for a more popular audience at firms such as Gien and Sarreguemines. The revival of the styles of the eighteenth century was another feature of the epoch, particularly within the imperial circle, inspired in part by Empress Eugénie's fondness for, and identification with, the tragic Marie-Antoinette. In objects created for popular consumption, distinctions between historic styles were often

blurred, leading to a stylistic pastiche that is only now beginning to be unraveled by scholars. At the same time, reproductions of eighteenth-century "antiques" flourished; it was in this period that the retailers of furnishings offered a full range of styles from Henri II to Louis XVI.

While revival pieces were acknowledged by the industry and the public for what they were—finely crafted objects of traditional taste and quality—a small but highly influential group of collectors began to make a practical and philosophical distinction between "true" antiques and "false" reproductions. And, as the first true collectors and connoisseurs of antiques appeared, so, too, did some of the first deliberate forgeries of antiques.

The revival of classicism—whether based on sixteenth-century Renaissance examples or eighteenth-century classicism—was but one popular theme to which artists and industry responded in the second half of the nineteenth century. A fascination with exoticism, made possible through the reopening of contact between Japan and the West and the appearance of Japanese art in French collections and galleries, found an especially appreciative audience among artists, both the "fine" and "applied" variety, ranging from glassmakers such as Gallé to ceramic artists like Deck. Unique works of art in the "humble" materials of the crafts were touted at exhibitions and in galleries, such as that opened by Siegfried Bing in 1895 bearing the name L'Art Nouveau. In addition, Japanese art was often based on direct study of natural forms—flowers, plants, and even insects—and this taste found a receptive audience among both the traditional and the innovative. Commercial firms recognized the potential of the mania for *Japonisme* and for naturalism, creating a wealth of designs, carried out in bronze or base metals, silver plate, earthenwares, porcelains, and glass, that reflected the new Oriental influence and also a French taste for nature that recalls the similar early nineteenth-century phenomenon. Also woven into this complex picture of Art Nouveau is the return of the human figure (particularly female) as a motif in the decorative arts, a tradition kept alive in the nineteenth century by way of the Renaissance revival.

By the beginning of the twentieth century, the decorative arts in France were acknowledged as a vital symbol of the overall health of the nation, both from an economic and a cultural point of view. The luxury industries that had flourished in the nineteenth century had proven their monetary and cultural power in the history of France. Even independent artists who rebelled against the industrial system found themselves involved in production as well as creation. Witness the growth

**Designs for chairs,
late 19th century**
Maison Poirier et
Rémon, Paris (active
about 1862-1900)
Gouache
Musée des Arts
Décoratifs, Paris

**Teapot and sugar
bowl, about 1875**
Christofle & Cie
Silver plate
Musée Bouilhet-
Christofle, Paris

29
**Chair in Louis XV
style, about 1860**
Ebonized wood,
mother-of-pearl,
needlework
Musée national du
Château de Compiègne

of art industries in Nancy, for example. The city
had been the birthplace and home to many of the
most independent spirits of the late nineteenth
century, such as Emile Gallé and Louis Majorelle,
whose "art industries" had become
mass-production systems by the early years of the
twentieth century. They were joined in the Ecole
de Nancy by others who saw creation and
production as sympathetic allies, most notably the
two brothers Auguste and Antonin Daum, whose
glass workshops produced thousands of "unique"
vases and vessels. By combining the mystique of
the unique object with efficient production
techniques within the workshop setting, furniture,
glass, and ceramics were made available and
affordable to the middle classes. A respect for
materials and craftsmanship was embodied in such
semi-industrialized workshops, as well as those of
the luxury industries in Paris. A part of the appeal
of French decorative arts has always been an
intangible element of irreplaceability or
uniqueness, and the luxury industries in France
successfully capitalized upon this attraction by
combining traditional quality with innovative design
a union that has been maintained even in the
twentieth century.

By the first decade of the twentieth century, the
Art Nouveau style had been popularized to the
point of exhaustion, and designers and industries
explored new sources of inspiration, ranging from
African art to the bold and surprising forms and
colors introduced to Paris by way of the Ballets

30
Design for incense burners, about 1875
Faïencerie de Gien
Pen and ink, watercolor
Musée de la Faïencerie de Gien

31
Wallpaper, about 1860-80
Jules Riottot et Pacon, manufacturer
Printed paper (3 colors)
Bibliothèque Forney, Paris

32
Vase, 1853
Manufacture Nationale de Sèvres
Porcelain
Musée National de Céramique, Sèvres

33
Fabric, about 1900
E. Bouvard & Cie, Lyon,
manufacturer
Silk
Musée des Arts
Décoratifs, Paris

34
Vase, about 1910
René Lalique
(1860-1945)
Glass (*cire-perdue*)
Glenn and Mary Lou Utt
Collection

Russes; the arts of ancient Egypt and China; and contemporary developments in painting and sculpture, such as Cubism. The dialogue between tradition and innovation, and that between creation and production, was intensified with the growth of industry and the continued expansion of the international marketplace through improved communications and transportation. On one side of the debate were the luminaries of the so-called Art Deco style, epitomized in the costly and richly crafted furniture of Ruhlmann and Süe et Mare, in the crystal of Baccarat and Saint-Louis, in the jewels of Van Cleef & Arpels, Cartier, Boucheron, and Mauboussin, in the porcelains of Sèvres, and the silver of Christofle and Ercuis. Recognition of the

changing face of production and marketing also led to changes in the careers of some designers, such as René Lalique. Lalique achieved fame as an extraordinary artist-jeweler in the latter part of the nineteenth century, creating one-of-a-kind masterpieces of jewelry that depended upon design and craftsmanship for their value, rather than on the monetary worth of precious stones. By the early years of the twentieth century, Lalique began designing glass for serial production and by 1909, he possessed his own factory. Lalique, along with the silversmith Jean Puiforcat, serves to symbolize a new attitude toward design in France in the twentieth century, in which creation is seen not as the antithesis of production, but as an inseparable part of the design process.

The voice of tradition resounds in many of the French decorative arts of the early twentieth

century: the furniture of Ruhlmann acknowledges its ancestry in the craftsmanship and proportions of the eighteenth century; the seemingly radical fashions of Paul Poiret are often inspired directly by fashion from the Empire period; and the stylized floral ornaments carried out on the furniture of Süe et Mare, the wallpapers of André Groult, and the textiles woven for interiors created by Ruhlmann find their roots in the self-assured classicism of the Louis-Philippe era.

In counterpoint to these traditions are the modern designs of Le Corbusier, Charlotte Perriand, and Robert Mallet-Stevens, in which refinements of rich materials and labor-intensive craftsmanship are secondary to efficient designs for

36
Ewer, about 1890-95
Clément Massier (about 1845-1917)
Earthenware, luster glaze
Private Collection

35
Design for a brooch, about 1898-1904
René Lalique (1860-1945)
Pencil, pen and ink, gouache
Collection Cristal Lalique, Paris

37
"Crown of Thorns," vase, 1911
Cristalleries Daum, Nancy
Glass
The Corning Museum of Glass, Corning, New York

industrial production. Only recently has the work of these designers, as well as many others who formed the cadre of the Union des Artistes Modernes, been regarded with the respect due to them by the French, outside of a small coterie of design historians. Ironically, it is this second voice in French design of the twentieth century that is now being reevaluated for its significance to the continuing creative traditions in France.

World War II, which ended the Third Republic in 1939, was yet another rupture in the social, economic, and cultural fabric of France. Many trends in design that were beginning to appear in the decorative arts in the late 1930s were interrupted, only to resurface in the late 1940s. New challenges were presented to traditional luxury industries, particularly in relation to the expansion of their markets in other countries. By the 1960s, many industries saw direct sales as essential to survival, and by the 1970s the finest products of the Parisian houses—fashion, porcelains, crystal, silver, jewelry—were available in specialized boutiques from Tokyo to Beverly Hills.

In an effort to introduce new designs, industry invited distinguished artists such as Alexander Calder at the Sèvres factory, Van Dongen at Bernardaud of Limoges, and Raymond Loewy at Le Creuset to contribute designs. Other industries made efforts to compete in international industrial expositions such as the Milan Triennale, where firms like Christofle were among the award winners. A new generation of designers for industry such as Olivier Mourgue, Pierre Paulin, and Roger Tallon, whose work has ranged from furniture and interior architecture to table glass, also began to make its presence felt in the field of French industrial design.

During the same decades a major revival of the crafts occurred in France, as it did in many countries, recapturing a sense of the traditional respect for materials and craftsmanship. This phenomenon had its popular side in the revival of "provincial" furniture and in textiles such as the printed fabrics of Souleïado, whose patterns were directly inspired by eighteenth-century printed textiles and have remained popular since the mid-1940s.

In France today, tradition continues to be maintained among firms involved in the luxury market, but efforts to revitalize the design traditions are not wanting. Philippe Starck, probably the best known among French designers today, has created designs for production at Daum, and Hermès, a traditional manufacturer of leather goods, has recently introduced carbon-fiber luggage into its line. Activity in the field of design is now experiencing a resurgence in France. Government

40
**Wallpaper, about
1925-30**
André Groult
(1884-1967), designer
Printed paper
Cooper-Hewitt Museum,
New York, Gift of Jones
and Erwin, 1945-13-3

41
**"Persia" door, about
1923**
Edgar Brandt (born
1880)
Wrought iron
The Metropolitan
Museum of Art, New
York, Purchase, Edward
C. Moore, Jr., Gift, 1924

42
Mirror, about 1922-23
Louis Süe (1875-1968)
and André Mare
(1887-1932), designers,
for Compagnie
des Arts Français
Painted and gilded
wood
The Metropolitan
Museum of Art, New
York, Purchase, Edward
C. Moore, Jr., Gift, 1923

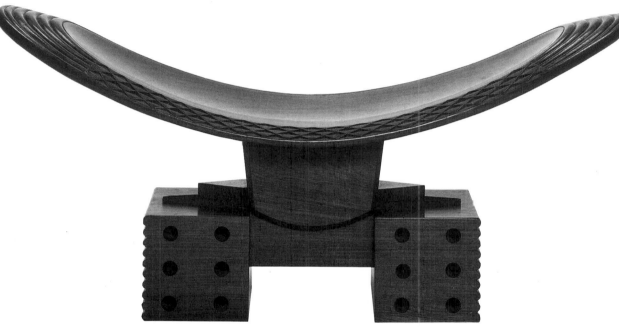

43
"Alhambra" wallpaper, 1929
Stéphany, designer, Desfosse et Karth, manufacturer
Flocked paper
Musée des Arts Décoratifs, Paris

44
"Fountains" glassware service, 1924
Georges Chevalier (born 1894), designer
Cristalleries de Baccarat
Glass
Musée Baccarat, Paris

45
Desk and chair, about 1925
Louis Süe (1875-1968) and André Mare (1887-1932), designers, for Compagnie des Arts Français
Ebony, gilt bronze, pigskin
The Metropolitan Museum of Art, New York, Edward C. Moore, Jr., Gift, 1925

46
Stool, 1922-29
Pierre Legrain (1888-1929)
Rosewood
The Metropolitan Museum of Art, New York, Fletcher Fund, 1972

47
Vase, about 1937
Aristide Colotte (1885-1959)
Glass
Collection of Miles and Lyn Lourie

48
Armchair with tilting back (model B 301), about 1928
Le Corbusier (1887-1965), Pierre Jeanneret (1896-1967), and Charlotte Perriand (born 1903), designers, Thonet, Germany, manufacturer
Chromed tubular steel, metal, fabric
Barry Friedman Ltd., New York

49
**"Milano" dressing
case, 1925**
Louis Vuitton,
manufacturer
Leather, ivory, glass,
silk, silver, brass, other
metals
Collection Louis Vuitton,
Paris

50
**Console from the
oceanliner
Normandie, 1935**
Charles, manufacturer
Bronze
Collection Charles
Bronze d'Art, Paris

51
**Tea and coffee
service, about 1936**
Orfèvrerie d'Ercuis
Silver plate, ebony
Collection Orfèvrerie
d'Ercuis, Paris

52
**Traveling case of
Karen Blixen, 1930**
Hermès, manufacturer
Crocodile, leather, glass,
silver
Collection Hermès,
Paris

53
Coffee service, 1932
Jean Luce (1895-1964)
Earthenware
Private Collection

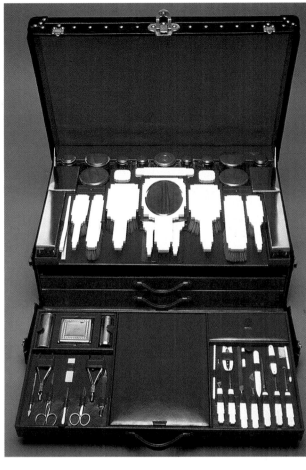

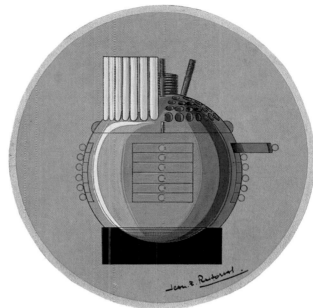

sponsorship remains significant; the attention focused on the work of Philippe Starck, Ronald Cécil Sportes, and Jean-Pierre Wilmotte by way of official commissions has helped to reassert France's role in the international design community, as have exhibitions organized by the Musée des Arts Décoratifs and the Centre de Création Industrielle at the Centre Georges Pompidou. Independent craftsmen have likewise maintained an active role, even when opportunities for exhibition and sale through galleries are few. It can only be hoped that the larger industries will see promise in the new generation of designers and continue to foster new creation by bringing industry and designers together.

Any survey of French decorative arts over a two-hundred-year period must necessarily highlight certain individuals and firms, particularly those that have played a significant role in the development of design during a large section of the chronology. However, a purely biographical approach to the history of the decorative arts in France can only provide glimpses into the aesthetic and social contexts in which these objects functioned. It is equally important to search for those features of any style that give a period or a moment in time its distinctive cast and flavor, and in so doing to illuminate the complex interaction of forces that stimulate creativity in design. In a review of the

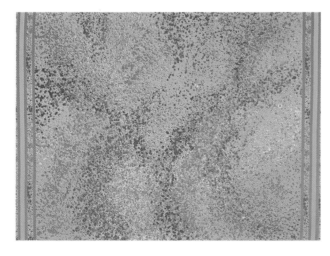

material and cultural history of French decorative arts from the Revolution to the present day, certain ideas and themes become apparent. In both the nineteenth and twentieth centuries can be heard a distinctively French conversation between tradition and innovation, a dialogue that is expressed in the assimilation and transformation of forms and systems of ornamentation that signify an epoch or a style; in the choice and use of materials by artists and industries, as well as in the attitudes toward craftsmanship implied by those choices; and in the contradictions and collaborations that comprise the relations between creation and production in France.

Tradition and innovation have continued their provocative relationship in France in the two hundred years since the French Revolution; often sympathetic partners, they have also provided one another with the stimulus for change. Upon the occasion of the bicentennial of the Revolution, it seems appropriate to reflect on this history, but to avoid nostalgia. Tradition can be a creative force in the decorative arts, bringing experience, wisdom, and confidence to the process of design. It can also impede innovation when maintenance of traditional values becomes an end in itself. Decorative arts and design are always faithful barometers of culture, and they have proven their economic and cultural value in France over the course of two centuries. It is to be hoped that the

61
**"Trois Etrangétés"
Table, 1988**
Philippe Starck (born
1949), designer
Daum Cristal,
manufacturer
Glass
Collection Daum Cristal,
France

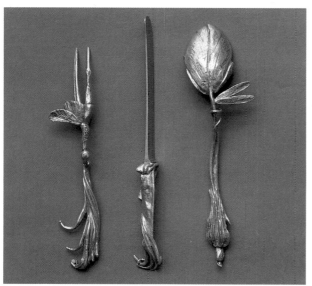

"art of living" that France has made manifest in its history will continue to inspire, delight, and inform in the next century.

62
**Fork, knife, spoon,
1966**
Claude Lalanne
Silver, steel
Marisa del Re Gallery,
New York

YVONNE BRUNHAMMER

NATIONAL, INTERNATIONAL, AND UNIVERSAL EXPOSITIONS AND THE FRENCH DECORATIVE ARTS

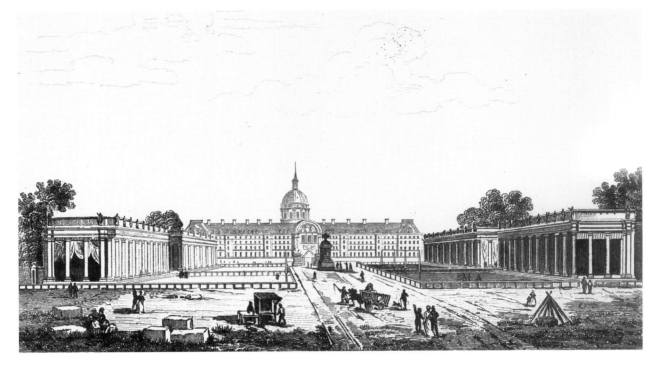

The art of living *à la française* can be studied across various forms of government and over many decades, but there is another history born of the Revolution of 1789. Its milestones are exhibitions of the products of French industry, invented under the Directory and appropriated by successive governments in the first half of the nineteenth century. The intent of the exhibitions was to stimulate the industrial arts, which had initially been thrown into disorder, rather than enfranchised, by the suppression of the guilds; and to bring them face to face with, and make them known to, the public. These exhibitions, national in scope until 1849, nurtured a new and closer understanding between producer and consumer.

It was the British, stalwart exponents of free trade, who, in 1851, led the way in opening their expositions to all the world's manufactures. A new chapter began, richer and also more competitive because its arena was the entire universe: all the products of man and his machines (as well as those very machines) were now brought together, and men and women came from all continents to see them. The story is a familiar one; it has itself been the subject of several exhibitions, including one in 1983 at the Musée des Arts Décoratifs in Paris whose catalogue was entitled *Le Livre des expositions universelles*.

EXPOSITIONS OF THE PRODUCTS OF FRENCH INDUSTRY

Exhibitions based on industrial products were a post-Revolutionary development and, according to

historians, a consequence of the suppression of the guilds. Under the Ancien Régime, the "brotherhoods" not only oversaw the professional activities of workmen and masters alike, but regulated the production that fell within the jurisdiction of the guild mastership. Jurors passed judgment on the "master pieces" of candidates for master status and watched over product quality. Each guild, within its narrow area of specialization, jealously guarded its prerogatives. For example, an armchair might pass through the hands of no less than four guilds, depending on whether it was constructed of molded, turned, carved, painted, or gilded wood, before reaching the upholsterer, who was usually also the final seller.

Although standards of craftsmanship were upheld, the system was not without its disadvantages. The fact is that not everyone could aspire to mastery; no craftsman could operate outside the guild, which did not stop at protecting its members, but actively prosecuted those who sought independence of it or who set up shop in unauthorized locations; and privileges were accorded by the monarchy to certain craftsmen.[1] When, on the passionate night of August 4, 1789, the privileges of the guilds were abolished, their suppression inevitably followed. More than a year later, on March 2, 1791, d'Allarde's Law (so called after its sponsor) established the voluntary contract as the new basis of social relationships. At the same time, all state regulation of production was abolished; manufactures were no longer to be hallmarked or inspected. This new freedom of commerce was matched by a new freedom of employment "even for masters." The Le Chapelier Law, passed by the Constituent Assembly on June

14, 1791, forbade "associations," that is, any organization, whether formal or ad hoc, of either workers or employers.[2] Thus, during a period of abrupt transition, craftsmen and manufacturers were left to their own devices and were among the first to sustain the impact of social and economic change.

Comte Léon de Laborde, official reporter on the fine arts at the Great Exhibition of 1851 in London, produced an analysis of the condition of the industrial arts that became virtually a reference text and was recapitulated in most of the reports on the universal expositions in the latter half of the nineteenth century. Today, we can see this report in the context of the Second Empire, which, if it did not actually reject the events of 1789, at least repudiated the ensuing period of instability and its "lugubrious and impracticable Utopias."[3] But for its historical content the report is invaluable: it affords us the earliest account of art exhibitions from the reign of Louis XIV, beginning when the Academy of Painting and Sculpture, founded in 1648, first exhibited the work of its members to the public. These salons, initially held at the Palais-Royal, were moved to the Grande Galerie of the Louvre and then, after 1737, to the Salon Carré (hence the word *salon*). Such "salons" were reserved for the members of the Academy—painters, sculptors, and engravers—and excluded craftsmen and manufacturers who belonged to shopkeeping guilds, since the keeping of shops was forbidden to Academy members. The specialization that the guilds imposed on their members became

segregation when it came to the distinction between "liberal" and "useful" arts.

The abolition of the Academy did not put an end to the series of annual exhibitions in the Salon Carré of the Louvre, which in 1795 became the "Museum," and later the Palais des Sciences et des Arts.

The suppression of the guilds, and the simultaneous disappearance of aristocratic patronage, inevitably threw the situation of the craftsmen into confusion. In Laborde's dramatically negative formulation, industry "had lost both its traditional techniques and its workers, driven from their benches; there was no longer the guidance of an elegant court, the natural arbiter of good taste, nor of those artists risen from the workshop who could all the better direct its aspirations in that they understood its problems as well as its duties." Denying to the "parvenu" any legitimate function in the formation of 'taste,' he saw arts and crafts fallen to be "the plaything of everyman," drifting "at the whim of a fashion that every day sets its sights lower." Even more serious was the defective training of the new craftsmen: the suppression of the guilds had entailed the disappearance of those long-established families from which the artists in each trade would naturally spring. "Now a young man born to a trade would lightly leave it if he were so inclined and thought he had the ability, taking his work and his aspirations into some different sphere that he perceived as more exalted. Industry was delivered into the hands of unenterprising, uninspired practitioners; if it turned

64
Exposition of the Products of French Industry, in the courtyard of the Louvre, 1801
Anonymous
Watercolor, gouache
Musée Carnavalet, Paris

for its designs to artists, they would provide them but with no real understanding of the purpose of the product or the processes of its manufacture. On one side was the creative artist, on the other the artisan."[4] Here Laborde underlines a problem that is still pertinent today: in a system that classifies the arts according to a table of precedence, a talented young man would sooner become an artist than an artisan.

The objective of the Minister of the Interior, François de Neufchâteau, in proposing a "Public Exposition of the Products of French Industry" was to bring together the various trades that "were no longer in communication" and to familiarize the public with their wares, as had been done for more than a century and a half for the fine arts. The event would coincide with the sixth anniversary of the proclamation of the republic, which the Directory was eager to celebrate with festivities. The ideas of exposition and festivity were linked by an established tradition. We know that such events were customary in the Middle East, where precious objects and articles for everyday use were displayed—and sold—on festive occasions. The trade fair was the descendant of such markets and bazaars. The competitions and prizes that were offered at the trade fairs were an incentive to exhibitors and served to raise the standards of the exhibits, but the primary objective of these events was always to sell.[5] Nevertheless, the exposition had goals that were not exclusively commercial. Speaking of the first Universal Exposition in Paris in 1855, Taine wrote: "All of Europe is on the road to come and look at goods."[6]

The first public exposition of the products of French industry has been dated to the last days of the year VI (October 1798), but a booklet printed by A. Poilleux at Neuilly and preserved in the Bibliothèque des Arts Décoratifs in Paris mentions two earlier expositions organized by the marquis d'Avèze, "Commissioner of the Manufactories at Gobelins, Sèvres and Savonnerie."[7] Confronted with "the misfortune heaped on" these manufactures, "the deserted workshops," the starving workers, the warehouses bulging with inventory, d'Avèze proposed to the Minister of the Interior, the previously mentioned François de Neufchâteau,[8] that an exposition of the wares of all the state-owned factories be organized at the Château de Saint-Cloud, along with public festivities and games in its park. The idea was approved and implemented with the help of the various factory managers and the architect Peyre. The opening, intended for the 18 Fructidor of the year V (September 4, 1797), was canceled on account of the antiroyalist coup d'etat. The marquis d'Avèze, who was compelled to leave the country, decided on his return at the beginning of the year VI (1798) to relaunch the project in a new setting at the Maison d'Orsay on the rue de Varennes. He recounts how he assembled there precious artifacts, "the products of the state-owned factories," and organized, in the manner of classical antiquity, athletic contests and intellectual games, as well as literary assemblies.

A few months later there opened on the Champ de Mars, under the sixty-eight arches of a portico designed by the painter David, the exposition that was to elevate "the peaceful victories of industry to the same eminence as the trophies of heroism." The comte de Laborde rightly commends this new departure by the Directory and its Minister of the Interior, for "there is nothing to suggest that they were aware of how great a movement they had initiated."[9] One hundred ten exhibitors from Paris and its surroundings, or the nearby departments, responded to the minister's appeal and were there on opening day, 24 Vendémiaire (October 15). Drapers, milliners, hosiers (these last all from Troyes), makers of cotton goods and handkerchiefs, including the eleven partners of the Chollet factory, occupied a place of importance among the gunsmiths and mechanics. The official reporters remarked on clocks by Breguet of Paris; earthenware by Potter of Chantilly and Villeroy of Moselle; and wallpaper by Petit and Daguet of Paris. The national porcelain factory at Sèvres had two archways to itself; the Paris house of Dihl and Guérard on the rue du Temple had one. The glassware of Le Creusot, formerly the manufacture of the queen, was displayed by its agent in Paris, Lebon. There were also printers, booksellers, casters, and typographers, including both Firmin Didot and Didot Jeune. The Martin foundry of Paris exhibited a full-length statue of General Bonaparte; Roby, pictures in Aubusson tapestry; Cicéri, "the artist, of Paris," a set of Republican tables of measurement with printed instructions for use.

The following year, political events in France precluded the hoped-for public exhibition of the "useful arts." The Consulate's new Minister of the Interior, Chaptal, submitted for the approval of the First Consul a decree dated 13 Ventôse of the year IX (March 1801), providing for an annual public exposition in Paris of the products of French industry as "part of the festival designed to celebrate the anniversary of the Republic's foundation." There was to be a competition open to "French manufacturers and artists," to be judged first by a jury appointed by the prefect of each department, then by a second jury of fifteen members chosen by the Minister of the Interior from among the leading figures of art, science, and industry. The jury for the second exposition included the chemist Berthollet, the painter Léonor Mérimée (father of the writer Prosper Mérimée), and one of the Montgolfier brothers, the paper manufacturers who invented the hot-air balloon (still known in France as a montgolfière). Article VII of the decree provided that a specimen of each product designated by the jury be deposited in the Conservatoire des Arts et Métiers, founded in the year III (1794), thus inaugurating in the nineteenth century the first public collection for the products of French industry.

The first exposition under the Consulate, in the year IX (1801), was held in the courtyard of the Palais des Sciences et des Arts (now the Louvre), and the 220 exhibitors were deployed beneath 104 romanesque porticos, which were not commissioned from David, to his great indignation. Awards were bestowed according to differing criteria. Some had to do with the exceptionally

67
Salon in the Louis XV style shown at the Exposition of the Products of French Industry, Paris, 1844
Georges Monbro (active 1832-53), designer
Published in *Les Beaux-Arts et L'Industrie*, vol. 3, Paris, 1844
Cooper-Hewitt Museum Library, New York

68
**Potpourri vase, about
1840**
Jacob Petit (1796-1868)
Porcelain
Musée des Arts
Décoratifs, Paris

high quality of the product or work: for example, the typographical work of Pierre and Firmin Didot, the vellum paper of Montgolfier and Johannot, the furniture of Lignereux and of the Jacob brothers on the rue Mêlée in Paris. In the case of Lenoir's precision instruments for mathematics and astronomy, it was originality that earned the jury's commendation. One of the main purposes of the exposition was served by providing incentive for competitive industries and for those that were only recently established on French soil. The jury awarded a gold medal to Conté, for example, for his "artificial crayons," which were adjudged one of the products of the future. For obvious reasons—the intensity of foreign competition—the textile

69
Porcelain and glassware from the Escalier de Cristal, exhibited at the Exposition of the Products of French Industry, Paris, 1844
Engraving, published in *Exposition de l'industrie française,* 1844
Cooper-Hewitt Museum, New York, Picture Collection

70
Centerpiece belonging to the Duc d'Orléans, exhibited at the Exposition of the Products of French Industry, Paris, 1844
Jean-Baptiste Klagmann (1810-1867)
Gilt bronze, glass, precious stones
Musée des Arts Décoratifs, Paris

industry received special attention. The jury was not indulgent to the *manufactures nationales*, but recognized that "their products were better finished and of higher quality than they were fifteen years ago." Apart from the goldsmiths and jewelers, all the art trades were represented in the Louvre courtyard: glassware by Le Creusot and Mont-Cenis; wallpaper by Jacquemart and Benard, successors to Réveillon; silk from Tours. Lyons sent nothing. The jury expressed itself satisfied: "This weighty and memorable exposition should dispel all anxiety concerning the future of our commerce."[10] A year later, the Consulate organized its second exposition, in an interlude of peace and prosperity. The number of exhibitors more than doubled. By 1806, in the euphoric days of the early Empire, their numbers rose to 1,422. The emperor appealed to "all the manufacturers and

artists of France," and their enthusiastic response required the organizers to move the exposition to the Esplanade des Invalides, a more spacious setting than the Louvre courtyard. All in all, it was an impressive tribute to the vitality of French industry. Textiles had benefited from protectionist measures introduced by the emperor in February 1806; in particular the cotton industry developed in Paris and around the three centers of Rouen, Lille, and Mulhouse. The official reporter, Costaz, deplored the vogue for cotton, which had inflicted "grievous harm" on manufacturers of jute, linen, and "lightweight wool."[11] The exposition catalogues offer a fascinating capsule account of the products chosen in Paris and the provinces; the account begins with a long list of textile manufacturers and continues with paper, printed fabrics, and wallpaper — a M. Zuber of Rexheim [sic] received a silver medal for the quality of his colors and "his landscapes, in which he has overcome technical difficulties in a way calculated to further the state of the art." [!] Leather and hides came from Paris and elsewhere in France; iron and steel were represented by more than one hundred fifty factories located in about forty departments. Producers of files seemed of particular interest to the jurors: they had been singled out in all the preceding expositions.

Following the order of the sections, the visitor passed on to various kinds of hardware; armaments, with a mention of the Saint-Etienne plant; mechanical engineering, where it was no surprise to encounter a significant number of specialized machines, many connected with the textile industry; and precision machinery, for which Breguet won a gold medal. After a group of "combustion devices," oil lamps, and a section

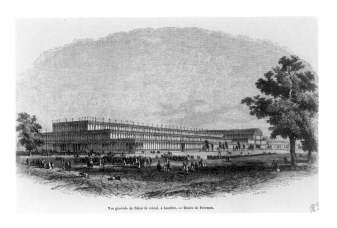

Vue générale du Palais de cristal, à Londres. — Dessin de Freeman.

displayed, particularly pieces bearing the signatures of Auguste, Odiot, or Biennais, and this was the first exposition of its kind for the bronze founder Thomire, who walked away with a gold medal.

There were not many cabinetmakers or joiners, and it is not surprising that the 1806 Exposition would give more prominence to developing industries than to traditional trades. The jury closely scrutinized the production of what had now become imperial factories, believing that they should serve as an example by "setting standards of beauty." Apparently the Gobelins tapestry works fared better than Sèvres, Beauvais, and Savonnerie; mechanization of its looms had made possible a more exact imitation, when desired, of the painted original, while its dyes were considered to be more light-fast. The long description ends with the work of the pupils of the Compiègne School of Arts and Crafts, here for the first time exhibited to the public; thus the Empire emphasized the importance it assigned to artistic instruction for the development of national industry.

The Empire's wars left little room for such

dedicated to "chemical arts and products," one came to glassware. Le Creusot crystal, which was under the patronage of Her Majesty the Empress, was awarded a gold medal; there was glass from Saint-Louis in Moselle, and mirrors and window glass from Romesnil. Dartigues of Vonêche received a silver medal for the quality of his glass. Ceramics (or, rather, "pottery," the word used in the 1806 catalogue to cover all ceramic products) were represented by Dilh and Guérard, Nast, Dagoty and Després, the porcelain factories that had successively opened in Paris after the Sèvres monopoly was abolished. The finest goldwork was

74

"The Garden of Armida" wallpaper, 1854, shown at the Universal Exposition, Paris, 1855
Edouard Muller (1823-1876), designer
Desfossé et Karth (1851-1948), manufacturer
Block-printed paper
Musée des Arts Décoratifs, Paris

peaceful celebrations as industrial exhibitions; the next was not to take place until twelve years later, on the initiative of Louis XVIII's Interior Minister, Comte Decazes, who urged on his sovereign the organization of a new exposition to underline the blessings of peace restored. After the scintillating display of industrial strength under the Empire in 1806, the object now was clearly to demonstrate the benefits of new legislation, the "progress of the exact sciences" and their implications for industry: "We do not owe the superiority of these industrial products solely to the intelligence, energy and tenacity of their manufacturers; it is due, no less,

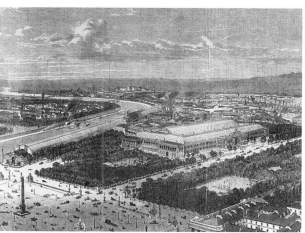

75

View of the Universal Exposition, Paris, 1855
Engraving, published in *The Illustrated London News*, September 29, 1855
Cooper-Hewitt Museum, New York, Kubler Collection

76
**Interior of the
Universal Exposition
building, London,
1862**
Engraving, published in
*Cassel's Illustrated
Exhibitor*, London, 1862
Cooper-Hewitt Museum
Library, New York

to the inventive genius of artists who have invented new machines, simplified the laborer's task, improved dyestuffs, and perfected weaving."[12]

Three expositions were held under the Restoration: those of 1819, 1823, and 1827. In 1819, 1,662 participants displayed more than 6,000 objects or, more precisely, products, on the ground floor of the Louvre. The number of participants dwindled to 1,642 in 1823 but swelled again, to 1,695, in 1827. The expositions lasted progressively longer—two months rather than the original five weeks—and were held always at the same time of year, August, September, and early October.

The industrial exposition had become an institution, but it was intended to celebrate technical advances rather than creative art, which

VIEW OF THE NAVE FROM THE EASTERN DOME, PREVIOUS TO THE INAUGURATION FESTIVAL ON MAY-DAY.

77
**Ewer and basin,
displayed at the
Universal Exposition,
London, 1862**
Joseph-Théodore Deck
(1823-1891)
Earthenware
Musée des Arts
Décoratifs, Paris

was now in a crisis of stylistic revival: first of classical antiquity, then, taking a cue from the Romantic novel, of the Middle Ages, which spurred a renewed interest in jewelry. There was, of course, no lack of personalities to impose their individual styles on the production of the times: Jacob Desmalter and his son Alphonse Jacob, Jean-Jacques Werner, Bellangé, and François Beaudry all helped to develop the "Restoration" style, characterized by the use of light native woods and inlays of exotic hardwoods, and shapes that, with the passage of time, lost their stiff outlines and were enriched by a return to the diversity of furniture types characteristic of the Ancien Régime. Porcelain makers, no longer under the shadow of the Sèvres monopoly, competed with glassmakers for pride of place on the

tabletop, and in 1827 the Baccarat exhibit evinced far greater significance and originality than those of the Le Creusot and Choisy-le-Roi factories.

The invention of the Jacquard loom, and of mechanical printing from a pattern on the roller rather than the plate, along with the development of chemical dyes, brought about a transformation in the manufacture of silks, printed fabrics, and wallpaper at precisely the moment when domestic demand was soaring. A new section appeared in descriptions of Restoration expositions: "Domestic Economy," including both lighting and heating appliances. Comfort had become a manufactured product.

Expositions now formed a competitive arena in which manufacturers were pitted against each other; the award of a medal sent an important message about the product to both domestic and foreign consumers. The royal factories—Sèvres, Gobelins, Savonnerie, Beauvais—were represented but "abstained from a contest for which their special situation endowed them with unfair advantages."[13] These advantages included equipment and a sophistication that set them above their competitors, even if some producers might set out to rival Sèvres porcelain (as did Nast) or Savonnerie carpets. In 1819, the jury singled out a carpet from the Sallaindrouze factory located at 3 rue des Vieilles-Andriettes, in Paris, as "equal in its weaving and in the brilliancy of its colors" to those from the royal manufacture.[14]

Under the July Monarchy, Louis XVIII's four-year cycle was replaced by an exposition in the spring of every fifth year; this was the decision of Louis-Philippe, who directed his Commerce Minister, M. Thiers, to introduce an executive order dated October 4, 1833, fixing the opening of the eighth exposition for May 1, 1834, on the Place de la Concorde.[15] As before, exhibits were submitted

French industry and from which he drew some interesting conclusions. Despite the generally favorable impression that he shared with other visitors, he deplored the hubbub in the two most popular pavilions, those devoted to machinery and to the fine arts: "It is a real hurly-burly.... The Exposition should not be reduced to the status of a grand bazaar, where manufacturers are free to come to make each other's, or the public's, better acquaintance. Nor should it be a showplace where

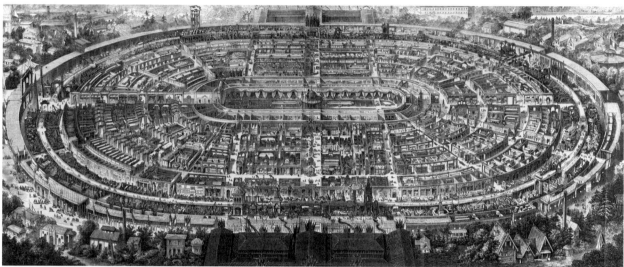

to a two-tier jury, the first appointed by the prefect of each department, the second, the central jury, commissioned to pass on "the relative merits of the objects exhibited" and to propose awards.

Here we encounter for the first time a phenomenon that was to be reiterated in the universal expositions of the second half of the century. Products were distributed among four temporary pavilions built on the central spaces of the Place de la Concorde, more or less according to classification by type and technology. Machinery, tools, metals, and fuels were in the first pavilion; chemicals and their derivatives such as wallpaper, glass, and clothing, in the second. Textiles and their raw materials had a pavilion to themselves — not surprisingly, in light of their importance to previous expositions, particularly the first, in 1798. The luxury trades, grouped together in the fourth pavilion, were: bronze, goldwork, jewelry, cabinetmaking, carpets, porcelains, and crystal, along with musical and scientific instruments, firearms, and lighting devices.

The overall effect was an assessment of scientific progress and its impact on industry since 1827, and an impressive one it was, notwithstanding the Revolution of 1830 and the accompanying economic crisis. How far did it show up in the "useful arts"? Here we may turn to a work by Stéphane Flachat written during the exposition, which he regarded as an audit of the condition of

Silverware exhibited by Christofle & Cie at the Universal Exposition, Paris, 1867
Musée
Bouilhet-Christofle, Paris

a few enthusiasts may come to study the products of industry.... The Exposition must be a national celebration, and as such, it must present the moral and useful character befitting the progress of ideas and manners."[16]

For the first time a contemporary complained that an exposition had fallen short of the goals that the public had the right to expect: useful instruction combined with "lively entertainment." It was also the first time that questions were raised about a "style of the times." Not only were the objects on display all jumbled together but, he complained, so were the show's aesthetic principles: "...where are the styles, where are the schools, where are the masters? Are we here in the Greek, or the Roman, or the Gothic? Are we recapitulating the style of the Renaissance, or of Louis XIV, or of Louis XV, or of the Empire? Have we a style of our own?"[17]

The "useful arts" were in the course of becoming "applied arts." Beginning in 1789, the term "product" was applied to everyday objects no less than luxury articles, and this usage was charged with significance. It reflected the concern of the organizers of this new type of fair to encourage the participation of craftsmen and to help them in assimilating the discoveries of science and adopting new technologies. Here began the debate on the role of art in industry. Flachat's conclusion was, "Art today is disorganized: industry makes use of it to serve its own needs, and waits for it to acknowledge the laws of industrial economics." But, in fact, the moment Flachat heralded was not yet at hand; not until the birth of the Werkbund in 1907 and the Bauhaus in 1919 in Germany, or later, in France, of the Union des Artistes Modernes in 1929, would industrial design be able finally to disengage itself from the

conscious imitation of earlier idioms. First it was necessary to accept the machine as a true extrapolation of the hand tool, and to accept the equation of material with form with function.

In 1834 the machine was new, the effect of the scientific advances of a society in the throes of change. Flachat, like the comte de Laborde a few years later,[18] imputed to the dominant middle class the responsibility for "this new hesitancy, this tiresome uncertainty as to form, this anarchy in the field of design" that characterizes "the industry of fine arts." Luxury "has ensconced itself" among the privileged classes and "the superfluous is big business"; while "those newly arrived at the pleasures of prosperity...have not yet reached the point where, for better or worse, they can leave their stamp on the history of art, determining its forms and fixing its preferences." These new "consumers" (thus early do we encounter a modern concept!) had not yet, he believed, exhausted "the possibilities of usefulness, of the *comfortable*...beauty has not yet presented itself to them as a need." The response of manufacturers to the prevailing uncertainty of "taste" is to seek to satisfy "*all tastes.*"[19]

Cabinetmaking in particular demonstrated "the uncertainty, nay, the anarchy that prevailed throughout the applied arts. One could encounter every period from Chinese to Imperial; every style from Greek and Renaissance to a style, as yet unnamed, that some have sought to dub the *comfortable style.* . . ." Along with stylistic vacillation there was a renewed vogue for exotic woods, particularly mahogany and palisander, that troubled

Silver dressing table and accessories exhibited at the Universal Exposition, Paris, 1867
Christofle & Cie, manufacturer
Engraving, published in *The Illustrated Catalogue of the Universal Exhibition*, August, 1868
Cooper-Hewitt Museum Library, New York

THE PARIS UNIVERSAL EXHIBITION.

82
**Silver dressing table
exhibited at the
Universal Exposition,
Paris, 1867**
Emile-Auguste Reiber
(1826-1893), designer
Albert-Ernest
Carrier-Belleuse
(1824-1887), modeler of
the caryatids
Gustave-Joseph Chéret
(1838-1894), modeler of
the ornaments
Christofle & Cie,
manufacturer
Silver, silver gilt, gold,
lapis lazuli, jasper
Musée des Arts
Décoratifs, Paris

Flachat. It must be remembered that native woods came into favor as a result of the Continental Blockade of 1807. What, Flachat asked, was to be done in the event of another war? And what would become of the workers in the furniture industries? Some exhibitors continued to use native woods; they included Jean-Jacques Werner, and Chenavard, who, in our author's eyes, had the additional merits of a partiality for the Middle Ages (a style of indigenous French origin) and a desire to make the production of furniture a true industry, from which the people at large might also benefit.

Eclecticism was not confined to furniture; it was to be found everywhere, in textiles, and in Jacob Petit's porcelains, as well as in the crystal of Baccarat and Saint-Louis. These two establishments exhibited pressed glassware, manufactured by a process very popular in the United States that "put crystal within the reach of the middle-class consumer." The fashion for fine faïence and earthenware reflected the growth of the domestic market. But the French factories of Montereau, Creil, Gien, or Choisy could not compete in quality, still less in price, with British products. At the time that Flachat was writing, French industry

protected itself from foreign competition by prohibition. Flachat, nevertheless, was among those who could imagine the advantage that a lowering of trade barriers could confer on domestic producers. As a faithful disciple of Adam Smith, he bewailed "the absence of the division of labor," which he saw as "one of our industrial shortcomings."

The July Monarchy, following Louis-Philippe's five-year cycle, staged two more expositions of the products of French industry before the Revolution of 1848: in 1839 and 1844. They were moved westward in the city, to the same Carré de Marigny on the Champs-Elysées where the Palace of Industry would be built for the Universal Exposition of 1855. They aspired ever higher, and the swelling enrollment of exhibitors — 3,381 in 1839 and 3,960 in 1844 — resulted in a change in the composition and functions of the central jury under the presidency of Baron Thénard, who was also president of the Société d'Encouragement à l'Industrie Nationale founded by Chaptal in 1802. The jury was now divided into commissions specialized according to product type: fabrics, metals and minerals, agricultural tools, musical and scientific instruments, chemicals, and domestic arts. Directly involved with the domestic arts was the Fine Arts Commission, presided over by the architect Fontaine; ceramic art was under Brongniart, director of the royal factory at Sèvres; and other arts came under the chemist Chevreul, director of dyestuffs at the royal Gobelins factory.

The Fine Arts Commission dealt with stained glass, bronze decorations, and furniture ornaments, all kinds of jewelry, all the crafts of bookmaking, cabinetmaking, and joining, but neither painting nor sculpture, which had their own annual salon at the Louvre. The Ceramics Commission (styled "Pottery Commission" in 1844) had jurisdiction over earthenware, glass, and enamel. Wallpaper and clothing accessories fell into the catchall category of "other arts." Here we have the beginnings of the "classes" (sections) of future universal expositions, which would also inspire the classifications of the decorative arts museums founded in England, France, Germany, and Austria in the hope of throwing some light on the confused state of the applied arts.

The growing diversity of the exhibits was at first a trial to the newly specialized juries. Their criteria were firmly handed down to them by the Minister of Agriculture and Commerce, who reserved to himself the direction of "these solemn occasions,"

which bring together "all the productive elements in the country," thus guaranteeing "an increase in employment." The juries were to consider "the products' nature," their "quality," and their "commercial and industrial value": the yardsticks were thus utility and cost-effectiveness. The directive dated December 15, 1843, which laid down the functions of the juries, cautioned them against the tendency of certain manufacturers "to create exhibition pieces at vast expense." It was the intention of the sponsors that the everyday should receive more attention than "the extraordinary."[20]

The official reports and the award citations indicate that the last two expositions under the July Monarchy presented an accurate picture of the state of French industry—attesting to encouraging scientific advance, but also to an inability to put the machine to work on designs that would make full use of its capacities. Indeed, the potential of the machine remained largely unexploited, despite the triumphant paeans of the official reporters.

The Second Republic, offspring of the 1848 Revolution, honored the undertakings of Louis-Philippe and in l849 mounted the eleventh exposition. Here agriculture made its first appearance, as well as a range of Algerian products: chemicals, marble, minerals, fabrics, silks, and so on. Charles Dupin, presiding over the jury,

83 84
Pair of candelabra, 1873
Christofle & Cie
Silvered and gilded copper and bronze, cloisonné enamel
Musée
Bouilhet-Christofle, Paris

inaugurated a special section for the work of Parisian industry, thus emphasizing both the superiority of Paris as "the metropolis of our most sophisticated industries and our most exquisite craftsmanship," and the feat of endurance whereby such industries had been able to survive the Revolution of 1848.

It appears that there was serious discussion of opening the exposition to "products of all kinds from all nations." According to the comte de Laborde, the minister Thouret pondered "a Universal exposition of Art and Industry. But the February Government, while it had survived and may well have been inured to political upheaval, turned tail before an upheaval of the cotton, carpet, ceramics, and glass industries. Creil and Baccarat, Mulhouse and Saint-Gobain, uttered loud lamentations; the great corporations insisted that if Britain, Switzerland, and Belgium were allowed to exhibit in France it would be all up with them and they would not exhibit themselves."[21]

On January 3, 1850, a decree from Queen Victoria announced to the whole world that "a Royal Commission had been formed, under the presidency of Prince Albert, to organize a universal exposition for May 1, 1851, in the capital of England, where are to be exhibited the products of the arts and industry."[22]

UNIVERSAL EXPOSITIONS

The Great Exhibition of 1851 sought to be truly universal and to assimilate the fine arts —

architecture, sculpture, and engraving — into industrial arts categories. Painting was excluded on the grounds that "it deals in orders of studies, subjects and feelings that are remote from industry." The comte de Laborde, representing France in London, tells of his fruitless quest in the studios: "...nowhere did I meet with understanding.... Art is not industry, our artists told me; what have we to do with a bazaar?" He encountered the same reaction at the Institut, where the "old quarrel between arts and trades flared up again."[23]

The Crystal Palace in which the Great Exhibition was housed, itself a shining example of the alliance between art and industry, contributed much to the event's success and influence. As for the exhibits, they asserted helter-skelter the revivalist trends in each country: the fifteenth century Renaissance in Italy, the medieval Gothic in England, the styles of Louis XV and of the Renaissance in France. Exhibits bearing witness to technological inventiveness were limited to the bentwood chairs of Michael Thonet from Austria, English papier-mâché furniture, and swivel chairs from the American Chair Company of New York.

The industrial arts were at a standstill — this was visible in the domestic exhibitions under the July Monarchy, and even more so in the limelight of the international competitions that alternated among the world's capitals until 1900, engendering a frenzy of imitation that ended only with the advent of Art Nouveau. New departures, and violent reactions to them, were frequent. When, in England and France, the first museums of

**Baccarat glassware
exhibited at the
Universal Exposition,
Paris, 1878**
Baccarat Archives, Paris

87

**Ceramics exhibited at
the Universal
Exposition, Paris,
1878**
Published in *L'Album de
l'exposition 1878*, Paris
Musée de la Faïenceries
de Gien

decorative art were opened not only to the public
view but to students and craftsmen as study
collections, the result was a polemic: the falsity and
mediocrity of everyday objects were blamed on the
machine. In 1861, William Morris led a movement
encouraging a return to handicrafts, of which he
saw the best examples in the art of the Middle
Ages. The movement, formally christened in 1888
"The Arts and Crafts Exhibition Society," evolved to
a less radical posture, and accepted the need to
come to terms with the modern world. The
interwoven strands of a complex period can be
traced in the development of the Arts and Crafts
movement, divided as it was between the return to
handicrafts that ultimately led to Art Nouveau and

the adoption of techniques that presaged the
coming of industrial design.

The first universal expositions oscillated between
two capitals: London in 1851 and 1862, Paris in
1855 and 1867. Then the scene changed, to Vienna
in 1873 and Philadelphia in 1876, the centennial
year of American independence. The French came
to Philadelphia, and there encountered the
"American Renaissance," with its great industries,
powerful press, and independent women with their
own pavilion! Paris (or more properly, France,
since these were official occasions) returned to the
fray every eleven years, in 1878, 1889, and 1900.

At universal expositions, which take all human
activity as their province, the industrial arts enjoyed
a special preeminence for reasons that can readily
be imagined. They were aesthetic in nature, having
to do with the need to develop new forms and
decorative styles adapted to contemporary
techniques of production. They also had a social
significance: industry was altering the balance
between town and country, drawing toward the
great cities the labor force it required. Housing
was needed for the new proletariat, and the right
goods to sell to the new consumers. One gallery
of the 1855 Exhibition, under the auspices of the
Société d'économie charitable de Paris, was
devoted to "Domestic Economy"; by 1867 it had
become the famous "Group X," where the exhibits

were "carefully chosen with a view to improving the physical and moral condition of the masses."[24] The bourgeoisie of the Second Empire, obsessed as they were with luxury wares, could thus assuage a guilty conscience.

It was the luxury trades that loomed largest at Napoleon III's two expositions. In 1855, Christofle, Sèvres, and Gobelins drew crowds to the rotunda of the Palais de l'Industrie, where their products were displayed alongside the Crown Jewels. In 1867, the galleries displaying Christofle table settings and the exhibits of the jewelers Froment-Meurice and de Fannières were among the most popular. This, according to the report of the international jury on Group III, was out of keeping with the "considerations of art in its industrial applications."[25] These observations dealt severely with artists, manufacturers, and customers.

Garde-Meuble must be opened to the public so that "our artists may study the almost unknown masterpieces of a bygone age housed in that institution." Guichard's reflections and suggestions were incorporated into the program of the Union Centrale des Arts Appliqués à l'Industrie of which he was president.[26] They also inspired the Museum of the History of Labor, housed in the Galerie du Palais, built in 1867 on the Champ de Mars by the architect Frédéric Le Play, with the creed that the creative arts could be rejuvenated only through the study, indeed the imitation, of the masterpieces of the past.

The remedies proposed ran counter to the essential purpose — the development of a contemporary style — and total confusion ensued. The presence of Japan at the 1867 Exposition suggested a new direction, which artists and

88
Case for liqueur bottles exhibited at the Universal Exposition, Paris, 1878
Cristalleries de Baccarat
Glass, metal
Musée des Arts Décoratifs, Paris

It is no longer fitting for the industrial arts to "live on the capital bequeathed by our forefathers." Such copies, easy to make and attractive, are not appropriate to their purpose; they reflect "a foolish fashion" and the "compulsion to sell that has taken possession of, and corrupted, the manufacturers." The degenerate taste of the consumer was, in the opinion of the writer Ernest Guichard, one of the main reasons for "the pretentious insipidity and disingenuous opulence" of so many of the exhibits. The remedy must be education at all levels: of future consumers in the high schools, of workers in the schools of fine arts. The collections of the

craftsmen were the more willing to follow in that it coincided with two contemporary vogues: "Orientalism," which had done much to restore esteem for handicrafts, and naturalist (more specifically, of the French soil) "Gothicism." The tenets of Japanese art included a lively sense of the value of everyday objects, a technical approach that left room for imperfections of form, and a repertory of ornament derived from nature. With a strong inherent tradition and deep respect for the craftsman and his work, Japanese art attained an authentic perfection of its own. The Japanese participation in the universal exposition held in

89
**View of the Universal
Exposition grounds
with the new Eiffel
Tower, Paris, 1889**
George-Felix Garen
(born 1854)
Etching
Cooper-Hewitt Museum,
New York,
Picture Collection

industrial setting. Artists in glass, for example, rarely produced their own designs: those of Eugène Rousseau were made at the Clichy plant belonging to the Appert brothers, while Emile Gallé, who had been an apprentice at the Meysenthal glassworks, conceived new techniques, designs, and decorations but did not actually make the pieces that bear his signature. He thought of himself rather as a sort of chief executive.

The end of the fashion for all kinds of decorative art came at the end of the 1870s. The gulf between industrial art and handicrafts widened yet further as manual work attracted even such painters and sculptors as Gauguin, Levy-Dhurmer,

France in 1878 was more extensive than it had been in 1867, and there were now distinct traces of *Japonisme*. By 1878, divergent trends in the domestic arts could clearly be seen: industry imitated and copied, always referring back to historical styles; craftsmen found their identity through a recapitulation of the Japanese experience and a rediscovery of national tradition.

The return of the craftsman was evident first (and for a long time only) in the field of ceramics, beginning with the Japanese and Korean wares exhibited in 1878, and with the work of such pioneers as Ziegler and Avisseau in the years before 1850. Thus there grew up a ceramic studio art practiced by independent craftsmen who threw or molded their wares by hand, and themselves undertook the risky business of firing, preferring the natural material and glazes to painted decoration. Like Chaplet and Delaherche, they set up shop in and around Paris, while others sought out centers long associated with ceramics such as Beauvaisis, Puisaye, and Haut-Berry. The vogue for ceramic work was so great that Jean Carriès gave up his career as a sculptor and opened a pottery studio at Saint-Amand-en-Puisaye, while Gauguin went to Chaplet's studio to make pots—which sold even more poorly than his paintings.

Other crafts were mostly practiced in an

90
Two views of the Universal Exposition, Paris, 1900: the Château d'Eau and the Alexander Bridge with the Petit Palais in the background
Cooper-Hewitt Museum, New York, Picture Collection

91
The antique furniture gallery at the Universal Exposition, Paris, 1900
Cooper-Hewitt Museum, New York, Picture Collection

92
Vase, exhibited at the Universal Exposition, Paris, 1889
Ernest Chaplet (1835-1909)
Porcelain
Musée des Arts Décoratifs, Paris

and the Nabis, a reality reflected in the 1889 Exposition.

The *industries diverses* were given a place of honor in the Palace that ran parallel to the Galerie des Machines at the foot of the Champ de Mars. As

l'Art Nouveau on his return to Paris. Opened in December 1895, its inaugural catalogue is an honor roll of the greatest artists of the age — painters, sculptors, graphic artists, glassmakers, ceramists, and architects.

After the Centennial Exposition of 1889, that of 1900 in Paris was to "constitute the synthesis, and represent the philosophy, of the nineteenth century.... Every branch of human activity will benefit equally from drawing up this balance sheet, which will illustrate the material and moral conditions of contemporary life."[27] This ambitious, if slightly moralistic, aspiration was at variance with contemporary reactions to the exposition. The

usual, Gobelins and Sèvres were conspicuous under the central dome. Emile Gallé's booth was flanked by Haviland porcelains, and silks from Lyons were to be seen in the 100-foot Galerie d'Honneur. The thematic galleries, identified for visitors by their symbolic porticos, were open to manufacturers as well as to independent craftsmen. A contemporary style was beginning to emerge, though eclecticism was still in favor and antiques were newly, and greatly, in fashion. It was a contest that has yet to abate.

As the century wound down, expositions were held at various cities. In 1893, Chicago commemorated the discovery of America by Christopher Columbus, and European visitors discovered a new civilization, based on the steel-framed skyscrapers that William LeBaron Jenney had developed after the city's disastrous fire in 1871. It was here, too, that the dealer S. Bing discovered Louis Comfort Tiffany and his company, which would inspire him to found the Galeries de

exposition reiterated a point first raised by observers in 1867: "Too many visitors will be distracted by the delights of the park.... What is intended to round out the great exposition runs the risk of detracting from its essential identity; it could become a plaything rather than an instrument of edification."[28] The cross between a "bazaar and a fairground" would continue and gather momentum to the point where "industry is

EXPOSITION UNIVERSELLE & INTERNATIONALE
DE St. LOUIS (ÉTATS-UNIS)
DU 30 AVRIL AU 30 NOVEMBRE 1904. 73468

DE PARIS A St. LOUIS
6 JOURS DE STEAMER
ET 1 JOUR DE CHEMIN DE FER

IMPORTANCE DE L'EXPOSITION

PHILADELPHIE	1876	95 HECTARES		CHICAGO	1893	240 HECTARES
PARIS	1900	135 HECTARES		St. LOUIS	1904	500 HECTARES

IMP. F. CHAMPENOIS . PARIS

97
Reinforced concrete "trees" exhibited at the International Exposition of Modern Industrial and Decorative Arts, Paris, 1925
Robert Mallet-Stevens (1886-1945) and Joël Martel
Musée des Arts Décoratifs, Paris

no more than a pretext; the real purpose is entertainment."[29]

In one of the essays from *Paris capitale du xixème siècle*, the German writer Walter Benjamin (1892–1940) analyzes this "merchandise cult," "merchandise as fetish" and the "glittering entertainment surrounding it," which are the themes of the universal expositions of the nineteenth century. He points out that they "wholly modify the exchange value of consumer goods, creating a new framework in which utility as a measure of value is relegated to second place."[30]

By the turn of the century, when both people and goods could travel more and more readily, there was even some questioning of the argument for universal expositions: "All markets are today one great worldwide market. As to products, they are no sooner made known than they are sold and often copied at all ends of the earth."[31] This somewhat jaded observation is not surprising considering that its author was the deputy Jules Méline, leader of the protectionist movement in 1892.

As for decorative arts they had become, in the words of the painter Maurice Denis, "a precinct of snobbery," torn between the authenticity of Art Nouveau, which was untrammeled by any reference to the past, and a confusion of pastiche on the other. At the same time there arose a "Faubourg Saint-Antoine" corruption of Art Nouveau, which

lured away a part of its following. Art Nouveau, since it came into being, has provoked two opposing schools of thought that persist to this day. The writer Paul Morand thought that "taste had never been so debased." He could find nothing to admire in the decorative arts of 1900; they were "the outward manifestation of an age endowed with great resources of money, technology, materials and labor, but capable of creating only the pretentious, the delirious, the anarchical.... It is a tentacular style of raw, ill-fired pots, of forced, drawn-out, sprawling lines, of senselessly distorted materials...."[32] Le Corbusier, unlike most of his contemporaries in the 1920s, recognized the revolutionary significance of the movement, even though it ran counter to his own aesthetic principles: "Around 1900 came the magnificent gesture of Art Nouveau. We stripped

98
Brooch exhibited at the International Exposition of Modern Industrial and Decorative Arts, Paris, 1925
Lucien Hirtz (1864-1928), designer
Bréthiot and Bisson, carvers, for Boucheron
Gold, lapis lazuli, onyx, jade, enamel, coral, pastes
Collection Boucheron, Paris

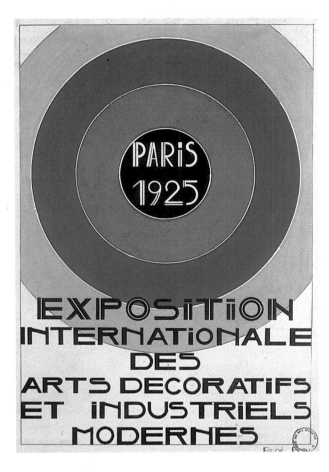

off the hand-me-downs of an outworn culture....In Paris, in 1900, could be seen a dizzying array of objects whose shapes, eschewing the salutary discipline of straight lines, wrung the inherent vitality out of their substance. But it was a magnificent effort, a true act of courage, a great feat of boldness, a real revolution.... People began to speak of 'Decorative Art,' and the battle was joined: fine arts, lesser arts. Two camps."[33]

THE TWENTIETH CENTURY

A debate on the decorative arts ushered in the first decade of the twentieth century. In 1901, the Société des Artistes Décorateurs gathered around a painter, Guillaume Dubufe, a sculptor, Louis Carrier-Belleuse, and a graphic artist, illustrator, and furniture designer, Eugène Grasset — all "true workmen in the arts," menaced by the reactionary forces intent on crushing Art Nouveau.
In the words of Raymond Koechlin, who wrote in the *Gazette des Beaux-Arts* at the time of the opening of the 1925 Exposition des Arts Décoratifs in Paris:

All the special interests threatened by innovation banded together; those manufacturers (the great majority) who had remained faithful to their Renaissance buffets and pseudo-eighteenth-century *bergères* were unhappy with the prospect of soon replacing their outmoded product lines, so they declared war on the "young lunatics" whom they saw as their eventual competitors. The antique dealers moved up in support: what would become of the trade in contemporary "antiques" if totally new designs were to come into fashion? It would be prudent to divert collectors in advance, and easy to persuade them that — just as with "blue chips" in the stock market — their interest would best be served by buying seasoned, old-line

merchandise that was sure to keep its value, rather than the modern stuff that was no sooner in fashion than out again. With the assistance of some gossip in the press, these voices prevailed; little by little the public turned away, discouraging the innovators who needed a measure of speedy success if they were to persist in their innovation. The Exposition of 1900, where the artists had looked for the triumph of their cause, ended in stalemate.[34]

The stakes were high. Art Nouveau was now to be confronted not with an art of pastiche based on myriad past styles, but with an opponent more formidable, because authentic — the real antique; the conflict continues to this day.

The history of the decorative arts in the twentieth century is framed within a twofold dialectic where creation evolves into the opposition of old and new. Its platform is the Salon and the international exposition, which after 1900 adhered to a thematic principle rather than striving for a universality for which there could no longer be a justification.

From 1904 on, the young Société des Artistes Décorateurs organized annual exhibitions in, and sometimes outside, France, not only to familiarize the public with its work but to bring pressure on industry to produce artists' designs. The idea of an international competition originated in 1909, but the object was essentially national: to recover for France the leadership lost to Italy in 1902 at the exhibition of Turin and to affirm the primacy of a French style — a task all the more pressing after the exhibition of the Deutsche Werkbund at the

Grand Palais in 1910. The *Style Nouveau* was to continue "the French tradition, it should be a natural evolution from our last traditional style, that of Louis-Philippe."[35]

After several postponements on account of the Great War, the Exposition Internationale des Arts Décoratifs et Industriels Modernes opened in Paris in 1925. It was a celebration of the decorative art that had evolved fifteen years earlier from movements that originated between 1905 and 1909: Fauvism, Cubism, and Futurism. Firmly rooted in the bourgeois tradition of nineteenth-century France, it steadfastly ignored the social and economic changes of the postwar world. Some of the exhibitors, recognizing the social changes at work and the impact of modern technology, aspired to the declared purpose of the event—to encourage a "social art." But they were few, and of marginal import; Le Corbusier's Pavilion de L'Esprit Nouveau was concealed behind palisades on the day of the official opening. The differences among

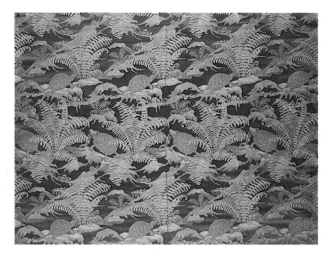

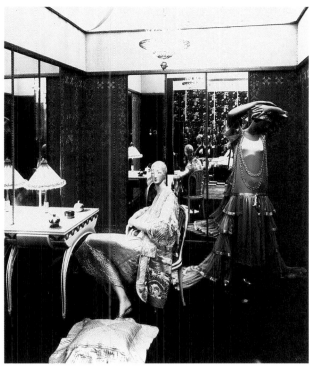

103
"Earth," "Air," "Fire," "Water" woven fabrics exhibited at the International Exposition of Modern Industrial and Decorative Arts, Paris, 1925
Mlle Clairinval, designer
Tassinari and Chatel, Lyon, manufacturer
Silk and rayon
Cooper-Hewitt Museum, New York, Gift of Susan Dwight Bliss, 1931-1-1, 2, 7, 14

104
Artist's dressing room exhibited at the International Exposition of Modern Industrial and Decorative Arts, Paris, 1925
Jeanne Lanvin (1867-1946) and Armand-Albert Rateau (1882-1938), designers
Musée des Arts Décoratifs, Paris

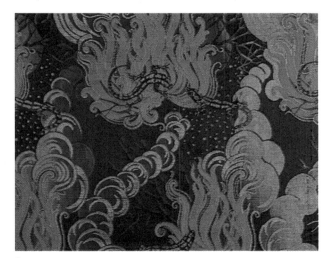

the Artistes Décorateurs themselves were revealed within the "French Embassy" program, which, according to the journalist Marie Dormoy, confronted the "colorists and decorators" like Henri Rapin with the "engineers and constructors," one of whom was Pierre Chareau. No sooner was the 1925 Exposition opened than it provoked attacks centered on the term "decorative." "Decorative art," the architect Auguste Perret announced to Marie Dormoy, "should be abolished. I'd like to know who first brought together the words 'decorative' and 'art'; it's a monstrosity. Where there is real art, there is no need for decoration."[36] For Le Corbusier, who published in 1925 a collection of essays on *L'Art décoratif d'aujourd'hui* that had appeared a year earlier in the periodical *L'Esprit Nouveau*, "decorative art is equipment, beautiful equipment."[37]

The debate on decorative art yielded to the battle on ornamentation: at the Exposition of 1937

105
Festival hall of the Grand Palais at the International Exposition of Modern Industrial and Decorative Arts, Paris, 1925
Louis Süe (1875-1968), architect
Jaulmes, decorator
Cooper-Hewitt Museum, New York, Picture Collection

106
Interior of the "Pavillon de l'Esprit Nouveau" at the International Exposition of Modern Industrial and Decorative Arts, Paris, 1925
Le Corbusier (1887-1965) and Pierre Jeanneret (1896-1967), architects
Musée des Arts Décoratifs, Paris

107
Exterior of the "Pavillon de l'Esprit Nouveau" at the International Exposition of Modern Industrial and Decorative Arts, Paris, 1925
Le Corbusier (1887-1965) and Pierre Jeanneret (1896-1967), architects
Cooper-Hewitt Museum, New York, Picture Collection

the Union des Artistes Modernes (UAM) was pitted against the champions of national tradition. On one side was a group of architects, decorators, and artists, convinced of the need to devise forms properly adapted to their function and sensitive to the demands of the contemporary world: "Beauty is to be found, above all, in form. We love balance, logic, purity. In our homes we prefer light to shadow, bright colors to somber hues. We seek to offer man's eye, and his spirit, some relief from the taxing haste and confusion of our daily hecticness."[38] The UAM had their own pavilion at the Paris Exposition of 1937, an international occasion that, having vainly sought to revive the concept of "decorative arts" after the lapse of a decade, chose the more ambitious theme of "art and technique in the modern world." "Art and technique is a good program," wrote Le Corbusier on his return from New York in 1935. "It has aroused expectations. Is the door to the future now to be thrown open? Not so soon; there are some state funerals to be conducted first. We shall see baldachinos erected to Art and Technique...." Just before the exhibition's opening Robert Mallet-Stevens, president of the association, still believed that the exposition as a whole would fulfill the hope for a new way of life, accessible to all. "The 1937 Exposition is the Union des Artistes Modernes—our ideas, our effort, our spirit,

modified and often distorted but none the less always there."[39] This was the theme of G. H. Pingusson's pavilion, taking the form of a bazaar of everyday objects; it presaged the UAM's first postwar project, the 1949 exposition *Formes Utiles: Objets de notre temps.*

The subtitle of the 1937 Exposition might well have been "Ornament: For or Against?" In the face of the UAM's resolute opposition to the decoration that "camouflages"—to use Le Corbusier's term—stood the exponents of a "modern art" where "reason and beauty can join hands," where "planes

are enlivened by relief and surfaces are rounded."[40] In such elegant periphrases, official art concealed its true intent: to exalt French nationalism rooted in the eighteenth century.

The 1937 Exposition was the last of such great international occasions mounted in France. There is no place in today's world for these "kermesses" where, during the nineteenth century, industry and amusement park were side by side; we already have Disneyland. The story of "the French at home" must today be culled from art exhibitions: those of the Arts Ménagers until 1984, and those of the Artistes Décorateurs which are regularly reborn according to the current mode. Since it was founded in 1969 at the Musée des Art Décoratifs, the Centre de Création Industrielle (CCI), now a department of the Centre Georges Pompidou, has re-initiated exhibitions of both national and international industrial products.

After World War II the history of "the French at home" oscillated between the constraints of Reconstruction (to which the UAM devoted its program) and the French tradition of the luxury trades, which took over the furnishing of state palaces, embassies, and ocean liners. Individualists, the French were not easily reconciled to postwar reality or to the requirements of industrial production — whether they were called "industrial aesthetics" or simply "design." France still continued to make room for luxury goods and handcrafted objects.

1. All these are historical facts, objectively set out by Pierre Verlet in his indispensable works on the eighteenth century; cf. *L'art du meuble à Paris au XVIIIème siècle* (Paris, 1958).

2. Cf. Michel Vovelle, *La chute de la monarchie, 1787-1792* (Paris, 1972), pp. 133 and 173-174.

3. Alain Plessis, *De la fête impériale au mur des Fédérés 1852-1871* (Paris, 1979), p. 21.

4. *Exposition Universelle de 1851, Travaux de la Commission Française, VIème groupe, XXXème Jury, application des arts à l'industrie, Beaux-Arts, par M. Le comte de Laborde* (Paris, 1856), pp. 197-199.

5. Cf. G.-Roger Sandoz and Jean Guiffrey, *Arts appliqués et Industries d'Art aux expositions* (Paris, 1912), pp. I-II.

6. Walter Benjamin, *Essais, II, 1935-1940*, French ed. (Paris, 1971-83), p. 43.

7. Documents relating to the first expositions of French industry in the Bibliothèque des Arts Décoratifs, case S 159.

8. François de Neufchâteau was twice Minister of the Interior, after a short spell on the Directory following the coup d'état of 18 Fructidor (September 4, 1797), from Thermidor to Fructidor of the year V, and again from Floréal of the year VI to Thermidor of the year VII. He contributed to the recovery of French industry by encouraging, inspiring, and publicizing innovation.

9. Laborde, op. cit., p. 217.

10. Documents relating to the first expositions of French industry in the Bibliothèque des Arts Décoratifs, case S 159.

11. *Notices sur les objets envoyés à l'Exposition des Produits de l'industrie française; rédigées et imprimées par ordre de S.E.M. de Champagny, Ministre de l'Intérieur* (Paris, 1807).

12. Comte Decazes, *Rapport au Roi, April 9, 1819*, in *Rapport du Jury Central sur les Produits de l'industrie française* (Paris, 1819), p. 385.

13. *Exposition de 1827: Rapport du Jury Central sur les Produits de l'industrie française par M. Le Vte Héricart de Thury et M. Migneron* (Paris, 1828), p. 152.

14. *Exposition de 1819: Rapport du Jury Central sur les produits de l'industrie française par M. L. Costaz* (Paris, 1819), p. 149.

15. See *Rapport du Jury Central sur les produits de l'industrie française exposés en 1834, par le Baron Charles Dupin* (Paris, 1836), Vol. I, pp. XLIV and XLV.

16. Stéphane Flachat, *L'industrie: Exposition de 1834,* (Paris, n.d.).

17. Ibid., pp. 33-34

18. Laborde, op. cit., note 4.

19. Flachat, op. cit., p. 35.

20. *Exposition des produits de l'industrie française en 1844. Rapport du Jury Central,* vol. I (Paris, 1844), p. xxii.

21. Laborde, op. cit., p. 233.

22. Ibid., pp. 233-234.

23. Ibid.

24. *Exposition Universelle de 1867 à Paris. Rapports du Jury International publiés sous la direction de Michel Chevalier* (Paris, 1868), Group X, Class 91, pp. 775-776.

25. Ibid., Vol. III, Group III, Classes 14-26, pp. 5-17.

26. Founded in 1864 around the architect-decorator Guichard, the Union Centrale des Beaux-Arts Appliqués à l'Industrie united figures in the world of art, practicing artists, and manufacturers who sought to "develop in France a discipline within the arts which attempts to achieve beauty through utility." In 1882 it merged with the Société du Musée des Arts Décoratifs, founded in 1877, to become the Union Centrale des Arts Décoratifs, with Antonin Proust as president.

27. *Expositions Universelles Internationales de 1900 à Paris, actes organiques* (Paris, June 1896).

28. Victor Fournel, "Voyage à travers l'exposition," in *Le Correspondant* (April and May 1867).

29. Alphonse de Calonne, in *Revue des Deux-Mondes*, January 15, 1895.

30. Benjamin, *Essais,* op. cit., pp. 43-44.

31. Speech by Méline in the Chamber of Deputies, in "débats parlementaires, séance du 16 Mars 1896," *Journal officiel*, March 17, 1896.

32. Paul Morand, *1900* (Paris, 1932), pp. 88-89.

33. Introduction to the first edition of "Le Corbusier et Pierre Jeanneret," from *Œuvre complète 1910-1919* (Zürich, 1929).

34. Raymond Koechlin, "L'Exposition des Arts Décoratifs Modernes. Les premiers efforts de rénovation (1885-1914)," in *Gazette des Beaux-Arts* (Paris, 1925), pp 258-259. Art lover and writer Raymond Koechlin was at this time chairman of the Council of National Museums.

35. André Véra, "Le Nouveau Style," in *L'Art Décoratif* (Paris, 1912), p. 31.

36. Marie Dormoy, "Interview with Auguste Perret on the International Exposition of Decorative Arts," in *L'Amour de l'Art* (May 1925), p. 174.

37. Le Corbusier, *L'art décoratif d'aujourd'hui* (Paris, 1925), p. 79.

38. "Pour l'art moderne cadre de la vie contemporaine," Manifesto of the UAM, 1934.

39. Le Corbusier, *Quand les cathédrales étaient blanches* (Paris, 1937; republished 1965), pp. 123-124.

40. *Exposition Internationale des Arts et Techniques dans la vie moderne* (Paris, 1937), (Imprimerie Nationale), vol. 6, p. 132.

Jean Béraud

SUZANNE TISE

LES GRANDS
MAGASINS

The construction in Paris in 1869 of Au Bon Marché at the intersection of the rue de Rennes, the rue de Babylone, and the rue de Sèvres marked the conclusion of a long process of commercial centralization begun during the second half of the eighteenth century with the *marchand de frivolités*, consolidated in the 1830s and 1840s with the development of the *magasin de nouveautés*, and culminating by the mid-nineteenth century in a modern form of merchandising—the

law of June 14, 1791, changed all that, in order to break the monopolies controlling production and sales (and the political power) held by the corporations. This law determined the abolition of "toute espèce de corporation de citoyens de même état ou profession," signifying that the market could now unify what production had traditionally divided, and that the fragmenting of production could be halted and reunified into a single commercial process with a unified realization of profit.[3] As this new situation developed during the

MAGASIN DE PAPIERS.

department store, or *grand magasin*. This process, however, was neither continuous nor predetermined. It was, rather, the result of an accumulation of various and often contradictory conditions.

The precondition to this revolution in retailing was brought about by Revolutionary legislation.[1] Traditionally, in France, the sale of goods was restricted to two distinctly separate groups: the corporation or guild that manufactured a specific item; and the tradesmen known as *merciers* (stemming from the Latin *merx*, meaning any item subject to commerce). The *merciers* could sell several kinds of merchandise, but were allowed to own only one shop.[2] However, the Le Chapelier

first decades of the nineteenth century, Commerce began to create a society in its image, and Merchandise became its sovereign.

A second factor that would contribute to the conditions under which the *grands magasins* appeared was new forms of financing. The first half of the nineteenth century witnessed the development of a modern structure of banking that would later be perfected during the Second Empire. This new financial system created a novel policy of investment and credit for commercial entrepreneurs, who were now able to compete with new industrial mass production. The department store can thus be considered as "one of the most characteristic forms through which the

114
**Poster: La Maison
Moderne, about 1900**
Maurice Biais
(1875-1929)
J. Minot, printer
Color lithograph
Musée de la Publicité,
Paris

industrial revolution sought expression."[4] Capital organized in widely varied forms of shareholding was behind the construction of the "cathedrals of commerce" that were the *grands magasins*—a capital that even looked for the financial participation of the store employees (however limited) lay at the heart of these "commercial factories," often conceived in the utopian spirit of the ideal city of the Fourieristes and of the socialist rationalism of the Saint-Simonians.[5]

A third essential condition lay in the radical modification of the urban structure of Paris. The centralization of commerce meant the centralization of merchandise and of the buying public. For this, big spaces and high mobility were needed. Paris, during the second half of the nineteenth century, entered into an era of great public works as its old quarters, with their often chaotic network of narrow streets, were opened up to a more rational

form of circulation consisting of wide boulevards organized in straight lines and *ronds-points* (traffic circles) whose starlike dispositions permitted access to many directions.[6] This new form of urbanism offered the more dynamic shopkeepers magnificent possiblities for expansion that the former urban structure had denied them.[7] In addition, after 1828, Paris was served by a system of public transport that would continue to expand as the century progressed and as the working population was pushed toward the suburbs. But people still came to the center of the city to work and to buy. The new routes passed by shops full of merchandise and the display of merchandise inevitably led to the consumption of merchandise.

This is only a brief outline of the essential innovations in modern commerce that brought about the development of the *grands magasins*. Their success, however, was not based solely on these exceptional conditions. It also stemmed from an entirely new phenomenon: a revolution in and manipulation of the behavior of the client.[8] It was no longer the merchandise that came to the client, as had been the case in the past; the client now made a "pilgrimage" to the merchandise.[9]

THE PILGRIMAGE TO THE MERCHANDISE

Customers were drawn to the department stores by publicity. Beginning in 1840, advertising in all its forms was accepted and promoted by Parisian newspapers. The *grands magasins* quickly learned how to use it to promote products, and of course sales, and their methods would become increasingly sophisticated and resourceful between 1900 and 1945.[10] Posters, catalogues, and calendars constituted the most important means by which the department stores attempted to create and direct the buying habits of the public, inducing people to visualize new styles in home decoration, clothing, and personal appearance. Posters advertising the stores could be found in trains, buses, subways, and in the streets. Catalogues seduced and flattered their readers through careful production, painstaking research into settings to present

merchandise, and elegant covers designed by renowned artists and illustrators of the day: Jules Chéret, Adolphe Willette, Paul Iribe, René Vincent, Drian, Cappiello, Brunelleschi, and Jean Carlu, to name just a few.

The catalogues of the *grands magasins* propagated the image of the Parisian bourgeoisie across the nation through their illustrations of the ideal family, the proper way to dress, to decorate the home, and so on, thereby constituting de facto guides to living (*savoir-vivre*) for the middle classes.[11] Further, avant-garde art movements such as Art Nouveau and Cubism were widely diffused by the posters and catalogues published by the department stores. These publications were intended to be works of art in themselves, with their abundant and elegant illustrations, high-quality paper, originality, and typographic innovations. By the 1920s, the department-store catalogue reached its zenith; no expense was spared to dazzle potential customers. The Grands Magasins du Louvre published a catalogue in the form of a fan in 1925, while the Grande Maison du Blanc turned selection and buying into a luxurious experience in catalogues illustrated with Cubist drawings and texts by well-known authors.[12]

All this, of course, transpired before the clients

117
Clock and jewelry shop, rue St. Martin, about 1850, from Edmond Texier, *Tableau de Paris*, vol. 2, Paris, 1853
Wood engraving

118
**House of L. T. Piver,
Perfumer, Paris, 1863**
Bertrand and Chervaux,
illustrators
Wood engraving
Cooper-Hewitt Museum,
New York, Kubler
Collection

120
**Corner view of
Maison du Bon
Marché, Paris, late
19th century**
Cooper-Hewitt Museum,
New York, Picture
Collection

Often the staff had the opportunity to participate in the capital of the enterprise, and in any case they benefited from its social programs, such as employee cafeterias and boardinghouses for unmarried female employees inside the store itself—in sum, a set of circumstances designed to encourage a sacerdotal dedication to the

even entered the store. After they arrived, often on public transport, they were drawn into the giant machine for selling, a metropolis of commerce where they were overwhelmed by a complex commercial strategy: fixed prices, the opportunity to browse, the possibility of returning or exchanging merchandise if it proved unsatisfactory, special exhibitions and weeks devoted to specific items, sales, bridal registers, and hundreds of other innovations. Attention was also devoted to the staff, who were given training, incentives, and above all special bonuses for selling specific merchandise.

merchandise and a modern devotion to the customer.[13]

At the same time, new forms of socialization were being constructed as the old forms of pre-Revolutionary society—corporate and aristocratic—were in the process of disintegrating, and as the bourgeoisie and the new industrial proletariat formed between the civil wars of 1848 and 1871. Walter Benjamin emphasizes just how radical this movement into the collective unconscious of the nineteenth and the twentieth centuries was: "With the birth of the *grands magasins* for the first time in history, consumers began to consider themselves as masses."[14]

businesses through which passed all the most recent frivolities of fashion, from notions to ready-made clothing. The wooden structures seemed more worthy of a country fair than a bourgeois boutique. Nevertheless, it was here that everything started. In the years that separated the end of the First Empire from the beginning of the Second, there are many indications that the Revolutionary spirit born in 1789, and beaten down on the battlefields, still continued in society. In industry and commerce, economic development was in fact very strong, and an entrepreneurial spirit was active at all levels of society.[16] Saint-Simon and other intellectuals of the period

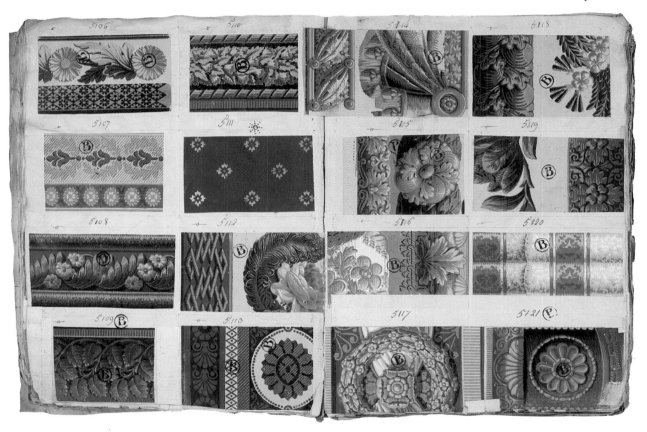

121
Volume of wallpaper samples, 1822-30
Billot, retailer
Block-printed paper
Cooper-Hewitt Museum, New York, Purchase, The Decorative Arts Association at Cooper-Hewitt Museum, and General Funds, 1986-34-2

FROM THE *MARCHAND DE FRIVOLITÉS* TO THE *GRAND MAGASIN*

The process of commercial centralization began in Paris at the Palais-Royal, whose galleries also housed some of Paris's most luxurious boutiques. It was in the Galerie de Pierre of the Palais-Royal, about 1813, that the Escalier de Cristal was founded. One of the most fashionable boutiques selling fine porcelain and crystal, this was the first store to manufacture ornamental objects and furniture in crystal decorated with gilded bronze.[15] The Galeries de Bois, constructed in the gardens of the Palais-Royal in 1784, was less luxurious. "Ce sinistre amas de crottes," as Balzac called it when he visited the Galeries de Bois in the 1830s, was an ensemble of tiny boutiques—a beehive of small

understood this, and it was here that French capitalism took its first steps uniting the country's enterprising spirit, cooperative efforts, individualism, and family structures.

In the 1820s hundreds of *magasins de frivolités*—carrying everything from notions to ready-made goods—lined the quays of Paris. By this time the practice of selling at fixed prices instead of by more traditional bargaining, and the principle of reimbursement for returned merchandise were already established.

It was in this confusion of boutiques between the Galeries de Bois and the shops on the quays that the first commercial innovations were experimented with. The novels of Balzac describe the atmosphere of these boutiques in minute detail. He wrote of the Petit Matelot: It was the first

122
Buildings in the new section of the Faubourg Saint-Denis, Paris, 1869
Bertrand and Lacoste Aîné, illustrators
Cooper-Hewitt Museum, New York, Kubler Collection

123
Delivery wagons, Au Bon Marché, rue Velpeau, Paris, about 1890-1900

establishment of a type which has since become common in Paris, with a greater or lesser profusion of painted signs and floating banners, displays of shawls draped across the pans of scales, neckties arranged on cardboard castles, and hundreds of other theatrical devices or optical illusions. The low prices of all the so-called "novelties" on display at the Petit Matelot won it unprecedented popularity, despite its location in a district less attractive to customers than almost any other in Paris."[17]

In addition to the amazing spectacle of such new riches, something else was being attempted: a direct relationship between commerce and the textile industry. Pierre Parissot, who in 1824 opened the boutique A la Belle Jardinière, introduced mechanized production of die-cut

Paris; and in 1844, A la Chaussée d'Antin. This was not yet the *grand magasin*, but we are close to the point where all these elements would culminate in something new.

The growth of associations, of Saint-Simonian ideology, and after 1848, the influence of Fourier and the cooperative movement were all essential factors contributing to the development of the modern department stores. They are worth examining here in more detail since this ideological impetus was the source of actual experiences that permit us to define the *grand magasin* as the product of a new mass subjectivity.[19] La Ménagère (1850), le Palais d'Auteuil (1862), and above all Les Magasins Réunis (1865-67) represent this cooperative experience in the most direct way.[20] Take the last example. In

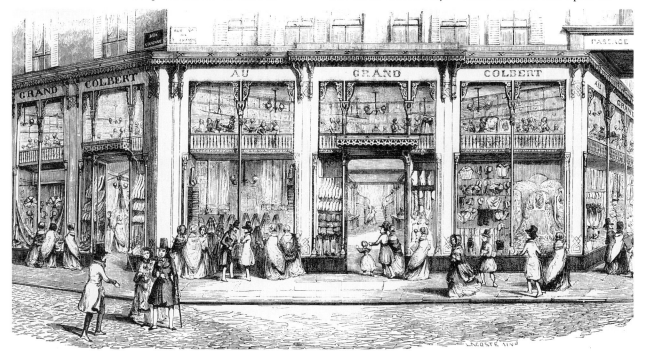

124
Au Grand Colbert, about 1850, from Edmond Texier, *Tableau de Paris*, vol. 2, Paris, 1853
Wood engraving

clothing patterns.[18] In the same year, the sewing machine was invented and rapidly adopted. Parissot managed to develop an industrial production-line system that organized nearly six thousand worker-cutters supplying his Belle Jardinière.

Growing mechanization encouraged a commercial system adequate for the sale of mass-produced goods; throughout the first half of the nineteenth century, textile production and marketing remained closely associated and became factors in the development of the *grands magasins*. During the years of the Restoration and the July Monarchy, numerous new commercial organizations were founded, constructing ever larger stores: in 1825, Le Grand Bazar; in 1827-29, Bazar de l'industrie; in 1829, Bazar de Boufflers; in 1830, Bazar Montesquieu; in 1838, Galeries du commerce et de l'industrie; in 1843, A la Ville de

the large building located in the Place de la République, a group of independent merchants united on the basis of a common commercial policy: fixed prices, to be kept as low as possible. Besides selling those goods necessary to life, there was a higher aim in this enterprise—that of providing merchandise that would further the process of civilization by the moral and spiritual elevation of the masses through the sale of products devoted to comfort, taste, and art. Thus, these "proto-*grands magasins*" would serve a highly democratic function unknown to previous generations: that of placing all sorts of articles within the reach of a broad public, and of satisfying the tastes for elegance and comfort of a new society whose needs and habits were rapidly changing. In addition, the Magasins Réunis offered a new venue for socialization in an interior street

125
Au Printemps, boulevard Haussmann, Paris, 1874
Daudenarde and Varget, illustrators
Wood engraving
Cooper-Hewitt Museum, New York. Kubler Collection

126
Central hall of Au Printemps, Paris, about 1885
E. Alix, illustrator
Wood engraving
Cooper-Hewitt Museum, New York, Kubler Collection

127
Dome of Les Galeries Lafayette, Paris, about 1940

THE *GRAND MAGASIN*: A TOTAL INSTITUTION

The *grands magasins* basically had the ability to make money circulate rapidly. Even more than today, fixed prices at that time were synonymous with low prices. But the relatively low level of retail prices (that is to say, the reduction of profit on single items) was compensated for by speed of turnover and by the large quantities of goods sold. This resulted in high profits that were absolutely extraordinary for the times.[23] Turnover at Au Bon Marché between 1852 and 1863 rose from 450,000

of boutiques that ended in an enclosed garden where customers could stroll and meet one another. Here the designers' explicit intention was to create a permanent universal exposition.

In less than a century, the warren that constituted the Galeries de Bois had become the model for a form of marketing that was extremely dynamic—and also the model for a specific architectural structure. In the shops contemporary with the Galeries de Bois, the customer had been assaulted by the owner as soon as he stepped in the door; in addition, the merchandise was piled up on high shelves separated from the customer by a long counter, entailing a moral obligation to buy after each item had been individually displayed. Prices were capricious, and lengthy bargaining was the inevitable result. The *grands magasins* did away with all that, making goods directly accessible to the customer and thus becoming a veritable *panoptique* of merchandise.

The 1850s and 1860s witnessed experimentation with iron and glass, new architectural materials that permitted new forms—and construction that met the needs for space, light, and ventilation required for large-scale commerce. The triumph of iron and glass permitted a new freedom in planning, substituting masonry walls and columns with lightweight cast-iron supports, and allowed for larger shop windows and glass ceilings so that light and transparency could be exploited to their fullest. Au Coin de la Rue, founded in 1864 in the rue Montesquieu, was the first Paris department store to be built totally with these new materials. It consisted of galleries on three floors, organized around a large central hall, and illuminated through a glass roof. It was to become the prototype for many subsequent stores.[21] Soon afterward, the new Belle Jardinière was built (1866-67) on the Quai aux Fleurs. It housed the production workshops and sales floors in the same building, all set around an illuminated central hall, and including, for the first time, a system of artificial ventilation, and water piped to every floor.[22]

to 7,000,000 francs.[24] This was the key to the fortunes made by the great entrepreneurial visionaries and planners of the second half of the nineteenth century, people like Aristide and Marguerite Boucicaut, Jules Jaluzot, Ernest Cognacq and Louise Jay, who were responsible for founding Au Bon Marché, Au Printemps, and La Samaritaine, respectively.

In *Au Bonheur des Dames* (1883), Emile Zola depicted this financial mechanism in his description of a new and rapidly changing world, a babble of signs controlled by a grand, all-powerful

128
**Reading room at the
Grands magasins du
Louvre, Paris, about
1880**
Cooper-Hewitt Museum,
New York, Kubler
Collection

organizing mechanism as in nature—he even called them "magasins de la Nature." French philosopher Michel Serres expanded on Zola's interpretation even further: "The store is an engine, a machine. It glows, it heats, it burns, and is perceived as doing so by everyone. It consumes and destroys its suppliers, its competitors and the buildings which adjoin it. It consumes, sucks dry and spits out its saleswomen and its customers.... The motor revolves at increasing speed; inventory turnover is faster; retained earnings accumulate and swell the

129
La Samaritaine, Paris, about 1925

130
The Boucicaut stables, quarters for Au Bon Marché livery, Paris, late 19th century

capital that is daily transmuted into new stock—curtain fabrics, umbrellas, children's clothing—and this increment, in turn, accelerates the system further. It is a perfect mechanism for making products, and symbols, go round and round."[25]

In this extraordinary acceleration, all the constituent elements—capital, commercial organization, architectural struture, and the organization of labor—came together in a synthesis that resulted in the exultation of merchandise, the ephemeral, and fashion. It was as if between the weight of this organization and its volatile elements there existed a profound affinity. Perhaps this was the first sign of modernity.

The "great cathedrals" rose one after the other

131
Bazar de l'Hôtel de Ville, rue de Rivoli, Paris, about 1900-05

in the years that followed the Commune to the years just after the turn of the century—in 1869-72, Au Bon Marché; in 1877, Les Grands Magasins du Louvre; in 1881, Au Printemps; and in 1903, La Samaritaine. Each had specific characteristics that their managements tried to underline. In any case, Au Bon Marché was the first in which the principles and experiences tried in the preceding period arrived at a synthesis.[26] Opened by Aristide Boucicaut in 1852 as a *magasin de nouveautés*, the new building was constructed between 1869 and

1872 at the intersection of the rue de Sèvres and the rue Velpeau according to the plans of Alexandré Leplanche. The monumental entrance was flanked by sculptures and large display windows, while the interior was organized around a series of glazed courts, the largest containing an elegant double staircase. The iron structure was concealed, however, by traditional masonry. In 1872-74 the building was extended, this time to a design by Louis-Charles Boileau, an ardent exponent of metal architecture. Here, the remarkable iron structure was left exposed, in particular the delicate columns supporting the galleries and glass roof.[27]

The participation and the sense of responsibility of committed salespeople at Bon Marché was encouraged through the concession of a small percentage of the management profits, and above all by incentives, which for difficult-to-sell merchandise could go as high as 30 percent. But the real novelty lay in another practice instituted for the first time in a department store: that of virtual absorption of the client into the life of the enterprise. In addition to the merchandise counters that were raised on five floors in the new building of Au Bon Marché, there could be found a billiard room, a reading room where customers could rest, read, and write letters, and a buffet that offered complimentary refreshments. For women, "cabinets de lumière" were provided for modeling special party clothes and undergarments. The store also offered concerts, as well as courses in music, foreign languages, and fencing.[28]

If all these attentions were intended for a middle-class clientele, Au Bon Marché, especially after the death of its founder Aristide Boucicaut, also felt an obligation to help the least favored members of society. Boucicault's wife, Marguerite, put into action philanthropic works ranging from distributing shares in the enterprise to the staff, to building an institute for the poor, to her "Mystical Testament" of 1887 that made public assistance the sole benefactor of her fortune. The Boucicauts represented at both the commercial and philanthropic levels the highest example of the utopia of participation. The *grand magasin* as a "total institution" answered the needs of its employees as well as those of its customers. It is a classic incarnation of the ideology of participation, and one that Zola described explicitly, with great perception.[29]

Each *grand magasin* strove to distinguish itself from the others. The Grands Magasins du Louvre first opened in 1855, coinciding with the inauguration of the first universal exposition held in Paris. Its founder, Alfred Chauchard, had been an employee of the *magasin de nouveautés* Pauvre Diable. He used the same commercial policy and the same system of merchandising and personnel as the other *grands magasins*, but aimed at a more wealthy and sophisticated clientele.[30] With buyers in Albania, Syria, Guadeloupe, Mauritius, and Martinique, the Grands Magasins du Louvre was the home of exoticism, where one could find Eastern silks and carpets, and all the products of the French Empire. It was the Fauchon of clothing and interior decoration.

Here the attitude toward the client was more skeptical and less protective than in the other department stores. Fashion was presented as a way of life, a way of decorating the home—a

framework of the imagination. If Zola's naturalistic style was perfectly adequate to express the "totalizing machine" of Au Bon Marché, Baudelaire would have been the perfect poet for the functioning of the Grands Magasins du Louvre, an "haut lieu métropolitain" where the *flâneur* was in his element, and where *flânerie* was the mood. As with Bon Marché, "Le Louvre" offered a lavish salon and reading room for its customers. Chauchard used his fortune to build a collection of classical and modern paintings. On his death, the collection was bequeathed to the Musée du Louvre, thus instituting a new form of philanthropy.

Au Printemps, directed by Jules Jaluzot, must be considered as a Minerva sprung fully grown from the head of Jupiter.[31] Jaluzot had been a department manager at Au Bon Marché. He then married into a fortune that permitted him to open his own business, thus differentiating him from his predecessors; already in possession of great wealth, he specialized in commerce. The progressive construction of Au Printemps and of its commercial organization was based on a project that he developed as his capital increased. In 1881, the *grand pavillon* of Au Printemps was constructed by the architect Paul Sédille on the boulevard Haussmann, which had become the center of modern life after the hiatus of the Commune. Au Printemps was a modern setting—the most modern to date. Here, electric lighting made its triumphal entry into commerce (160 arc lights and 112 Edison lamps). Its great central dome lent a sense of majesty to the store that few small shops, even the most luxurious, could rival, and it was one of the most audacious examples of iron and glass architecture, leaving even the smallest rivet exposed.[32]

The interior space was animated by the brilliant colors of the painted iron structure, and by the addition of decorative elements in bronze, marble, and glazed terra-cotta, rendering it a masterful mise-en-scène where space, light, and color were orchestrated to perfection.[33] The evolution of iron and glass construction here reached its apogee—an enormous and brilliant metallic womb in which commerce took place:

It was like the concourse of a railroad station, surrounded by two floors of galleries, punctuated by spiral stairways, knitted together by overhead footwalks. The iron stairways formed daring cubes that emphasized the galleries; the footwalks made straight lines high above empty space. And all this ironwork, under the white light of the windows, was spun into an airy architecture, a complicated lacework through which the daylight shone, the modern version of a fairy palace, of a many-layered Tower of Babel whose great halls seemed to extend into an infinite series of other floors and other halls.[34]

The construction of Au Printemps marked the profound transformation of Paris. The center of social life passed from the Left Bank to the grand boulevards, initiating their years of greatest glory and completing the transfer of luxury commerce from the Palais-Royal that had begun under the reign of Louis-Philippe.[35] Balzac described these boulevards with marvelous accuracy:

136
**At the Milliner's,
about 1883**
Edgar Degas
(1834-1917)
Pastel on paper
Royal Academy of Arts,
London

What heady, enticing air breathes from the area between the Rue Taitbout and the Rue de Richelieu.... Once he sets foot there, the man of active mind might as well write off his whole day. It is a dream of gold, a distraction which you cannot hope to resist. You are in a crowd, yet all alone. The print-sellers' engravings, the day's buskers, the sweetmeats in the cafes, the diamonds in the jewelers' windows—all are calculated to stimulate, indeed intoxicate you. All the finest, costliest wares of Paris await you here: jewels, fabrics, engravings, books.[36]

As the cathedrals of commerce successively moved to these great routes, they marked the emerging point of fashion and the emerging point of social life.

The *grand magasin* would initiate an extremely persuasive promotion aimed at its female clientele. At Au Printemps, Jaluzot concentrated on women as the exclusive potential clients of his enterprise.

Though the concept was modern, the store still catered to the age-old needs of women for fashion and luxury. "How fortunate you are, ladies! At the Printemps we spoil you, with posies of violets, with shimmering fabrics, handled by discreet, eager, courteous clerks who make every effort to please you!"[37] Au Printemps exalted the eroticism of fashion and capitalized on women's needs. More than one critic of the great cathedrals of commerce would insist that the *grand magasin* lay at the heart of a whole gamut of modern female neuroses—the most prevalent being the new pathological impulse toward kleptomania.

Other observers would affirm that the department store was a terrestrial paradise of the modern age, where by means of a potent "cocktail" of fabrics, music, light, and color, women were drawn in, overpowered, and encouraged to spend beyond their means: "Observe the women as they come out of the great store. Their pupils are dilated, their gazes vacant. As they find themselves

once again on the sidewalk, in the street, back in
everyday life, their faces are agitated for a moment
as if by some great nervous convulsion. It is
because they had left reality, and wore the faces of
dreamers. They had to make an effort to re-adapt
themselves, to resume their everyday masks."[38]
Indeed, the power of attraction of the department
store was considered so great that it could even
jeopardize the morality of honest women. A certain
Doctor Dubuisson would testify before the
Tribunal de la Seine that one of his female patients
was so addicted to the ambience of the *grand
magasin* that she got up from her sick bed to
make her habitual pilgrimage to the department
store and subsequently died.[39]

In 1883 Ernest Cognacq, who since 1867 had
been the owner of a *magasin de nouveautés*
named La Samaritaine, on the rue Turbigo, met the
architect Frantz Jourdain, whom he asked to
renovate a series of buildings around his shop, as
he continued to acquire surrounding property to
expand his enterprise. The project was completed
between 1895 and 1905. It was during this "work
in progress" that La Samaritaine became the
synthesis of all the experiments conducted in the
grands magasins over the preceding fifty years.[40]
This was true from a commercial and architectural
as well as a social and philanthropic point of view.
Frantz Jourdain's Samaritaine was a masterpiece of
Art Nouveau architecture, with its ornate iron

skeleton, circular corner tower, and elegant cupola.
A rationalist architect, Jourdain masterfully
incorporated the decoration of the building into
the structure: the exposed iron structure was
painted a brilliant blue, and he called on the best
decorators of the day to design the display
counters, stained-glass windows, ceramic tiles,
electric lamps, and decorative grillwork.[41]

In commercial terms, the innovation at La
Samaritaine consisted of a perfect organization of
the merchandise according to the functional
necessities of clothing, home furnishings, sports,
and so on. This stratification and functionalization
of retailing would be reorganized in the various
buildings of the Samaritaine during the 1920s.
These new display methods demonstrated the
remarkable capacity of the organizational machine
to reach the customer—above all, the petit
bourgeois and proletarian client who was, so to
speak, taken by the hand into the world of
merchandise, educated to new needs, and taught to
appreciate ever-changing fashions. In this way, La
Samaritaine represents the perfecting of exhibition
techniques and sales methods that prefigured
modern techniques of merchandising. Ideologically,
La Samaritaine synthesized all the earlier
experiences. Louise Jay, Cognacq's wife, organized
a large number of philanthropic associations
around the enterprise for the benefit of the
employees and their families. Half the capital was

138
**Au Bon Marché
home furnishings
catalogue, 1868**
Bibliothèque des Arts
Décoratifs, Paris

a cathedral of commerce but a place where the determination of new sensibilities, and the production of new needs, was central. The Samaritaine was the modern popular institution.

By the early 1890s, reform movements in the applied arts had sprung up in major cities all over Europe. Various new forces in production and commerce fostered by the Industrial Revolution lay at the heart of these movements that attempted to reconcile art and industry, beauty and utility. The division of labor had resulted in a division in the design process: artists had no knowledge of how their designs could be adapted to machine production and were therefore separated from the manufacture of their designs. Workers involved in the production process had little or no artistic training and were therefore incapable of respecting the integrity of an artist's designs. At the same time, a traditional prejudice against the decorative arts as "minor arts" encouraged painters and sculptors to shun them as unworthy of their attention. Applied-arts training had not kept up with advances in technology, and the rapidly expanding middle classes, avidly imitating the fashions and manners of the aristocracy, preferred the reproduction of historical styles in the decoration of their homes. Thus we find throughout the second half of the nineteenth century a booming furniture trade in copies of French furnishings from the seventeenth and eighteenth centuries, as well as more contemporary furnishings that were a chaotic mixture of classical,

divided among the store employees, and the other half went to the Fondation Cognacq-Jay, which administered social works.

Through this extraordinary and complex organization, La Samaritaine was no longer simply

Annexe de l'Ameublement. - Rayon des Meubles Anciens

139
**Postcard: antique
furniture department
in Au Bon Marché
furniture annex,
about 1905**

140
Sitting room, 1900
Edward Colonna
(1862-1948), designer,
for L'Art Nouveau
Musée des Arts
Décoratifs, Paris

141
**Interior of Siegfried
Bing's shop, L'Art
Nouveau, 22 rue de
Provence, Paris, 1895**

142
**Trade card: Au Bon
Marché, Paris, 1903**
Collection Au Bon
Marché Archives, Paris

Gothic, and Renaissance styles. Finally, an enormous increase in the production of goods by machine engendered new and highly competitive forms of international trade, as European nations vied with one another to renovate their applied arts industries and to conquer new export markets.[42]

In France, all these circumstances led to the development of a broad-based movement for the reform of the applied-arts industries—one that was supported by the government and by resourceful entrepreneurs who wanted to raise standards of public taste and to stimulate the national economy by breathing new life into the decorative-arts industries. The cause would also be taken up by artists and intellectuals with socialist sympathies who believed that the artist, by concerning himself with the most common objects, could infuse beauty into everyday life and thereby improve the environment for all.[43]

Where did the *grands magasins* stand in relation to the reform movement and this new attention to the arts of the home? Typically, furniture manufacturers were obliged to sell to a middleman who then sold the merchandise to the boutiques. Thus, to maintain profits, prices were augmented for the consumer. The *grands magasins* employed the same commercial policy toward furniture as they did toward the rest of their merchandise—buying and selling in large quantities and at reduced prices. They would quickly establish fixed contracts with manufacturers, particularly in the provinces, where labor was much cheaper than in Paris. The *grands magasins* also sold large quantities of furnishings produced in Italy, Belgium, and Germany, where labor was frequently even less expensive.

The capacity of the big stores to buy directly

143

Compagnie des Arts Français, at the corner of avenue Matignon and rue de Faubourg du Saint-Honoré, Paris, about 1925-30
Thérèse Bonney (1897-1978), photographer
Cooper-Hewitt Museum, New York, Bonney Collection

144

Tablewares in the shop window of Au Printemps, Paris, about 1925-30
Thérèse Bonney (1897-1978), photographer
Cooper-Hewitt Museum, New York, Bonney Collection

from manufacturers, thus eliminating the middleman, permitted sales at prices far lower than those that smaller dealers in the Faubourg Saint-Antoine, the furniture center in Paris, could offer. In addition, the fact that the *grands magasins* sold a wide variety of merchandise permitted them to hold enormous end-of-the-year clearance sales of furnishings, often at a loss that could be recouped in other departments. At the same time the emergence of department stores meant that inexpensive reproductions of French *meubles de*

145

Poster:
Les Grands Magasins du Louvre White Sale, 1929
Thérèse Bonney (1897-1978), photographer
Cooper-Hewitt Museum, New York, Bonney Collection

style—copies of past styles—could be marketed at prices only slightly above those of contemporary pieces. The furniture catalogue for Au Bon Marché in 1878, for example, listed the price of an ordinary armchair at 78 francs, while one could purchase an armchair in the "Pompadour" style for only 95 francs, or a carved "Louis XII" chair at 125 francs.[44] Around 1900, Au Bon Marché even opened its own antiques department, entering into competition with still another important branch of Parisian commerce in the decorative arts.

If the efforts of the department stores to make decent furnishings at low prices available to a large audience could be applauded, their growing capacity to undersell their smaller competitors in furniture and decorative arts could make them the target of attacks by decorative arts reformers and leaders of the furniture industries. On the occasion of the Universal Exposition of 1889, the reporter for the furniture section attributed the general decline in quality and design of French furnishings to the influence of the department stores that

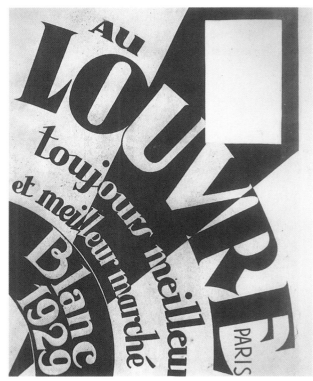

94

claimed that department stores were a major contributor to the decadence of French furniture and decoration:

The economic organization of these enterprises exacerbates yet further the existing situation in the industry. Since their only object is to beguile customers with low prices (or more precisely, the illusion of them), they demand from their suppliers only products that will serve this purpose. The importance of their business forces

146
Oriental rugs in the shop window of Au Bon Marché, Paris, 1925

147
Lace display in the shop window of Au Bon Marché, Paris, about 1925-30
Thérèse Bonney (1897-1978), photographer
Cooper-Hewitt Museum, New York, Bonney Collection

demanded from their suppliers goods that only had the appearance of quality, when in fact they were badly constructed. That more and more manufacturers were turning to lower-quality production to meet the increasing demands of the department stores, detractors argued, meant the general abasement of the entire French furniture industry.[45]

Other spokesmen for furniture and the decorative arts claimed that the general public was completely uneducated in matters of style and taste. They argued that the department stores separated the client from the artisan, and thus from the artistic direction that the average buyer badly needed in order to decorate a home properly. Thus, furnishing a home became an entirely anonymous action, leading to an even greater confusion in domestic decoration, a lack of originality, and a general lowering of public taste.[46] In his social and economic study of the furniture industry published in 1894, Henri Fourdinois, one of the leading furniture manufacturers in Paris,

on their suppliers a dog-eat-dog competition that results in a continual lowering both of prices and of technical standards throughout the industry. A concern with progress of any kind is wholly foreign to them; they have but one goal: to buy from the producer at the lowest possible price so that they can resell at the lowest possible price.[47]

In spite of these undoubtedly exaggerated charges by embittered industry representatives,[48] the department stores in fact played a decisive role in the movement for a revival of the applied arts. During the 1890s, for example, Monsieur Honoré, director of the Grands Magasins du Louvre, sat on the board of directors of the important Union Centrale des Arts Décoratifs—the union of artists and industrialists founded in 1864 that was devoted to the improvement of the nation's industries through education and exhibitions.[49] Under the direction of Monsieur Honoré, the Grands Magasins du Louvre encouraged innovation in the decorative arts by holding a series of annual

95

innovative aspects of Bing's enterprise was his realization that it was the general ambience rather than the individual objects that would make a lasting impression on potential customers. So he installed a series of model rooms, each under the artistic direction of a single artist, that proposed design solutions to home furnishing in the modern style.[54] In addition, hoping to reestablish a unity in the design process and to ensure the quality of the designs that he produced, Bing built his own ateliers and brought together a group of innovative craftsmen such as Eugène Gaillard, Edward Colonna, and Georges de Feure, who worked under his close supervision to create harmonious ensembles for interiors: furniture, fabrics, wallpaper, friezes, tableware, ceramics, and art objects, all in the new style.[55] Based on models such as this, between 1900 and 1914 numerous boutiques of modern decorative arts were established in Paris: Paul Poiret's Atelier Martine (1911), Louis Süe's Atelier Français (1912), and Francis Jourdain's Les Ateliers Modernes (1912) are among the best known. All were founded on the principal of producing an entire line of home furnishings, from furniture to wallpaper, under the careful attention of a single artistic director.[56]

The department stores were quick to join this trend. Sales records demonstrate that during the nineteenth century a substantial part of the high-income population bought its bed linens and kitchenware in the *grands magasins*, but reserved the most important purchases of dresses, suits, coats, and furnishings for couturiers and decorators.[57] The department stores tried to reach a higher-income clientele by opening their own *ateliers d'art* (design workshops) within their stores, each directed by an eminent decorator. Au Printemps, the most modern of the big stores, founded its own *atelier d'art* in 1912. Primavera, which was directed by Mme Chauchat-Guilleré, and organized as a special boutique within the department store, hired its own team of artists and sold a wide range of domestic furnishings marked with the exclusive Primavera stamp. Spokesmen for Primavera

contests for the design of models that would later be manufactured and sold by the store—in 1893, a lamp and an embroidered lace handkerchief, and in 1894, a bedroom and a piano drape.[50] At the Universal Exposition of 1900, the *grands magasins* were permitted to participate for the first time; Les Grands Magasins du Louvre and Au Bon Marché both sponsored important displays of modern furnishings.[51]

After 1900, department stores in Paris became increasingly important as popularizers of the modern style. Au Bon Marché, the Grands Magasins du Louvre, and Au Printemps had already opened their own factories, which competed with the Faubourg Saint-Antoine in quantity of production.[52] But aside from the competition presented to manufacturers, the *grands magasins*, continuing to diversify, now entered into competition with specialized boutiques of decorative arts.

As Art Nouveau developed in Paris between 1895 and 1900, dozens of new boutiques opened, aimed at promoting an artistic modern look to home furnishings. La Maison de l'Art Nouveau, opened by Siegfried Bing in 1895; La Maison Moderne, directed by the German art critic Julius Meier-Graefe; and L'Art dans l'Habitation, opened by the craftsman Serrurier-Bovy and his collaborator René Dulong, were but three of the most successful examples.[53]

Of these, the best known was Bing's Maison de l'Art Nouveau, located on the rue de Provence in the ninth arrondissement. One of the most

emphasized its democratic initiative in putting the artist at the service of the people, and its seminal role as educator of taste in introducing the public to the notion of decoration, to the "joy of personalizing one's interior," and in promoting the modern style to a public that had always preferred furnishings in traditional styles.[58] Much of the merchandise sold by Primavera was mass produced, but its artists also executed designs commissioned by clients, and produced one-of-a-kind pieces.

Les Galeries Lafayette (founded in 1895 by Alphonse Kahn and Théophile Bader) was the next to open its own *atelier d'art moderne* in 1921,

from the great craftsmen of the past—a heritage that was explicitly and strikingly French:

Continuing development of the true principles of the ancient crafts, the decorative artists of La Maîtrise strive to work in the finest French traditions. Like their predecessors they seek to conceive and create appropriately to their age, to build untrammeled by outworn formulas, and to make the fullest use of not only methods that have survived from the past but also reinvigorated techniques and new materials. In accordance with the age-old virtues of the race—reasoned audacity, befitting taste, good sense and order—they seek to

BAINS DE MER VILLES D'EAUX

AU BON MARCHÉ

MAISON A. BOUCICAUT. PARIS

PUBLICITÉ WALLACE, PARIS

Imp. DUVAL & BEDOS 14 Av. Félix-Faure. PARIS

150
Poster: Au Bon Marché, 1925
René Vincent
(1879-1936), designer
Duval & Beods, printer
Color lithograph
Musée de la Publicité,
Paris

directed by Maurice Dufrêne (1876-1955), a leading decorator of the period, and a supporter of new techniques and materials who had made his debut in 1899 in Meier-Graefe's Maison Moderne.[59] Promising "le meilleur au meilleur marché" they named their ateliers "La Maîtrise" in reference to the title of master artisans of the Middle Ages. Their first catalogue, featuring furnishings, fabrics, carpets and accessories in the Art Deco style, was prefaced by a quote from the poet Octave Mirbeau: "The people too have a right to beauty."

Les Galeries Lafayette took great care to underline both its modernism and its inheritance

accomplish new, sound things, making them as beautiful as possible and, loyal as ever to their highest ideals, putting them within reach of all, be their means small or great.[60]

The furnishings sold by La Maîtrise were created by Dufrêne or executed under his direction. While many of the designs were manufactured in the store's own workshops, Dufrêne did not hesitate to turn to the finest French manufacturers to achieve the quality he desired. The decorative glassware that he designed for La Maîtrise between 1922 and 1924, for example, was executed by the prestigious Cristalleries de Saint-Louis and sold under the name Art-Verrier.[61]

The *ateliers d'art* displayed home furnishings in the ambience of a sensuous dream world, where the experience of visiting was as important as the act of purchasing. The display windows were "museums for the people" that provided precious indications as to the proper way to decorate the home.[62] Far more than creating a mirror image of bourgeois culture, the ateliers created the image of how people should live and how they should furnish their homes, thereby revising the very definition of the bourgeois way of life. La Pomone, the atelier founded by Au Bon Marché and directed by the decorator Paul Follot, published a

annual salon of the Société des Artistes Décorateurs and the Salon d'Automne, and their displays were regularly featured in highly popular magazines such as *Art et Décoration* and *Art et Industrie*. But with master cabinetmakers such as Jacques-Emile Ruhlmann acting as artistic consultant to Au Printemps's Primavera, apprehensions over compromised standards of quality in an era of mass production could be allayed. The art critic Raymond Cogniat even praised the efforts of the *grands magasins* to further the evolution of public taste and a general understanding of modern art.[64]

The importance of the *ateliers d'art* would be affirmed at the Paris Exposition internationale des

luxury catalogue in 1925 that suggested in poetic text for potential customers the importance in everyday life of beautiful furnishings and curios:

One cannot come into contact with these French furnishings and curios without becoming intimately attached to them, without understanding how much they are impregnated with sensibility and charged with significance. They contain our souls, they assume the most exquisite form of our thoughts. It is the virtue of the curio that it secretly influences our ways of feeling, and perhaps acting. Thus, our love of curios, far less futile than we might imagine, seems to be one of the manifestations of whatever is most profound and essential within us.[63]

The success of the *ateliers d'art* provoked consternation among private decorators who were losing clients, and representatives of the art industries who questioned standards of quality. The ateliers even had their own stalls in the prestigious

Arts décoratifs et industriels modernes of 1925, their moment of greatest glory. The four most important stores in Paris erected their own pavilions at the four corners of the vast architectural ensemble located on the Esplanade des Invalides.[65] One of the most striking was the pavilion for Au Bon Marché's La Pomone (architect, L. H. Boileau), with its monumental geometric forms and modernistic surface decoration in a decorative Cubist style. The displays of furnishings and decorative arts by Dufrène, Gabriel Englinger, and Suzanne Guiguichon for La Maîtrise, of Paul Follot for La Pomone, of Louis Sognot and Guillemard for Primavera, and of Etienne Kohlmann and Djo-Bourgeois for the Studium of the Grands Magasins du Louvre were undeniably stylish and modern, rivaling in luxury Jacques-Emile Ruhlmann's "Pavillon d'un riche collectionneur." The library designed by Maurice Dufrène for La Maîtrise was characterized by a whimsical combination of Cubism and traditional

"PRIMAVERA" — MEUBLES

UN COIN DE CHAMBRE
AYANT FIGURÉ AU
" SALON D'AUTOMNE "

COIN DE BOUDOIR AYANT
FIGURÉ AU "SALON DES
ARTISTES DECORATEURS"

Voici dix ans que le " Printemps " a
fondé l'Atelier Primavera en lui donnant
pour tâche de créer des modèles artistiques
ou d'ajouter une note de bon goût à tout
ce qui compose le décor de la vie moderne,
et répond à ses besoins. Depuis cette
époque, si l'on comprend tous les modèles
créés par Primavera pour le meuble,
les étoffes, la céramique, le bronze,
le total dépasse aujourd'hui 8.500.

Primavera renouvelle continuellement ses
modèles. Il réalise des objets pratiquement
étudiés dans une destination d'utilité.
Leur qualité de matière, leur forme et
leur décoration en font des œuvres qui
embellissent toujours la pièce ou le meuble
qu'ils ornent. Pourtant ces modèles sont
réalisés aux prix les plus abordables.

104200. Spécimen de
nos LANTERNES
" PRIMAVERA "
en soierie peinte,
orange, jaune ou
vieux rose. 55 fr.
45 fr. et 29.50

104202. Spécimen de
nos CRETONNES
"PRIMAVERA",
desains et coloris variés,
largeur 0m.80.
Depuis 7,90 le mètre.

104202

104203. LAMPE ÉLECTRIQUE bois naturel ou peint,
en gris ou noir, abat-jour soie, hauteur 0m.35. 25 fr.

104201. FRISETTE
lamé or, décor grosse rose
" PRIMAVERA ",
noir et or, bleu et or,
jade et or, brique et or,
largeur 1m.35,
Le mètre. . . 65 fr.

104201

Au
PRINTEMPS
Paris

104204. BOITE MARQUISE en
carton peint. 12.50

104205. CRUCHE en poterie
d'Alsace, décor "PRIMAVE-
RA" sur fond bleu, brun ou jaune.
1 litre   2, 3 litre   1/3 litre
9.50   6.50   4.50

104206.
Spécimen de nos
VASES en poterie
rustique. 29 fr.

BONBONNIÈRE en
faïence à émaux de
Longwy, décors variés
"PRIMAVERA",
d'am. 0m.10. 10.50

104207.
104208.
GUÉRIDON bois
peint rouge et noir,
noir et or, ou
gris et bleu. 85 fr.

104209.
SERVICE A CAFÉ "PRIMAVERA",
en faïence à ayures, vert et noir.
La tasse à café 2.25, à thé 2,75,
à déjeuner 3.75, l'assiette à lunch 1.90

104210. VASE
meplat
"Cléopâtre", en faïence
de Longwy, décor bleu
sur fond blanc craquelé,
hauteur 0m.30. 50 fr.

104211. Spécimen de
nos PLATS DÉCO-
RATIFS, en poterie
d'Alsace, décors variés.
Depuis 12 fr.

153
**La Maîtrise, pavilion,
Galeries Lafayette, at
the International
Exposition of Modern
Decorative and
Industrial Arts, Paris,
1925**
Jean Hiriart, Georges
Tribout, and Georges
Beau, architects
Collection S. Tise

8 - PARIS — EXPOSITION DES ARTS DÉCORATIF
PAVILLON «LA MAITRISE» Atelier des ARTS APPLIQUÉS des GALERIES LAFAYETTES
(par Jean Hiriart, Georges Tribout, et Georges Beau, architectes)   A. P

154
**Pomone pavilion,
Grands Magasins du
Bon Marché, at the
International
Exposition of Modern
Decorative and
Industrial Arts, Paris,
1925**
L. H. Boileau, architect
Collection S. Tise

9 - PARIS — EXPOSITION DES ARTS DÉCORATIFS
PAVILLON «POMONE» (par L. H. Boileau, architecte) Grds Magasins du BON MARCHÉ   A. P

155
Primavera pavilion, Grands Magasins du Printemps, at the International Exposition of Modern Decorative and Industrial Arts, Paris, 1925
H. Sauvage et Wybo, architects
Cooper-Hewitt Museum, New York, Picture Collection

156
Studium Louvre pavilion, Grands Magasins du Louvre, at the International Exposition of Modern Decorative and Industrial Arts, Paris, 1925
A. Laprade, architect
Cooper-Hewitt Museum, New York, Picture Collection

101

157
Boudoir for L'Atelier Primavera, 1925, Plate 35 from Léon Deshairs, *Intérieurs en Couleurs*, Paris, 1926
Louis Sognot (1892-1970), architect
Boris Grosser, illustrator
Cooper-Hewitt Museum Library, New York

158
Boudoir for La Maîtrise pavilion, at the International Exposition of Modern Decorative and Industrial Arts, Paris, 1925
Maurice Dufrène (1876-1955), artistic director
Bibliothèque des Arts Décoratifs, Paris

French style, while the bourgeois *petit salon* by Dufrêne's associates Gabriel Englinger and Suzanne Guiguichon was a theatrical space with its simple, yet carefully crafted curvilinear forms in rare woods. Moreover, the ateliers at the 1925 Exposition served as a training ground for numerous artist-decorators such as Sognot, Djo-Bourgeois, and Kohlmann, who from their debuts with the department stores would go on to pursue individual careers as some of the most important decorators in Paris.

By the mid-1920s, the era of great expansion of the department stores was coming to a close as an increasing number of specialty shops, in an effort to compete with their larger competitors, adopted some of their most successful features, such as modern methods of merchandising, sales promotions, and innovative and artistic display techniques.[66] At the same time, the department stores were upgrading their merchandise, and prices were often equal to those of smaller specialty shops.

With the worldwide depression of the 1930s, the department stores fell on hard times when the buying power of a large sector of the population drastically decreased. Au Printemps was the first to

respond to the economic depression with the development of its Prisunic stores—five-and-dime stores based on the model of New York's Woolworth's.[67] The Prisunic of the 1930s offered to the classes of society that were the hardest hit by the Depression a wide assortment of products at low prices, produced in large quantities. Here display techniques had little to do with the cathedrals of commerce; the merchandise was arranged according to price in large bins, and for the first time foods were sold alongside notions and household goods. The Prisunic stores were an immediate success—there were forty in France on the eve of World War II.

During the thirties, the low prices offered by Prisunic corresponded with merchandise of rather low quality. This was to change after the war, and particularly during the 1960s, as the store adopted a new mission: low prices, quality, and style, relying on new materials and new technology—plastics, steel, and synthetic fibers. It opened its own "bureau de style" and called on young designers from all over Europe to create youthful, modern, and functional clothing and

home furnishings. Prisunic introduced Parisians to the first Swedish tableware in steel; to bold, color-coordinated plastic kitchenware; and to motifs adapted from Pop Art and Op Art in textiles and bed linen, a revolution for the traditionally conservative French buyer. In 1964, under the careful eye of its advertising and style director Denise Fayolle, the store published its first catalogue of home furnishings, offering designs by Terence Conran, Marc Berthier, and Gae Aulenti, and even sold original lithographs by such artists as Alechinsky, Matta, Messagier, and Bram Van Velde, thereby exposing a broad sector of the French population to modern art and to "good design" that previously had been reserved for an initiated elite.

Denise Fayolle and her partner Maïmé Arnodin, doyenne of French ready-to-wear, were behind yet another innovation in a different domain of French retailing. Beginning in 1968, through their marketing agency Mafia, they brought a new image to the biggest mail-order house in France: Les Trois Suisses. Advising on what goods to produce, when, where, and how, Fayolle and Arnodin have brought the biggest names in fashion and design into more than 25 million homes by asking couturiers such as Sonia Rykiel, Agnès B., and Azzedine Alaïa, and designers such as Gae Aulenti and Philippe Starck to design special lines for the Trois Suisses catalogue.[68]

159
Window display of tennis equipment, Paris, about 1925-30
Thérèse Bonney (1897-1978), photographer
Cooper-Hewitt Museum, New York, Bonney Collection

160
Windows of Louis Vuitton shop, avenue des Champs-Elysées, Paris, about 1925-30
Thérèse Bonney (1897-1978), photographer
Cooper-Hewitt Museum, New York, Bonney Collection

If today the *grands magasins* have lost some of their specific character and the overwhelming charm of their original architectural conception, they have continued their search for innovation, making even greater efforts to obtain the most exclusive and unusual items from all over the world. And now we can find the products of some of the most luxurious and exclusive French industries in the stores; Chanel, Hermès, and the Cristalleries de Saint-Louis among others have their own stalls staffed by specially trained personnel. In spite of these changes, one basic reality will remain: by reducing the differences between life-styles, appearances and even outlooks of the various classes of society, the *grands magasins* have initiated profound transformations in our way of life and can be considered one of the great social forces of the last century.[69]

1. Bernard Marrey, *Les Grands Magasins* (Paris: Picard, 1979), p. 11. Marrey has made the most complete study of the history and architecture of French department stores. I would like to thank him for his suggestions during the preparation this essay.

2. Paul Jarry, *Les magasins de nouveautés* (Paris: André Barry et Fils, 1948), p. 9.

3. For corporations, see Eugène Müntz, "Corporations," *La Grande encyclopédie*, vol. 12 (Paris, 1885-1902), pp. 1025-32.

4. H. Pasdermadjian, *The Department Store, Its Origins, Evolution and Economics* (London Newman Books), 1954, p. 7.

5. For Saint-Simonisme, see B. Gille, *La Banque en France au XIXe siècle* (Paris: 1970); S. Charlety, *Histoire du Saint-Simonisme* (Paris, 1931); and F. Manuel, *The Prophets of Paris* (Cambridge, Mass., 1962).

6. The *grands boulevards* were not introduced by Haussmann, but in fact date to Louis XIV. See *Les Grands boulevards*, exhibition catalogue, Musée Carnavalet, Paris, 1985, p. 5.

7. For the urban transformation of Paris during the nineteenth century, see François Loyer, *Paris XIXe siècle: L'Immeuble et la rue* (Paris, 1987).

8. Vicomte G. d'Avenel, "Le mécanisme de la vie moderne: Les grands magasins," *Revue des Deux Mondes* 124 (July 1, 1894): pp. 367-9.

9. Referring to Taine's statement on the occasion of the Paris Universal Exposition of 1855: "L'Europe s'est déplacée pour voir des marchandises." Walter Benjamin wrote in his essay "Paris, Capitale du XIXe siècle (1935)" that the universal expositions were the new pilgrimage places for the "merchandise fetish." For further reference, see Walter Benjamin, *Essais II, 1935-1940*, translated by Maurice de Gandillac (Paris, 1983), p. 43.

10. Pasdermadjian, op. cit., p. 44.

11. See *Pages d'or de l'édition publicitaire*, exhibition catalogue, Bibliothèque Forney, Paris, 1988, p. 13.

12. See, for example, "Variations sur le blanc," text by Pierre Mac Orlan, La Grande Maison du Blanc, 1927.

13. D'Avenel, op. cit., pp. 337-9.

14. Benjamin, op. cit., p. 449.

15. For the Escalier de Cristal, see Yolande Amic, *L'opaline française au XIXe siècle* (Paris, 1952), pp. 140-148.

16. Honoré de Balzac, *Les Illusions perdues*, quoted in Marrey, p. 12.

17. Quoted in St. Martin Saint-Léon, *Le petit commerce français, sa lutte pour la vie* (Paris, 1911), p. 7.

18. François Faraut, *Histoire de la Belle Jardinière* (Paris, 1987), chap. 1.

19. On associations, see Joseph Prudhon, *Projet de Société de l'exposition perpétuelle* (Paris, 1855), and Jean Gaumont, *Histoire générale de la corporation en France* (Paris, 1924).

20. Marrey, op. cit., pp. 36-7.

21. Ibid., p. 48.

22. For the development of iron architecture in France, see Bertrand Lemoine, *L'Architecture du fer: France XIXe siècle* (Paris, 1984).

23. Pasdermadjian, op. cit., pp. 13-4.

24. D'Avenel, op. cit., pp. 335-6.

25. Michel Serres, *Zola, feux et signaux de brume* (Paris: Grasset, 1975), p. 282.

26. The information that follows on Au Bon Marché is drawn from Michael Miller, *The Bon Marché* (Princeton, N.J., 1981).

27. The original structure has been concealed by successive transformations. See Lemoine, op. cit., p. 194.

28. See, for example, the advertisement for Au Bon Marché in *Exposition universelle de Turin, Section française*, exhibition catalogue, Paris, 1912.

29. One of the most penetrating accounts of how the department store functioned can be found in Emile Zola's *Au Bonheur des dames*, published in serial form in *Gil Blas* in 1882 and as a book in 1883. To prepare his novel, Zola undertook an extensive social and economic inquiry into two of Paris's most important department stores, Au Bon Marché and Au Printemps. His research would serve as the basis for much of what has subsequently been written on the phenomenon of the department store.

30. D'Avenel, op. cit., pp. 339-42.

31. For Jaluzot, see "Jules Jaluzot," *La Grande encyclopédie*, vol. 20 (Paris, 1885-1902), p. 1190.

32. Lemoine, op. cit., pp. 194-5, and Marrey, op. cit., pp. 97-109.

33. Lemoine, op. cit., pp. 197-8.

34. Zola, op. cit., pp. 275-6.

35. For more on the grands boulevards, see *Les Grands boulevards*, exhibition catalogue, Musée Carnavalet, Paris, 1985, pp. 5-8.

36. Honoré de Balzac, *Histoire et physiologie des boulevards de Paris* (Paris: Le Cadratin), 1980, cited in *Les Grands boulevards*, p. 181.

37. Cited in Marrey, op. cit., p. 98.

162
Living room for Prisunic, about 1964-70
P. Bacou and P. Molier, designers

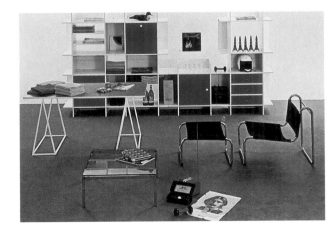

38. Francis Ambrière, *La vie secrète des grands magasins*, 2nd ed. (Paris: Les œuvres françaises), 1938, p. 198.

39. Ibid.

40. Michel Zahar, "Les grands magasins," *L'Art Vivant*, vol. 4, 1928.

41. On Jourdain and the Samaritaine, see Arlette Barré Despond, "Frantz Jourdain," in Arlette Barré Despond and Suzanne Tise, *Jourdain* (Paris, 1988).

42. These issues are treated in greater depth in my doctoral thesis, "Entre deux expositions 1925-1937: The Politics of the Applied Arts in France," University of Pittsburgh (in preparation).

43. During the 1890s, the decorative arts reform movement was incorporated into a broader movement for popular education. See, for example, Marie-Laure Albertini, *Les politiques d'éducation populaire par l'art en France: théâtres et musées, 1895-1914*, vol. 1 (Paris, 1983).

44. Maison Aristide Boucicaut, *Au Bon Marché, Album de l'ameublement* (Paris, 1878).

45. Alfred Picard, *Exposition universelle de 1889, groupe III, Mobilier* (Paris, 1891), p. 59.

46. See, for example, Arthur Maillet, "Causerie," *L'Art décoratif moderne*, December 1894, pp. 41-42.

47. Henri Fourdinois, *Etude économique et sociale sur l'ameublement* (Paris, 1894), pp. 17ff.

48. The attacks fall within a larger current of protest by small merchants against big business around the turn of the century. See Philip Nord, "The Small Shopkeeper's Movement and Politics in France," in *Shopkeepers and Master Artisans in 19th Century Europe* (London and New York, 1984), pp. 185ff.

49. The Union Centrale founded the Musée des Arts Décoratifs in 1887.

50. Maillet, "Causerie," p. 43.

51. Gabriel P. Weisberg, *Art Nouveau Bing* (New York, 1986), p. 163.

52. See the debate on the situation of the department stores by members of the Chambre Syndicale de l'Ameublement in "Suite de la discussion sur l'admission des grands magasins au Salon du Mobilier de 1905," *Bulletin de la Chambre Syndicale de l'Ameublement*, October 1903, pp. 186-9.

53. For Serrurier-Bovy, see Jacques-Grégoire Watelet, *Gustave Serrurier-Bovy, architecte et décorateur, 1858-1910* (Brussels, 1975).

54. Weisberg, op. cit., p. 66.

55. For more on Bing, see ibid.

56. For further references, see Yolande Deslandres, *Poiret* (Paris, 1986); on Süe, see Susan Day, *Louis Süe, Architectures* (Brussels, 1985); and on Jourdain Barré and Tise, eds., op. cit.

57. Pasdermadjian, op. cit., p. 27.

58. *Au Printemps Paris, 1865-1965* (Paris, n. p., 1965). Unfortunately, Au Bon Marché, Galeries Lafayette and Printemps no longer possess the archives of their *ateliers d'art*. I have drawn most of my information from contemporary store catalogues and decorative arts periodicals.

59. On Dufrêne, see "Notre enquête sur le mobilier moderne: Maurice Dufrêne," *Art et Décoration*, January-June 1921, pp. 129-143.

60. Catalogue of La Maîtrise, Les Galeries Lafayette, Paris, 1922.

61. Dufrêne's original drawings are kept in the archives of the Cristalleries de Saint-Louis in Saint-Louis-les-Bitche. I would like to thank M. Armand d'Humières and M. Claude Bromet for generously opening the Saint-Louis archives for consultation.

62. For window displays of Parisian department stores and boutiques, see for example *Présentation 1927* (Paris, 1927).

63. *L'Amour du bibelot*, Au Bon Marché, Paris, c. 1925.

64. Raymond Cogniat, "Défense des grands magasins," *L'Amour de l'Art*, 10 (December 1932) :339.

65. *Exposition internationale des arts décoratifs et industriels modernes, Rapport général*, vol. 4, Paris, 1927, p. 31.

66. Pasdermadjian, op. cit., p. 46.

67. The first was opened in 1931. See *Prisunic 1931-1988*, exhibition catalogue, Centre Georges Pompidou, Paris, 1988, p. 20.

68. For more on Fayolle and Arnodin, see Marie-Françoise Leclerc, "Derrière la Mafia," *Elle*, 15 November, 1976, and Michel Leloup "Les caprices de Marianne," *L'Express*, 17 September, 1982. I would like to thank Mme Arnodin for the information she provided on Prisunic and Les Trois Suisses.

69. Pasdermadjian, op. cit., p. 124.

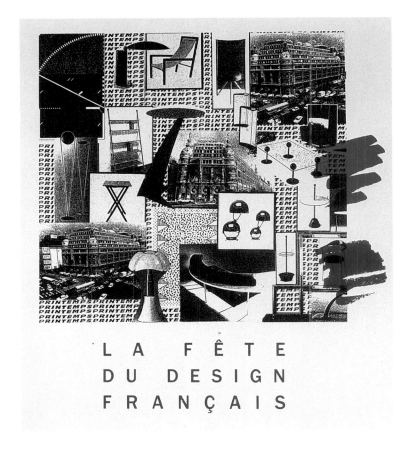

LA FÊTE DU DESIGN FRANÇAIS

163
Advertisement: Printemps, La Fête du Design Français, 1987
Hervé Le Douarec (born 1952), artistic director

MADELEINE DESCHAMPS

DOMESTIC ELEGANCE :
THE FRENCH AT HOME

Between the Revolutionary era and the present day, France has lived through periods of remarkable creativity and refinement, of grandeur and influence, alternating with periods of devastation, searching, and imitation. From the conquering years of the First Empire through the comfortable bourgeois nineteenth century, from the tragedy of World War I through the long and difficult aftermath of World War II, a new society was born, another disappeared, and yet another came into being. Paramount throughout these periods has always been a sense of history, which developed during the last century and has shaped French taste well into this one, leaving its mark on the social evolution of the country as well as on its arts and way of living—a feeling for history that has both sustained and hampered French creation through two centuries.

Furthermore, the middle class had grown far wealthier through the development of commerce and nascent industries, but it still had no access to power. The French Revolution was essentially a *révolution bourgeoise* that put an end to centuries of Ancien Régime—in the political sense at least, for it would take almost a century for the old life-styles to fade. Indeed, the Revolution meant the overthrowing of a monarchy that had reigned in France for eight hundred years, giving the country its territory, its political and social structure, and its culture. Only very slowly in the course of the nineteenth century would the old structures evolve into new patterns.

The change in regime accentuated a vogue that had appeared in the arts in the late eighteenth century—a passion for history that was rooted in the classical past. Renewed interest in antiquity had followed the discovery of Pompeii and

164
Design for a painted ceiling about, 1810
Anonymous
Pen and black ink,
watercolor
Cooper-Hewitt Museum,
New York, Gift of
Eleanor Garnier Hewitt,
1903-12-48

On page 106
Ministerial office commissioned by Jack Lang, minister of Culture, Paris, 1983
Andrée Putman,
designer
Produced by the
Mobilier National

The Revolution was a major breach in French history. In the course of the eighteenth century, under the influence of the *philosophes des lumières*, Voltaire, Diderot, and Rousseau, it had become clear that the social and political system perpetuated privileges for the aristocracy and the Church that were no longer acceptable.

Herculaneum in the middle of the eighteenth century, and classicism now seemed a desirable diversion from the *style rocaille* of this frivolous and aristocratic century. Artists and architects spent more time than ever in Rome, returning with notebooks filled with motifs they later applied in their work; this influence is particularly evident in the Directory style, which brought new elements to the elegant Louis XVI style and opened the way for the Empire style. Young General Bonaparte's Egyptian campaign added further variety to a theme that in earlier centuries inspired French classicism but was now conceived of quite widely, and variously dubbed *à l'antique, à la grecque, à l'étrusque, retour d'Egypte*. Bonaparte had taken with him a large group of scholars whose studies and drawings started a new fashion throughout Europe. When members of the aristocracy lost all power and were forced to flee the country during the Revolutionary years, the bourgeoisie came to the fore and adopted these antique styles, which served to distinguish it from the banished class.

The first significant example of the new style was seen when, in 1798, the architect Charles Percier redecorated the mansion of the very successful banker Récamier, whose twenty-two-year-old wife Juliette was known as far as Russia for her beauty. In the new and affluent district of the Chaussée d'Antin, the Hôtel Récamier attracted many luminaries to its famous dinners, balls, and literary evenings. Marble, mahogany, gilded woods, bronze and silks, spectacular beds, candelabra—these were the elements of the Empire version of the eighteenth-century *appartement de parade* where even the bedroom was on view to guests. The style of this particular mansion was novel, but interiors generally were still close to former tastes.

Until the end of the eighteenth century, rooms had loosely defined functions. Tables and chairs could be brought in at any moment; major spaces were organized with little attention to privacy, and the emphasis was on the large reception rooms, while the private *appartement de commodité* was neglected. Little by little the main rooms became smaller and more distinct in their use, and the very feminine atmosphere of the boudoirs, cabinets, and later *petit salons* showed a new wish for privacy. But the Empire style remained majestic and luxurious in its rather masculine dignity, even when, for example, Josephine redecorated some of the smaller rooms at Malmaison and chose slightly milder colors for her own apartments. And despite the apparent ease of Madame Récamier's celebrated *méridienne*, the stiff beauty of her room left no place for many personal effects; such objects or paintings would have destroyed the overall harmony. The setting of Juliette Récamier's portrait by Gérard, though probably more poetic than accurate, reflects a taste for beautifully crafted furniture and rather theatrical decors, for gossamer muslins and distant foliage.

Theatricality, in fact, is one of the traits of the period. The popular "fêtes" of Revolutionary times organized and staged by the painter David, and

later the sumptuous ceremonies of the Empire, were influential in their display of emblems and symbols in the antique style. Napoleon preferred solemnity and grandeur, and the architects Percier and Fontaine, who had earlier designed opera sets, orchestrated the ceremonies as grandly as they designed the imperial furniture.[1] Their furniture for the châteaux of Fontainebleau and Compiègne or for the Palais des Tuileries was spectacular and of magnificent quality, since they collaborated with the finest cabinetmakers of their day, particularly Georges Jacob, whose sons Georges II Jacob and François-Honoré-Georges Jacob-Desmalter continued his business on an almost industrial level. Under the influence of Percier and Fontaine, Empire furniture was conceived as part of an ensemble: massive shapes and rather strict lines were contrasted with the verticality of the interior

165
Furnishing fabric made for the Palais de Saint-Cloud, about 1805
Seguin et Cie, Lyon
Silk
Cooper-Hewitt Museum, New York, Gift of Herman A. Elsberg on the Fortieth Anniversary of the Museum, 1937-63-4

MIDI

VUE D'ITALIE

RIVAGE PRES DE TIVOLI

169
Design for a bedroom, Plate 36 from *Receuil de décorations intérieures*, 1812
Charles Percier (1764-1838) and Pierre-François-Léonard Fontaine (1762-1853)
Engraving
Cooper-Hewitt Museum, New York, Gift of the Council, 1921-6-377

decoration; and in turn, the relative austerity of drapes and wallpapers enhanced the richness of gilded or painted wood or mahogany, the sphinxes and griffins, and the finely worked bronzes such as those of Thomire.[2]

More broadly, the Napoleonic conquest became an epic dream that lasted long after Napoleon had been defeated and exiled in 1815. In the decorative arts, military insignia were a frequent element: a good example of this could be seen in the Council Chamber at Malmaison, where the drapes formed a tent supported by pikes and insignia between which were suspended trophies of arms. Small boudoirs and dressing rooms were draped in this manner, as in the delightful boudoir of Queen Hortense, and wallpaper often imitated curtain and tent materials. Napoleon influenced decoration in yet another way: his numerous commissions for palaces gave new life to the Lyons silk industry and to national porcelain and tapestry

manufactures. In the midst of his campaigns, even during the Hundred Days of his return from exile, he was always attentive to such details as the dye of the silks he had ordered through the Mobilier Impérial, demanding that the quality be improved and worrying about the international reputation of the industry.[3]

Napoleon was the last monarch to be a tastemaker in the old sense. When he came to power, he inherited empty palaces, some of which had been devastated by the Revolution; they were to become part of the wealth of France's patrimony even as the Revolution dethroned the Monarchy. Yet despite the change in regime, the new social structure was still modeled on the former one. Napoleon instituted a *noblesse d'Empire*, and the imperial court became a new form of aristocracy. But the new middle class that rose to prominence was not yet confident in its tastes and stressed its status and wealth through imitation of Napoleon's interiors. Moreover, very little building was undertaken in the troubled period following the Revolution or during the costly Empire wars. Interior decoration thus became a way for the new class to distinguish itself. But cautious in its choices, needing the guarantees of past history, the bourgeoisie would for over a century shy away from any innovation and continue to rely upon known styles.

In the nineteenth century, stylistic changes occurred at different rates in different sections of France; in the provinces, the Paris style lingered on long after the fall of the Empire. "Whoever does not visit Paris regularly will never be really elegant," said Balzac.[4] When, with the restoration of the monarchy in 1815, the aristocrats were allowed back from exile (without, however, having their privileges reinstated), they found their mansions empty and tried to recreate the atmosphere they had known before the Revolution. While not totally rejecting the trappings of the Empire, they nevertheless renewed the charm and delicacy that had disappeared with this solemn and often pompous style. A new awareness of privacy, and a decor that was lighter both in volume and in color, gave more intimacy to the settings of social life. Delicate furniture filled the rooms in a less formal manner—blond wood inlaid with motifs in dark wood was favored under Louis XVIII; dark wood, mahogany and palissander, sometimes inlaid with lighter exotic wood was used under Charles X; and, finally, a return to heavier shapes and black wood took place under Louis-Philippe.

In 1830, after the advent of Louis-Philippe, the aristocracy was excluded from political power[5]. In an attempt to create an association with the remote times of their heyday, they adopted symbols of

170
Queen Hortense's boudoir, rue Cerutti, Paris, 1811
Auguste-Simon Garneray (1785-1824)
Watercolor
Olivier Le Fuel Collection, Paris

171
Wallpaper, 1810-20 (active 1804-27)
Joseph Dufour manufacturer
Block-printed and flocked paper (11 colors)
Cooper-Hewitt Museum, New York, Gift of Harvey Smith, 1968-111-1

medieval feudality, and a vogue for the Gothic style flourished in the decorative arts. The *"style à la cathédrale,"* or *"troubadour,"* paralleled themes in the arts and literature. The duchesse de Berry made this medieval style quite fashionable. She commissioned the Gothic interior decoration of Notre-Dame, and the balls she gave, the white ball of "l'Ange de la Monarchie" and the "Bal Marie Stuart," marked the fêtes at the Tuileries with a romantic note.

In contrast, the bourgeoisie, who were acquiring new wealth in industry, textiles, mines, metalwork, and sugar, were proclaiming their preeminence. Although they did not own châteaux in the provinces and mansions in Paris, as did the nobility, they inhabited large flats in some of the new, elegant districts such as the Parc Monceau. They did not always own these flats and for this reason the interior became a symbol of position, all the more so since this class, in order to feel it had become the equal of the aristocracy, needed to live in the same refined manner. Paradoxically, even as French society was reaching a new equilibrium, the ideal life-style remained—as it would until almost the end of the century—that of a waning class, the nobility.

Nevertheless, the new middle classes also needed to discover their own roots; and whereas the aristocrats went back to the Gothic period, the bourgeoisie preferred the art of the Renaissance, a period that had been modeled by exceptional individuals. Soon, however, both the Gothic and the Renaissance styles would be adopted throughout society in the new eclecticism.[6] New fashions spread rapidly, graceful Gothic arches and motifs copied from Renaissance castles adorned the furniture, and "scenic" wallpapers induced romantic and historical atmospheres in private rooms. But the setting of social life was still governed by former conventions.

The Empire style had retained the formal arrangement of rooms of earlier centuries: furniture was aligned along the walls; the many chairs (*chaises meublantes*) were left in place, while the lighter *chaises volantes* and smaller tables were brought to a particular spot in the room. When entertaining guests, a lady would sit by the fireplace with the women around her in a circle and the men standing in their midst or in another circle. As Queen Hortense put it: "A conversation in which everyone shone with wit was the sole preoccupation of the evening"—even though women often complained that they only saw men's backs. And even late into the nineteenth century, social gatherings followed this pattern, for example, in Victor Hugo's salon. Queen Hortense, however, proposed a radical arrangement that was

Design for wall treatment, early 19th century
Anonymous
Gouache
Musée des Arts Décoratifs, Paris

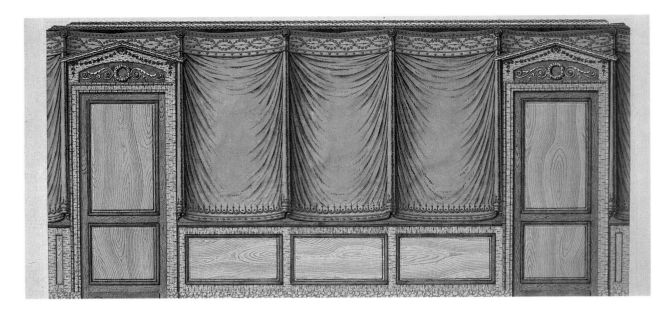

in fact an entirely new way of viewing social life. She wanted her evenings "to have an air of family reunion about them," and she claimed to have been "the first in France to place a round table in the center of the salon so that one could work or keep busy all evening, as one does in the country."[7] A technical innovation added a further new dimension: lighting in the home had changed little over the centuries. Candles, oil lamps, and the hearth were the only sources of light as soon as the sun went down. Now, an improved oil lamp was invented that gave a brighter light—the *lampe d'Argand*—and soon an even cleaner version appeared that could be set in the middle of the table, the *lampe Astral*. Despite this invention, until late into the century most elegant homes would use nothing but candles.

Around the middle of the century, as women took greater pleasure in the domestic bourgeois interior, a new sense of comfort shaped *le home* — and the English term testifies to the influence England had on a growing sense of privacy in France. This comfort would become a smothering plushness under the Second Empire, as prosperity increased and as the variety of choices multiplied in the decorative arts. Up to this point, an interior had reflected the position of its owner; now it became, within certain conventions, a mirror of individual taste: "You can tell the personality of a *maîtresse de maison* the moment you cross the threshold," Balzac remarked.[8]

After a brief republican interlude, France was ruled for a second time by a Bonaparte, Napoleon III, before becoming once again a republic in 1870. The state was exceptionally wealthy during the Second Empire and the Third Republic, and the urban projects and vast construction works undertaken by Gustave Eiffel and Baron Haussmann changed the pace of life in France. Napoleon III wanted to modernize the capital, and he entrusted Haussmann with this gigantic project: new avenues and boulevards were drawn across Paris, destroying old *quartiers* but giving broader perspectives and more light to a compact city. It also became easier for the city police to control popular upheavals than it had been in the narrow medieval boroughs — at a time when the bourgeois were increasingly afraid of the reactions of the underprivileged masses and when the bourgeois home represented a refuge against the noise and danger of city unrest.

Napoleon III had come to power after many years in exile, ready to impart a new splendor to the life at court. The receptions at the Tuileries were sumptuous, and in Compiègne the emperor and empress would invite guests of high rank to their cosmopolitan and much-sought-after "series," weeks when one was invited to the château for hunting, dances, and games. The Second Empire was the time of *la vie parisienne*, celebrated in Offenbach's operettas and *opéras bouffe*, when the ballet, the theater, and the opera were all extremely popular. The Paris Opéra, so lavishly designed by Garnier, was the epitome of gilded magnificence in interior design.

However, the nucleus of social life during this second half of the century was the family. Even Napoleon III and Eugénie gave their private life a domestic air that the well-to-do bourgeoisie could aspire to imitate. They maintained the habits of an affluent middle-class family, and in the provinces —in the large villa that Eugénie had built in Biarritz, for instance—the pace of life and entertainment was quite casual. It was to start an endless trend of *villas basques*.

But the life-style of the middle class was no longer exclusively modeled on that of the elite, even though Empress Eugénie was a major tastemaker. Lineage and culture were not the only arbiters of social life. Money and social climbing had become crucial features of life, as is shown dramatically in many of the characters created by Balzac and Stendhal. But what exactly was the bourgeoisie? Was it "simply the contented portion of the people," as Victor Hugo replied with disdain? Did it have a taste of its own?

More than ever, the possession of beautiful objects was a sign of affluence; it was not considered *de bon ton* to spend lavishly as the aristocracy used to. But a comfortable opulence was desirable, even morally condoned, for as the director of the Ecole des Beaux-Arts explained in one of his treatises, a strong family feeling flourishes in a warm and luxurious interior. The role of women had become central, both as

around meals and visits paid by and to friends. One no longer took one's guests around the house; only a few rooms were for public viewing, a change that had happened much earlier in England. However, despite the importance of the family, the art of conversation remained pivotal to French social habits. One custom, known as *le jour*, is an example of this emphasis. From the time of Louis-Philippe, a lady entertained her guests once a week—hence le jour. "Entertain" perhaps is not the word; rather she would "receive," which implies, as it does nowadays, that she invited a select company, the conversation flowing with ease if her selection was discerning.[9]

In earlier years it was thought pleasant for a woman to embroider while she sat to the right of the fireplace entertaining her guests—which

173
Salon of Princess Mathilde, rue de Courcelles, Paris, 1859
Sébastien-Charles Giraud (1819-1892)
Oil on canvas
Musée national du Château de Compiègne

beautiful ornaments of the home (as can be seen from Ingres's striking portraits) and as tastemakers. Their influence had always been felt in aristocratic circles, but now, as the child found a more important place in the bourgeois family, so, too, did the mother and housewife—though very gradually, as she grew older. Indeed, one particular custom might explain why interiors changed so slowly in these classes: when a man got married, so the many manuals tell us, he chose the decoration and furnishings of his future home with the help of his bride's mother, whose taste would probably still be rather conservative.

From then on, the *cercle de famille* cited by Hugo would be the woman's main concern, the necessary regularity of family life being organized

explains the delicately crafted workboxes that even appear in palatial interiors—and Madame Récamier is described at the center of her literary salon with an *ouvrage* always in her hands. However, toward the end of the century this seemed too private an occupation, and slowly even the custom of *le jour* disappeared.

In the average middle-class home, rooms were now set in a pattern that would not change for a century: vestibule, salon, *petit salon*, and *salle à manger*. The latter remained formal the longest, and it was usually decorated in the Renaissance style.

The sitting room was perhaps most characteristic of the period because it was the least formal of the rooms opened to the outside world. It was where the women met and where individual taste could bloom, where one felt protected. A midcentury article in *L'Illustration*, the most important newspaper of the middle class, describes its coziness: "You meet in the 'petit salon' tightly closed with heavy curtains hiding the doors, with silk padding and double drapes hermetically sealing the windows. . .a good carpet under your feet. . .the wood paneling and the cold marble hidden under velvet or tapestries. . . ."[10] This profusion of textiles of all qualities, textures, and colors was not refined—refinement was not a trait of the period—but it was secure, allowing neither light nor noise nor danger to penetrate from outside.

As for the drawing room, it was usually like the bedroom, in the Louis XVI style. Empress Eugénie

had the greatest admiration for Marie-Antoinette and a passion for eighteenth-century styles; hence the vogue of Louis XV and Louis XVI furniture that pervaded so many interiors during the Second Empire. Handcrafted or manufactured, such furniture was accepted even at court. The "style Louis XVI Impératrice" was thus considered a new style. Numerous little towns in the provinces turned out furniture that was sold in Paris, where the dealers pretended it came from one of the deft ateliers of the Faubourg Saint-Antoine in the east of Paris.

The decorative arts flourished in public buildings as well as in private homes, and the furniture industry, which had expanded at the beginning of the century, now benefited from new techniques that could imitate the craftsman's dexterity in lathework, veneering, and molding. The same held

true for the rapidly expanding metalwork industries that supplied mounts and ornaments to the furniture trade. But the design and quality of furniture suffered from this growing trend toward mechanization.

The new techniques answered a growing need for comfort: the upholstery was thick, the buttoned-down silk was rich, the many tables, chairs, and armchairs that had been the pride of the French cabinetmakers were now copied, often in heavy, dark, or gilded versions. Such was the style to be found in the empress's various residences or in luxurious hotels (hence the later term *le goût Ritz*), as well as in the middle-class home, in whatever interpretation one could afford.

An increasing interest in history had led to the opening of museums, archives and schools, to the restoration of historical monuments such as those Viollet-le-Duc was famous for, and to numerous redecorations including that of the Renaissance Château d'Anet, which set an example. At the same time, the thriving industry in imitations was matched by a new attention to antiques. Until now people had not attached any special value to authenticity, and contemporary copies appeared more comfortable and sturdy. But the *meuble d'époque* became an object to be collected as well as an investment—as Balzac's *Le Cousin Pons* dramatically illustrated. The first antique dealers opened businesses in the 1870s—and the first forgers around 1880 (until then people were only reproducing and improving). A significant trendsetter was Baron de Rothschild, who had the interior of his Château de Ferrières decorated in the most opulent manner by Eugène Lami and who assembled spectacular works of art; hence *le goût Rothschild*.

Eclecticism—or the mixing of styles—as it has been called, was the rule, because there were so many historical periods with which one could be infatuated in recent decades. Gothic, Renaissance, Louis XV, Louis XVI were joined by a vogue for chinoiserie and japonisme, which brought beautiful new patterns to the decorative arts, as well as a plethora of bibelots, lacquers, and fans. One might have thought that this melange of styles would lack any sense of unity, but the interior was the kingdom of the upholsterer (*tapissier*). He was the one who created an ambience by coordinating chintz, damask, lampas, leather, and wallpaper—the unifying factor often being a wealth of deep red and dark green velvets and thick red carpets. The drawing room in particular was crowded with seats of every kind—*le crapaud, le pouf, le confortable, la causeuse, le confident,* and *l'indiscret,* with some names evoking a moment in conversation—and weighty balloon-backed chairs.[11]

In the palaces, innumerable upholstered stools were also provided for the empress's friends, who sat around her in their crinolines.

Wherever possible, vases and ceramic ornaments were featured: on mantelpieces fitted out with *housses* of gold-fringed velvet or on tables covered with fabulous cashmeres or carpets. Since the Restoration period, when the duchesse de Berry and Princesse Amélie had collected dainty objects of glass, wood, or porcelain, people had delighted in objets d'art. Opalines, with their bright colors, were much sought after, and the fine creations of the Cristalleries de Saint-Louis reached a new perfection under the Second Empire.

In *Du côté de chez Swann*, Marcel Proust wonderfully evokes the intimacy that could be created in the midst of this abundance: "Odette

177
The apartment of the Comte de Mornay, rue de Verneuil, 1833
Eugène Delacroix (1798-1863)
Oil on canvas
Musée du Louvre, Paris

178
Design for a winter garden (*jardin d'hiver*), about 1830
Anonymous
Watercolor
Musée des Arts Décoratifs, Paris

received [Swann] in a wrapper of pink silk which left her neck and arms bare. She made him sit close to her, in one of the many mysterious recesses which were tucked in the dimness of the drawing room, protected by huge palm trees that grew in Chinese pots, or by screens onto which had been pinned photographs, little silk bows, fans."[12]

Proust also speaks of "a delicious passion for botanics"[13] that had invaded these very feminine homes. The men's smoking room might be in the Turkish or Moorish style, but the women had a love for flowers and plants, whether real or artificial, under glass domes or in woven patterns. The fashion for a winter garden had been set by Princess Mathilde, whose literary salon was unrivaled for half a century. Soon everyone had a *jardin d'hiver* according to their means—a fashion

still visible in the square metal bow windows of so many Parisian facades, their windowpanes of stained glass in floral motifs enhancing the exoticism of the winter dream.

However, in the midst of this comfortable splendor, a dream was coming to an end. Many years earlier, Alfred de Musset had sensed this, and his feeling was now becoming reality: "We have eclecticism in lieu of taste, we take everything we find...in such a fashion that we live off debris, as if the end of the world were close."[14] An entire society and life-style would soon vanish, never to return.

As the nineteenth century drew to a close, the Third Republic was going through rather confused changes of government and political disputes. This fact, however, did not hinder France's territorial expansion in Annam, Tonkin, and Africa, nor did it affect the consequent industrial and commercial prosperity. The country was now firmly established as a republic, and there would no longer be a monarch to set the pace of social life. The presidents of the republic were either disinterested in the decorative arts or markedly conservative in their tastes. Official decoration perpetuated the style of the last major tastemaker, who had also set

up all the institutions of modern France, Napoleon I.[15] Not until the Art Deco period and again in the 1970s would there be any major innovation in the decoration of public buildings.

Several factors were giving a new shape to the middle class. Social laws permitted the emergence of a petite bourgeoisie of civil servants and owners of small businesses, while a first serious blow was to strike older bourgeois fortunes in 1914 with the taxation of revenues. This date, the onset of World War I, more than any other rang the death knell of

179
Wallpaper, 1850-55
Unknown manufacturer
Block-printed and
flocked paper (11 colors)
Bibliothèque Forney,
Paris

180
Velvet, about 1869
Unknown maker, Lyon
Silk
Cooper-Hewitt Museum,
New York, Gift of
Richard C. Greenleaf,
1952-149-4

181
Wallpaper, 1845-50
Jean Broc, designer
Jules Riottot et Pacon,
manufacturer
Block-printed paper (30
colors)
Bibliothèque Forney,
Paris

a society which, even while effacing the nobility and creating France's economic power, had tried to preserve a way of life that was more or less consciously imitated from the ease and timeless elegance of the aristocracy. The facility with which professional, social, and family life had overlapped would be no more. The terrible *grande guerre* was to put an end to the social pleasures of a vanishing society, and fortunes would never again be made so comfortably. La Belle Epoque was the last efflorescence of a society that had cast a veil over the vast majority of its people.

Until that time, the interiors that the bourgeois created for themselves would not of course be recognizable as one went down the social ladder—or up the winding *escalier de service* to the miserable maids' rooms and garrets that were the "interiors" of the masses. Insalubrious and cold, these rooms and the city tenements were denounced by the *hygiénistes* of the late nineteenth century, who condemned the promiscuity, filth, and lack of light and even air of the lodgings of the poor. Under the Ancien Régime, the servants had been almost part of the family, and their quarters were less separate than they became after the middle class moved into apartments.

One element was even more sadly lacking in the dwellings of these classes — water and sanitation. France was notoriously late in this field. It seems hardly credible that when the young empress Eugénie moved into the famous Palais des Tuileries, there was no running water and the water carriers had to be called in every morning. By the turn of the century the situation was improving, and bathrooms were becoming more common, at least in the *appartements sur rue*, the flats of the more affluent families that overlooked the street. But in the wings of these same buildings, surrounding the courtyard and with no elevator, flats were built without proper bathrooms, even though they were decorated with charming hearths and moldings on the ceilings. These pleasant but more modest *appartements sur cour* were smaller and lacked the long winding corridors so typical of a bourgeois interior, where the kitchen was placed at the very end to prevent unpleasant odors from reaching the reception rooms.

The comfort and security of the home were beginning to weigh on the individual. André Gide put it vividly: "Families—I hate you! Closed homes, behind tightly shut doors: possessions of a jealous happiness."[16] Social life outside the home had, for women at least, been restricted to social visits, evenings at the theater, and promenades in the Jardin des Tuileries. Now, at the end of the century, greater freedom was possible, such as had probably always existed in the more popular classes where convention had not kept the woman confined at home. "Social life is going through a great evolution," wrote the brothers Goncourt. "I see women, children, households, families in the café [the Eldorado]. The interior is passing away. Life turns back to become public"[17]—as it had been in the lively cafés at the end of the eighteenth century.

Interiors were crowded with objects in every conceivable style, so that they looked like a museum. One person who was among the last to live in the grand aristocratic manner, Boni de Castellane, spoke of "a jay's nest adorned with peacocks' feather."[18] He married Anna Gould, and his own extravagant Palais Rose and fêtes contrasted with the gaudiness he deplored. Castellane also stressed that people now enjoyed meeting in garish hotels rather than in private homes.

All the same, the French middle class had no real desire to overthrow the reassuring conventions that had shaped the setting for its rituals. The split between tradition and innovation was widening, but the avant-garde in painting, literature, and the decorative arts was confined to very small groups. The style "le 1900" was in fact a gigantic recapitulation of all known styles, while the Modern style, or Art Nouveau, began only timidly, in furniture at least, by applying novel decorative elements to traditional pieces.

For many years, a few dissatisfied critics had castigated the lack of imagination and creativity of designers and decorators. As early as 1851, after visiting the Crystal Palace exhibition in London, Léon de Laborde called for a more rational approach to furnishings and decoration. And in 1863 a group of 130 technicians and craftsmen founded the Union Centrale des Arts Appliqués à l'Industrie. Nevertheless, despite their progressive ideals and their dissatisfaction with the interiors that were stifling them, they still subconsciously wanted to fend off the oncoming wave of modernism. During the last decades of the century,

architects, designers, and critics could not come to a clear decision. They knew the days of pastiche and clichés ought to have vanished, but they shied away from industrialized and serial production. Influenced both by the Gothic period—when craftsmanship was, so they thought, at its highest—and by the delicacy of the arts of Japan, they created an Art Nouveau lush with floral and natural motifs—which was also a tribute to the

184
Design for an interior in the Chinese style, 1850-70
Maison Pénon Frères
Gouache
Musée des Arts Décoratifs, Paris

185
"Abbaye de Jumièges" wallpaper, 1845
Leroy, manufacturer
Block-printed paper (8 colors)
Bibliothèque Forney, Paris

186
Design for a carpet, about 1850-70
Piat-LeFebvre et fils, Tournai
Gouache
Musée des Arts Décoratifs, Paris

122

187
Design for a boudoir in the Gothic style, about 1836
Anonymous
Watercolor
Musée des Arts
Décoratifs, Paris

188
Design for the atrium of the "Maison Pompéienne," Paris, 1860
Alfred-Nicolas Normand
(1822-1909), architect
Pen and ink, pencil, watercolor, gouache,
Musée des Arts
Décoratifs, Paris

189
**"Style Moderne,"
bedroom, 1902**
Majorelle Frères, Nancy,
designers
Cooper-Hewitt Museum,
New York, Picture
Collection

190
**Curtain (detail),
1900-15**
Unknown manufacturer,
France
Cotton velvet
Cooper-Hewitt Museum,
New York, Purchase S.C.
Hewitt Fund, 1988-42-1

191
**Dining room of the
Guimard's house, rue
Mozart, Paris, about
1910**
Hector Guimard
(1867-1942), designer
Photograph
Cooper-Hewitt Museum,
New York, Gift of
Madame Hector
Guimard, 1956-78-11

fabulous aspects of nature being discovered in the French colonies.

The change in decoration finally emerged, less threateningly, through objets d'art, which clearly enjoyed a wide audience of amateurs, connoisseurs, and collectors. In eastern France, Art Nouveau was nurtured in the workshops of a group of craftsmen who gathered around Emile Gallé in Nancy—remarkable men, soon known in Paris through the efforts of Siegfried Bing, a dealer in Japanese art, and, later, in French Art Nouveau furniture and objects, and through the various expositions. Gallé's superb glass pieces with floral and animal motifs were tremendously successful at the 1889 Expositions, and from then on Art Nouveau became *un snobisme*, as the painter Maurice Denis said. Thanks to Art Nouveau, the decorative arts came back to the fore, after long being held in contempt as "minor arts" by the Académie and the Ecole des Beaux-Arts, which seldom included them in official exhibitions. Splendid works in glass were produced by Daum Frères of Nancy, luxuriant with flowers, foliage, and grapes in sensuous colors. These extraordinary pieces—as well as glass by Eugène Rousseau,

ceramics by Ernest Chaplet, the exquisite jewelry of René Lalique—were all works that could be worn, collected, and displayed. They gave immediate visual and tactile pleasure.

But furniture and interior design of the kind that Bing showed in his own boutique or at his pavilion at the 1900 Exposition met with strong resistance in France, despite the efforts of

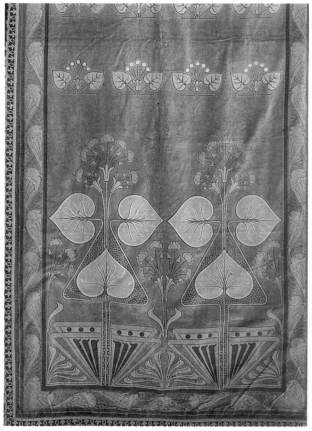

enlightened artists, collectors, and teachers to educate their compatriots. Louis Majorelle, Eugène Gaillard, Alexandre Charpentier, and Eugène Vallin designed furniture that ignored classical conventions and used ornamentation in a fluid, sculptural manner, curving the line of a mirror or a chair, inflecting the rigidity of a desk. Yet the Art Nouveau style was only fully accepted very late, when the public had become so used to seeing it in magazines that it could finally be produced in large series—by which time its quality had deteriorated so much that a new generation of designers was reacting vigorously against it. Many competitions for popular and affordable furniture had been launched to encourage the new style, but neither the manufacturers nor the department stores dared transgress the public's preference when cheap and sturdy replicas *de style* sold so well. Furthermore, the very concept of Art Nouveau, the sinuous lines worked into the wood itself, seemed to discourage industrialized production of quality.

Accustomed to the ornate warmth of thick dark velvets, the public did not appreciate the rather subdued colors used in Art Nouveau decoration: light gray, olive green, pale blue, or salmon appeared frequently in textiles and wallpapers such as the delicate patterns created by Hector Guimard, the famous architect who also designed the entrances to the Métro.

Despite Art Nouveau's short life and lack of influence, one often overlooked fact about the movement is significant: for the first time the creators of a French decorative style were neither theorists nor craftsmen but artists, however "minor" their art might be. They were not artisans working under the direction of an architect-designer like Percier or to the desires of tastemakers of high rank, as was the case for the wonderfully creative cabinetmakers up to the time of Louis-Philippe. They were conscious of being outside the official mainstream and knew that they were creating their own visions in glass, ceramics, or wood. Proof of this appeared when artists like Gauguin left their easels to work in these materials. The divergence between the traditionalists and an innovative group of creators who conceived of their art as part of the way they looked upon the world was now clear.

Art Nouveau interiors were rare, and admittedly they had not modified the French way of living. This, however, was not the reason for Art Nouveau's rejection by the new generation of architects and decorators. Very few were those who acknowledged its contribution and would say, with Le Corbusier, "Around 1900 came a magnificent gesture, Art Nouveau, shaking off the garments of an old culture." They criticized it for its "squirms, wriggles and blobs," and in typically French classical tradition, they resented Art Nouveau's exuberance, which they thought was often in bad taste. They also considered that it had drawn too heavily upon foreign sources, both English and Oriental. They found its ornamentation preposterous and called for simpler outlines; the fact that some of these spokesmen were architects may explain their attitude. But many really yearned to renew the grand tradition of French cabinetmaking, with its refinement and its subtle use of beautiful materials.

The term *Art Déco* originated after the Exposition Internationale des Arts Décoratifs et Industriels Modernes of 1925. Yet the attitude underlying the style was born long before World War I. The Exposition Universelle of 1900 had been the apotheosis of Art Nouveau but had also heralded its decline. In a similar way, the Exposition of 1925 was to reveal the most splendid achievements of Art Deco style at a time when it

192
Wallpaper, 1896-98
Hector Guimard
(1867-1942), designer
Le Mardelé,
manufacturer
Printed paper (3 colors)
Bibliothèque Forney,
Paris

193
Design for an interior, about 1900
Eugène-Samuel Grasset
(1841-1917)
Pencil, watercolor, gold
highlights
Musée des Arts
Décoratifs, Paris

was already reaching its zenith.[19] In effect, the style lasted for several decades, which is surprising. The first advocates of the future Art Deco style began working as the Belle Epoque was ending; the style went into decline during the war, then flourished during *les Années Folles*, the Roaring Twenties; it lingered on through the Depression and was timidly revived after World War II. Was this perhaps the first time a style weathered peace and war, affluence and decline, only slightly affected by historical circumstances? The fact that Art Deco was so close to French taste might explain this endurance.

In the early twentieth century, France was in the vanguard in many fields—in painting, sculpture, dance, and music—but a lag continued so far as the home was concerned,[20] and a modern interior was not enough to the middle class the sense of material and social success to which they aspired. Balzac's saying, "A man becomes rich, but he is born elegant,"[21] would have been lost on them. Nevertheless, experimentation in the arts was

intriguing and even amusing to the public, however critical they remained. World War I had been so cruel, and had destroyed so many beliefs, that it was impossible to cling to former values. Neither moral certainties nor political ideals nor economic prosperity had been capable of preventing the death of millions and the collapse of an entire world. So the age was frivolous, especially in fashion, where the new attitude seemed easier to accept since the evolution had started even before the war. The corseted silhouette of the nineteenth century had been modernized, the war had shortened and simplified dresses, and the couturiers were among the first innovators.

The couturier Jacques Doucet is a case in point. A discerning patron of the arts, he owned a superb collection of eighteenth-century furniture and objects that he suddenly decided to sell in 1912. He then furnished his flat on the avenue du Bois (now avenue Foch), and later his "studio" in Neuilly, in a resolutely modern style, and called

194
Salon on a houseboat, Plate 38 (detail) from Léon Deshairs, *Intérieurs en Couleurs*, Paris, 1926
Martine, designer
Cooper-Hewitt Museum Library, New York

195
Dining room from a house in Brittany, Plate 31 (detail) from Léon Deshairs, *Intérieurs en Couleurs*, Paris, 1926
Léon Jallot, designer
Cooper-Hewitt Museum Library, New York

upon some of the most creative designers of his time—Paul Iribe, Eileen Gray, Marcel Coard, as well as Pierre Legrain, who was responsible for the beautiful leather bindings in his famous library. Another influential couturier was Paul Poiret; he said he "dreamt of starting a movement that would spread a new fashion in decoration and furnishing", and in 1911 he created l'Ecole Martine, a school for young girls that accomplished just this. The work of "les Martines" was simultaneously fresh, naive, and ultramodern;[22] their creations were considered the latest thing and much in demand.

Two very different aesthetics were evident in the Paris Exposition of 1925, though the term *Art Deco* is sometimes used rather loosely, encompassing design of the twenties and thirties. The first was luxurious Art Deco proper, which renewed, before 1910, the French tradition of cabinetmaking. The second was that of the Modernes, or of the *Esprit Nouveau*, as Le Corbusier termed it, which was proposing a totally new vision of the home and even of contemporary living.

Both tendencies had been influenced by the bold colors of Fauvism and the stylized and geometric shapes of Cubism. Diaghilev's Ballets Russes, which dazzled audiences when it came to Paris in 1909, introduced a radically new sense of theatricality. Both the traditionalists and the modernists felt the need to create a unity in the interior that had been rare since the 1840s. They also had in common a love for beautiful materials, exceptional woods, and fine leathers, for smooth surfaces and textures. Conceptually, however, they were quite opposed.

196
Printed fabrics, about 1950
Souleïado, Tarascon, manufacturer
Cotton
Collection Souleïado, Tarascon

The traditionalists were far more precious in their use of materials. Jacques-Emile Ruhlmann's furniture in particular is exquisitely elegant in its mastery of exotic woods inlaid with ivory and tortoiseshell, of shagreen, of gilded or silvered bronzes. There is also a poetic quality, seen in Jules Leleu's furniture incorporating mother-of-pearl, and in the very names of the woods these craftsmen selected, evoking distant shores and wild forests—amaranth, amboyna, Macassar ebony, coromandel, palissandre de Rio, sycamore, zingana. The lines of their furniture were wonderfully sensuous, opulent, and quiet.

These works were conceived by decorators who also thought of themselves as *ensembliers*, designers of a whole interior. The purpose of Louis Süe and André Mare's Compagnie des Arts Français was to consider every aspect of interior decoration. Similarly, Armand-Albert Rateau created an original and delicate interior for Jeanne Lanvin that was definitely in the Art Deco spirit but totally persona in its choice of materials and colors. The best work of these decorators was on a par with the finest furniture ever made, as were the beautiful porcelains created by the Sèvres and Haviland factories, the stunning crystal and glass of Baccarat, Lalique, and Daum, or the silverware of Christofle.

Ruhlmann, Leleu, Süe and Mare, and Lalique were among those decorators who received prestigious commissions for official buildings, for the Elysée Palace and the ministries, and for the fabulous liners that crossed the Atlantic: the *Ile-de-France, La Fayette, Champlain*, the legendary *Normandie*—as well as for luxury trains, such as the equally legendary Orient Express. Some of these decorators were also conscious of the need to cater to a less affluent majority, and they created workshops in the *grands magasins*, such as the Atelier Pomone founded by Maurice Dufrêne at Au Bon Marché. Indeed, the department stores became trendsetters on a very large scale.

This concern for a more popular clientele was essential, but it did not solve the fundamental problem: would cheaper furniture always be but a cheap copy of an ideal model, or should modern design take into account the contemporary way of life and new technology? Apartments were smaller now, domestic help was getting scarcer, even women worked longer hours outside the house,

and the family was losing its role as the focus of social and even private life.

The Modern movement was less well known and less spectacular than Art Deco, but it was to be continuously influential. Le Corbusier's Pavillon de l'Esprit Nouveau at the 1925 Exposition epitomized this new spirit. An interior was no longer furnished by a decorator or even installed by an *ensemblier*, rather, it was conceived as a totality in which the architecture, space, light, fixtures, wardrobes—all

were integrated into a program adapted to smaller homes (the studio apartment was a recent concept) and a faster pace of life. Most of the proponents of this way of thinking were architects or "interior architects," a notion that appeared in the 1930s. They might not all adhere to Le Corbusier's creed that the house should be a "machine for living" and that the decorative arts should be free of all superfluous decoration as he stated in *L'Art décoratif aujourd'hui*. But like Pierre Chareau, the architect of the Maison de Verre (House of Glass) in Paris and later of Robert Motherwell's house, they believed that the task of the designer was to invent *formes utiles*, objects whose shapes were strictly adapted to their function. Le Corbusier, in collaboration with Pierre Jeanneret and Charlotte Perriand, created revolutionary furniture in chromed or painted metal, to be manufactured in

197
"Les Fruits d'Or" fabric, about 1925
Edouard Bénédictus (1878-1930), designer
Silk brocade
Musée des Arts Décoratifs, Paris

198
Furnishing fabric, about 1920
Maurice Dufresne (1876-1955), designer
Cornille Frères, manufacturer
Silk
Musée des Arts Décoratifs, Paris

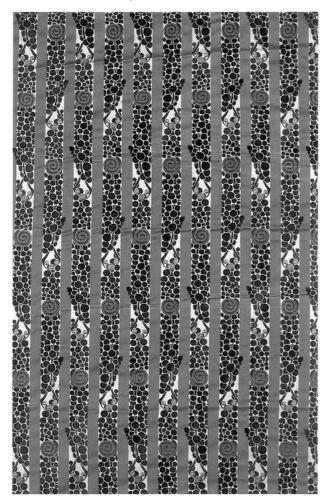

199
Bedroom shown at the International Exposition of Modern Decorative and Industrial Arts, Paris, 1925
Emile-Jacques Ruhlmann (1879-1933), designer
Cooper-Hewitt Museum, New York, Picture Collection

200
Furnishing fabric, 1925
Stephany, designer
Workshop of Emile-Jacques Ruhlmann (1879-1933)
Silk
Musée des Arts Décoratifs, Paris

series, such as steel *casiers-standard*, which could be piled up to form bookcases or to separate rooms.

Theirs was a totally novel way of envisaging the home, as was Francis Jourdain's concept of a "living room" (here again the English term being used), formulated as early as 1913, which later modified the traditional layout of the French interior. Pierre Chareau conceived of the interior space as a volume that could be transformed according to the varying needs of the family: sliding doors could close off a space or reduce it, lighting could lower a ceiling or reorient the center of activity. Because the modern way of living was his concern, Chareau also designed for the kitchen and the nursery, down to linen and broom closets. The architect Robert Mallet-Stevens, in his celebrated villa for the vicomte de Noailles in the South of France, in the same vein created a radically new decor, agreeing with his friend and collaborator Francis Jourdain: "You can most luxuriously install a room by unfurnishing it rather than furnishing it." Many of these modernists were unable to implement their ideas and have their furniture industrially made, but the foundations were laid for a new approach that would prepare the ground for *le design*.[23]

A passionate dispute now arose between the supporters of the Modern movement and those who believed that the home should offer what the agitation and impersonality of the city lacked—a warmth and serenity that these functional decors seemed to have forgotten, being in effect, closer to the spirit of the German Bauhaus than to the French sense of tactile pleasure and refinement. Some artists, though modern in their attitude, had felt this and let their sensibility speak. Jean-Michel Frank's designs showed an austere elegance, heightened by fine woods, unusual marquetries of split-wheat straw, and beautiful leathers, seen in his office decoration and chairs for Hermès. Similarly, Eileen Gray's furniture and carpet designs were as pure as her lacquerwork was delicate.

The abstract designs and bright colors of the artist Sonia Delaunay, who created very daring patterns, were also notable. One extraordinary artist was Jean Puiforcat, whose designs are among the most beautiful, sensitive, and sensuous of the period.

These years between the two wars were thus remarkably fertile and interior design expressed deeply rooted attitudes in French taste. A love of fine textures and form, a delicacy in the use of materials, an elegance of line that had been temporarily eclipsed during the second half of the nineteenth century by the need to flaunt one's riches and to protect oneself against change, were once again evident. Understandably, such qualities could more easily be found in a handcrafted work, and the traditionalists remained in vogue for a long time. Moreover, they spoke to the senses rather than challenging social and intellectual positions. Yet the modern current, rational and Cartesian, opened the door to what was to become a genuinely modern attitude toward both consuming and producing.

In 1945, when the war ended, the most urgent task was to rebuild the country, to plan cities and *grands ensembles* that would house the millions of homeless. With the Liberation came the dream of the American way of life, a new life made easy by cars and home appliances. But the reality of reconstruction and standardized design was not always cheerful, and budgetary concerns were foremost in the choice of building materials, fixtures, and furniture. The rift between architects and decorators, which, roughly speaking, corresponded to that between the Modern movement and the Art Deco of 1925, now became even clearer. Some of the best artist-decorators in the Art Deco style, which had been revived by the 1939 Exposition, continued to work for a small but select group. They received commissions from the Direction du Mobilier National for ministries and

embassies: Adnet, Arbus, Dominique, Leleu all did fine work, but it recalled an earlier epoch. Their concern was not with the circumstances of a society painfully emerging from the war, or with the technological advances that the war had confirmed in the use of rubber, plastic, or metal. On the other hand, modern architects like Le Corbusier and Auguste Perret, and designers like Jean Prouvé, René Gabriel, Marcel Gascoin and Charlotte Perriand, received important commissions from the Ministry of Reconstruction for severely bombed cities.

It was accepted that the layout of apartment buildings had eliminated at least one room in the home: the *salle de séjour* was a living room that combined drawing room and dining room and was sometimes, in more modest housing, also the parents' bedroom. This implied a rational use of space, of storage places and smaller pieces of furniture, with fitted shelving and cupboards, laminated surfaces, and sometimes tubular steel.

From these difficult postwar years until the end of the fifties, the French furniture industry was far from thriving, and its designs for molded plywood and plastics were rather bland, often a simple updated version of prewar designs adapted to the new materials. Still, the French were, as they had been for so long, timid about modernizing their interiors. Many official prestigious buildings in France date back to the seventeenth and eighteenth centuries, and commissions did not often permit plastic or metal furniture. Even in the fifties and sixties it seemed difficult to blend modern metal or Formica with family pieces passed down for generations.

Only a radical change could overthrow this caution. France in the sixties awoke to an international scene that was affluent, positive, fearless. These were wonderfully creative years, and they gave birth to diverse visions and life-styles. An interesting distinction in life-styles—or at least in opinions about them—became evident. In the twenties, in certain circles, a small house designed by Le Corbusier was a symbol equivalent to that of a large luxurious house in the past. In the mid-sixties, an awareness of contemporary trends compensated for an ebb in fortunes. And philosophies and even political preferences were mirrored in the interior, which is characteristic of a certain propensity of the French to translate life into psychological or social expressions.

The mid- and late sixties were also a period of "democratization," a term dear to both radicals and designers, when Prisunic, the chain of department stores, was publishing its first catalogue of affordable furniture.[24] Here was design for a public

201
Bedroom of a Paris apartment, about 1925
Pierre Chareau (1883-1950), designer
Thérèse Bonney (1897-1978), photographer
Cooper-Hewitt Museum, New York, Bonney Collection

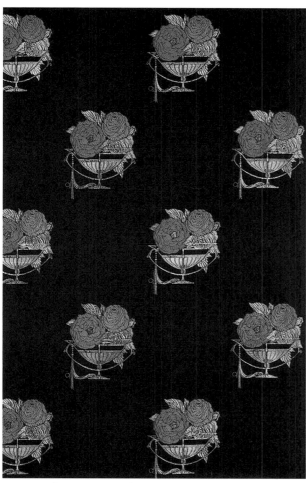

that was "young" in spirit—a new concept in France, where the authority of age was respected—and much practical and cheerful furniture was in fact created for children's rooms and for schools, by Marc Berthier in particular. A new magazine appeared, *La Maison de Marie-Claire*, which addressed a similar demand for an informal but pleasing way of life.

Some designers, such as Marc Held, who worked with Knoll, even entered the protected field of *"le contemporain,"* yet another style of the sixties and seventies. Modern in line, it was as elegant as the work of Jean-Michel Frank, of irreproachable quality, soothing in its refinement. Sofas appeared in white or beige textiles or leather, as well as thick altuglas or lacquered coffee tables, and lamps such as those of La Maison Charles. Such interiors tended to be favored by a cadre supérieur, an executive class.[25]

These years of enthusiasm for a still unfamiliar affluence were also years of reflection, if not rejection. Jean Baudrillard published *Le Système des objets*, questioning the consumer society. The students of May '68 discovered "under the cobbles, the beach";[26] and academics retreated to rural districts and mythical provincial *bergeries* to make goat cheese. In the city, young intellectuals opted

131

for a comfortable medley of furniture made of
dark wood, preferably bought at "*Les Puces*," the
flea market, with a few chairs from an exotic shop
that also sold Mao shirts, North African blankets to
be strewn over low couches with cushions in
Indian patterns, and the odd African stool brought
back from one's years in the Coopération, the
French equivalent of the Peace Corps. Dozens of
books were piled up on wooden shelves set on
bricks, and the television set was partly hidden
under a plant in a corner. The oil crisis and the
opening of shops such as Habitat (Conran's in the
United States) accentuated this use of natural
materials—wood, rattan, straw—and of sensible
furniture that could be bought in kits—bookcases,
desks and storage units of various shapes and
heights.

Textiles in the 1970s were of particular
importance, since they added a warmth and a
personal note to rather cool interiors where white,
beige, and later gray predominated. The delightful
patterns by Pierre Frey and Manuel Canovas are
often inspired from *documents*, fabrics that have
been handed down through history and adapted to
contemporary taste. Their floral motifs are poetic,
creating illusions of lushness in otherwise sober
environments, and they also radically changed the

use of textiles in decoration. The textiles of
Souleïado, inspired by eighteenth—century
documents, also perpetuated handsome patterns
from Provence, which in the seventies responded
to a renewed interest in folk traditions. Yet, even
in these dryer years of design, the taste for luxury
has never disappeared: finely crafted furniture and
leathers can be found nowadays at Rena Dumas's,
and the tradition of Puiforcat has been renewed
with a keen eye for the present.

In the exuberant eighties, a new wave of
historicity has crested—but it is totally unlike the
nineteenth-century historicism, which quenched
creativity. In the late seventies Andrée Putman
began reissuing furniture and objects designed by
Eileen Gray, Robert Mallet-Stevens, René Herbst,
and Pierre Chareau. This furniture is elegant and
looks remarkably modern without being "design."
And, strangely, despite the fact that some of the
chairs are mass-produced, these new editions seem
to have influenced a recent return to one aspect of
the Art Deco tradition believed long defunct: the
signed object intended to be repeated only in
limited series, which is, surprisingly, back in
fashion again. However, the return to history in the
eighties is also a vision of the end of history, the
postnuclear world without a past. Antiquity
reappeared—though not in the form of French
classicism, nor the triumphant Rome of the First

206
Salon from the house of the Vicomte de Noailles, Paris, about 1925-30
Jean-Michel Frank
(1893-1941), decorator
Thérèse Bonney
(1897-1978),
photographer
Cooper-Hewitt Museum,
New York, Bonney
Collection

207
Folding screen, made for Jeanne Lanvin, about 1930
Armand-Albert Rateau
(1882-1938), designer
Lacquered wood
Musée des Arts
Décoratifs, Paris

133

208
**View of the indoor
swimming pool, Villa
Noailles, Hyères,
1928**
Robert Mallet-Stevens
(1886-1945), designer
Musée des Arts
Décoratifs, Paris

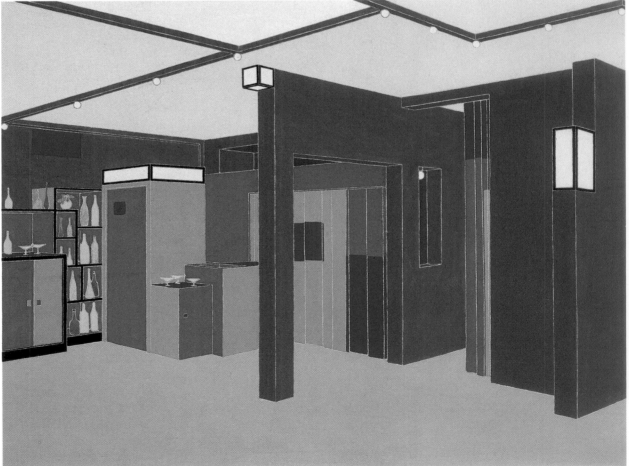

209
**Design for an entry
hall (detail), about
1925-30**
Francis Jourdain
(1876-1958), architect
Gouache
Musée des Arts
Décoratifs, Paris

210
View of the main hall of the "Maison de Verre" Paris, 1928-32
Pierre Chareau (1883-1950) and Bernard Bijvoet, designers
Musée des Arts Décoratifs, Paris

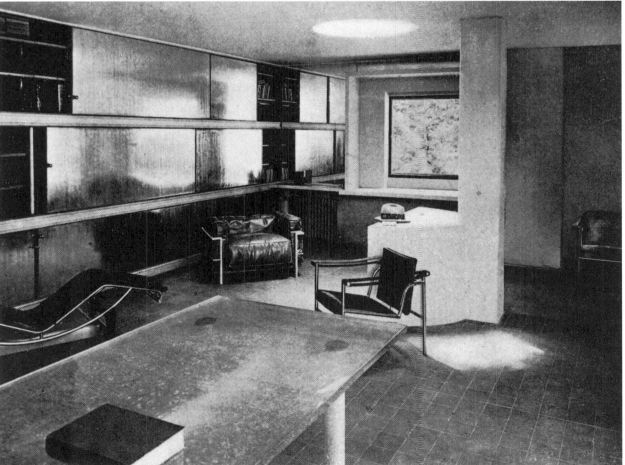

211
Living room in the Church House annex, Ville d'Avray, 1928-29
Le Corbusier (1887-1965), Pierre Jeanneret (1896-1967), and Charlotte Perriand (born 1903), architects/designers
Cooper-Hewitt Museum, New York, Picture Collection

Empire, but in the ruins of that world, the broken
columns, the heavy white drapes, and the delicate
urns, as in the work of decorator Jacques Grange.
Furniture designers (they call themselves *créateurs
de meubles*) also integrate the erosion of time into
their work, using materials apparently already

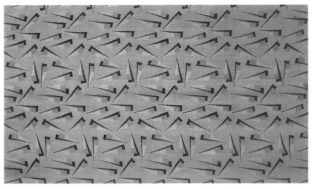

before function, must have "*un look*," however
comfortable that look may or may not be. At
home, of course, but above all in public
places—libraries, shops, nightclubs—the look is
essential; hence the success of the Café Costes in
Paris. Its creator, Philippe Starck, has synthesized
the spirit of the age: "I understood that furniture
and objects did not interest me.... But that these
objects should be vehicles of a meaning, of an
expression—absolutely, I feel totally concerned."
And when François Mitterrand and Jack Lang
commissioned new furniture for the government,
they were clearly promoting young designers but
they were also planting an image of the modern
France they wanted to encourage.[27]

At home, technology takes care of the
essentials—cooking, eating, washing. So, possessing
a piece of furniture or having one's interior
decorated by one of these fashionable designers is
a sign that one belongs to a certain elite—a sign
readily recognized by one's peers in a world of
speed, media, and advertising, where interiors are

weathered by the centuries, as Jean-Michel
Wilmotte has done. Indeed, the very names of
some of these groups—such as Totem or En
Attendant les Barbares—imply this expectation of a
reversed history.

There are no eternal or universal values. As the
end of the millennium approaches, an ironic look
is being taken at history, style, and French
standards of good taste especially. Of course taste
had already been rocked earlier: from kitsch to *le
rétro* (a feigned nostalgia for the forties and fifties),
from the blitheness of Archizoom and the
irreverence of Alchymia and Memphis to the wit of
High Tech. The young French designers have
reveled in this postmodern mood. Recently,
inspiration has sprung from all directions,
encompassing the Viennese Secession, Japan, and
Russian Constructivism, as well as cinema, painting,
and sculpture.

Does form still follow function? This is hardly a
contemporary concern. Decoration nowadays,

frequently redone. Is this an elite of money or class? Not really, for several of these designers create for mail-order catalogues. Is it an intellectual elite? Not really, or at least not in the former sense of an intelligentsia. Rather, it proves that one is "with it", "plugged in" to the future.

Owning an object sold in a catalogue is not demeaning, for the taste with which it is integrated into an interior will subtly change its meaning. Owning furniture by one of these designers is fun, which is central to the contemporary attitude: keeping a distance between image and wit, enjoying the creations of the eighties without prejudice.

So, a handsome wrought-iron table by Garouste and Bonetti can indeed be in the same room as an eighteenth-century armchair, and this implies that, after all, there is a continuity beyond the shocks of history. The French interior at its best has an ease and freedom that successfully blends styles beyond convention or fashion. The harmony lies in the refinement of materials and colors, in a certain quality of light, and remains timeless.

1. Percier and Fontaine began working exclusively for Napoleon in 1802. Their book *Recueil de décorations intérieures*, published in 1812, was immensely influential.
2. The Empire style was made more accessible to the public by publications such as the fashionable journal of the designer Pierre de la Mésangère, whose designs were copied well into the Restoration period.
3. The fashion for rooms hung with silks had become

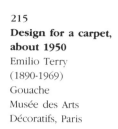

215
Design for a carpet, about 1950
Emilio Terry
(1890-1969)
Gouache
Musée des Arts
Décoratifs, Paris

216
Bedroom exhibited at the Paris Exposition of 1937
Maurice Barret, architect
Cooper-Hewitt Museum, New York, Picture Collection

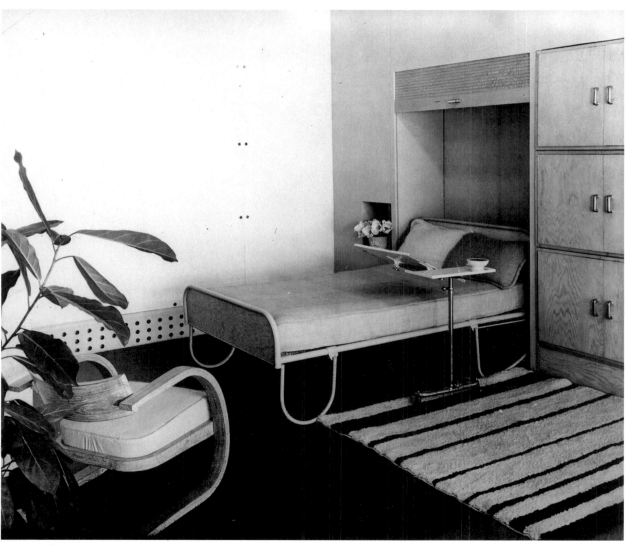

217
**"Vendages"
furnishing fabric,
1986**
Patrick Frey (born
1947), designer,
for Pierre Frey, Paris
Cotton
Collection Pierre Frey,
Paris

218
**"Falaises" wallpaper,
1976**
Alain Le Foll
(1934-1981), designer
Zuber, Rixheim, Alsace,
manufacturer
Cooper-Hewitt Museum,
New York, Gift of
Zuber et Cie, 1988

219
**"Maharajah"
furnishing fabric,
1965**
Manuel Canovas (born
1935), designer
Silk
Collection Manuel
Canovas, Inc., Paris

220
**Drawing room in the
apartment of Henri
Samuel, Paris,
designed 1975**
Published in *House and
Garden*, March 1984
Henri Samuel (born
1904), designer

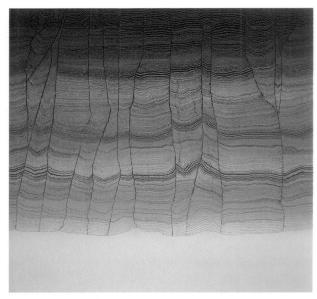

138

221
Bedroom the apartment of Jacques Grange, Paris, 1988
Jacques Grange (born 1944), designer

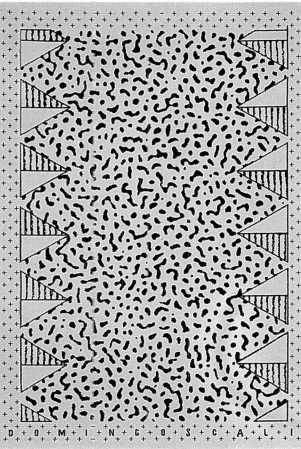

222
"Jardin d'Orient" carpet, 1986
Elizabeth Garouste (born 1949), Mattia Bonetti (born 1952), designers, for En Attendant les Barbares Wool Collection En Attendant les Barbares, Paris Courtesy V.I.A., Paris

223
"La Cienaga" carpet, 1988
Studio NEMO (active since 1981) Alain Domingo, (born 1952), and François Scali (born 1951), designers Wool, cotton, jute Collection Géométrie Variable, Paris

139

224
Private apartments of the President in the Elysée Palace, Paris, 1983
Ronald Cécil Sportes (born 1943), designer

widespread; and Charles IV, king of Spain, and the king of Bavaria were among the clients of the Lyons *soyeux*, the silk industrialists. However, for the less stately rooms of the palace, Napoleon ordered that less expensive damasks, satinades, or patterned cottons be used, as well as wallpaper. At this time the firms such as toiles de Jouy and wallpaper manufacturers flourished.

4. Honoré de Balzac, "Traité de la vie élégante," *La Mode*. 1830.

5. In opposition to Louis XVIII and Charles X, who were both Bourbons and still close to the old aristocracy, Louis-Philippe had lived as a bourgeois until he became king late in life. He always relied on the upper middle class of industrialists and bankers.

6. Someone who typified this eclecticism was Aimé Chenavard, who worked at the Sèvres factory and was the most influential ornemaniste (creator of motifs) of his time. Balzac nicknamed him the Hornet. From the endless hours he spent in the Cabinet des Dessins at the Louvre, studying drawings and prints of past centuries, Chenavard accumulated an extraordinary "grammar" of styles from every period, which he used in his decorations and which was copied by many a furniture maker after him.

7. The distinction Queen Hortense mentions between the two ways of life is of great interest: indeed, the interiors we know are those of the city and of the affluent classes, which have been documented. We may guess, chiefly from the contemporary literature, that these interiors could at best be distant models for the majority, who lived in modest lodgings or country homes and farms.

8. Balzac, op. cit., 1830.

9. At the beginning of the season, a lady sent out cards to relatives, friends, and acquaintances, indicating which day of the week she would be at home, from 3:00 p.m. to 7:00 p.m. in Paris and from 2:00 p.m. to 6:00 p.m. in the provinces. On that afternoon, brief visits, usually not exceeding half an hour, were paid, and husbands often made a point, in the midst of their day's work, of "passing by" the salons of their wive's best friends.

10. *L'Illustration*, 15 February 1851.

11. Quoted in Mario Praz, *L'Ameublement, psychologie et évolution de la décoration intérieure* (1964), p. 348.

12. Marcel Proust, *Swann's Way (Du côté de chez Swann.* (Pléiade Gallimard, Paris, 1987), p. 220).

13. Ibid, p. 592.

14. Alfred de Musset, *Confessions*, quoted by Praz, p. 60.

15. When Napoleon fell from power in 1815, the Mobilier Impérial had in stock 68,000 meters (68 kilometers!) of unused silks and fabrics, which later kings and presidents used for the decoration of official buildings until 1960. The main *soyeux* to work for the emperor was Pernon, whose company (Tassinari et Chatel) still supplies official palaces.

16. André Gide, *Les Nourritures terrestres* (Paris, 1897).

17. Quoted by Valerie Steele in *Paris Fashion*, 1988, p. 140.

18. Boni de Castellane, *Mémoires 1924-1925* (Paris, 1925).

19. The exhibition had first been proposed in 1906, in reaction to Art Nouveau, but was postponed several times. It finally took place in 1925.

20. Edith Wharton in *French Ways and Their Meanings* praises the French reverence for ancient forms and observances.

21. Balzac, op. cit.

22. The Martines initially received a little help from Raoul Dufy, who was designing textiles for Poiret, but Poiret left the girls totally free in their designs, which he then edited, used for his summer dresses, and sold in the Maison Martine on the Faubourg Saint-Honoré, where Fernande Olivier, Picasso's former lover, was one of the sales ladies.

23. In 1929 the Union des Artistes Modernes was created around Hélène Henry, René Herbst, Francis Jourdain, Robert Mallet-Stevens, and Raymond Templier. Over the years they were joined, more or less formally, by Jean Puiforcat, Pierre Chareau, Le Corbusier, Charlotte Perriand, and Pierre Legrain, among others.

24. The first furniture catalogue from Prisunic offered works by Marc Berthier, Olivier Mourgue, Marc Held, and Gae Aulenti.

25. Names of companies, such as Roset or Roche et Bobois, rather than of designers, seem to be attached to this permanent and timeless tendency of quiet French elegance.

26. "Sous les pavés, la plage" was one of the famous mottoes of the student revolt, implying that nature and true life were buried beneath the bourgeois city.

27. The task of decorating the private apartments of the Elysée Palace was entrusted to Jean-Michel Wilmotte, Philippe Starck, Marc Held, Annie Tribel, and Ronald Cécil Sportes.

225
Lobby Bar of The Royalton, New York, 1988
Philippe Starck (born 1949), designer

CATHERINE ARMINJON

THE ART OF DINING

In France, until quite recently, a passion for food could be considered vulgar. A passage by a member of the Club des Cent Gastronomes, quoted by the journalist Croze at the beginning of the twentieth century, testifies to this conventional reaction: "How extraordinary is the importance attached to the sense of hearing and the contempt in which that of taste is held. To have subtle tastebuds is ill regarded....What a dull-witted fellow, they say, his only pleasure is eating...." But actually everyone knows and Croze says, "There never was a true gourmet who was a fool." Yet the traditional attitude, current among the French for generations, has undoubtedly played a large part in the failure to give due consideration to the dining table—content and container alike—as an art in its own right.

Gonzague Saint-Bris defined dining as "a feast, a succession of codes that make their entrance like characters in a play... the feast of the palate demands a ritual in the presentation of the dishes...civilization clothes the needs of nature with the ornaments of art. It is not only the visual presentation of the food that enchants us; it is also the decoration of the objects...the form of the flatware...the play of references of the tools of the table that govern the feast." In the wake of the

upheavals of the Revolution, there followed a return to patterns of social behavior based on the Ancien Régime, to the great traditions acquired with such difficulty over previous centuries, which were to spread through the different levels of society. These traditions were seized on in the nineteenth century by the middle class, who often expressed their worldly ambitions at the dining table.

The twentieth century followed more modestly, with meals that no longer demonstrated status alone but also new living and eating conditions, in line with the development of the decorative arts. In the last few years there has been a revival of interest in the art of entertaining, though in a very different form. This has been sanctioned by institutions, state support, the creation of museums and research centers, contests, magazines and books, exhibitions, and finally by specialty stores selling both new and old tableware. Taken together, these factors have combined to restore the art of the table to a position of importance.

For one hundred and fifty years, from the Revolution to World War II, family life in France was guided by a detailed code of behavior in which objects and people had precisely defined roles. The image of a private life governed by and conforming to social norms was at the same time a

229
Le Grand Vefour restaurant, Paris, with early 19th century painted decoration, photographed about 1920
Cooper-Hewitt Museum, New York, Picture Collection

230
Café Frascati, about 1807
Philibert-Louis Debucourt (1755-1832)
Engraving
Musée Carnavalet, Paris

145

The *service à la française*, in which the dishes for each course were all laid out on the table at the same time, followed rules that could not be infringed. Meals consisted of a series of courses, which might comprise side dishes for the first, roasts and entremets for the second, and then a dessert course in which greater latitude was allowed. The overall plan for the table required dishes in specific numbers and sizes. Pairs of dishes were designed to be laid parallel to the sides and at the ends of the table. In the middle was a *dormant*, or *surtout*, an elaborate, decorative centerpiece. Unfortunately, the lavish and visually appealing aspect of such displays worked to the detriment of the food, which was difficult to keep hot when laid out in this spectacular fashion. In the first half of the nineteenth century, the *service à la française* was still used for state banquets—imperial, royal, or princely—but less and less frequently.

In the *service à la russe*, food was carved and garnished in the kitchen, and then sent to the dining room to be presented and served to the guests. For large cuts of meat that were too heavy or awkward to be passed, carving was done in the dining room or pantry, and the food was then served on hot plates.

Clearly, this system, though less satisfactory from the aesthetic point of view, had the advantage of allowing food to be served under the best conditions—cooked, carved, presented, and eaten without delay. Speed of service and the order of distribution were the first things to be affected by the system, giving it preference among gourmets. Today, *service à la russe* is the accepted practice, and most Anglo-Saxon countries have made it their own. The old French style of dining yielded to this foreign import with good reason. At the beginning of the nineteenth century, gastronomy had won out over spectacle—to reside henceforth in the gourmet's palate rather than in his vision, as it had done throughout the Ancien Régime.

factor in and a sign of middle-class success. In the nineteenth century, meals were governed by the three unities, learnedly enforced as they had been during the eighteenth century. First, there was the unity of place, the dining room. Originally ill-defined, this space was institutionalized over time until it became a fixed entity by the beginning of the nineteenth century, a place dedicated to the taking of meals in common and clearly dissociated from the reception rooms and from the kitchen quarters where food was prepared.

Second, there was the unity of time: dining was subject to schedules. In previous centuries, mealtimes varied enormously, depending on social class. Beginning in the nineteenth century and for almost two hundred years, the tyranny of schedule was to govern French meals. Indeed, it seems that the stomachs of certain French citizens frequently turned into clocks, making them particularly unreceptive to different eating habits in other countries.

The third and last unity, that of action, was to materialize in the *service à la russe*, which became widely accepted in the first decades of the nineteenth century. It progressively replaced the *service à la française*, whose usage dates from the seventeenth century in a carry-over from medieval practices.

GASTRONOMIC LITERATURE

French culinary literature and treatises have a long history. The earliest appeared around 1300 with the *Viandier* of Guillaume Tirel, better known as Taillevent, the first *maître queux* of Charles V. In 1651, La Varenne wrote *Le Cuisinier françois*. In the eighteenth century, the art of cookery began to command attention; important authors were Menon and, with his *Cuisinier moderne,* Vincent la Chapelle, noted predecessor of the famous chef Carême. The century was marked by the use of a built-in range, with several openings for charcoal

232
Dining room at the Hôtel de France, Biarritz, about 1864
Engraving
Cooper-Hewitt Museum, New York, Kubler Collection

233
Service à la française and *service à la russe*, 19th century
Engraving
Musée Bouilhet-Christofle, Paris

burners—the *potager*—which made it possible from then on to simmer sauces, glazes, and essences away from the flames of the open fire. This development engendered many new, complicated dishes, along with a need for cookbooks explaining how to prepare them.

Not until the nineteenth century, however, did true gastronomic literature (with engraved illustrations) appear. The very term gastronomy was created at this time by Joseph Berchoux, author of the poem *La Gastronomie et l'homme des champs.* The books were accessible to an elite in a period when a large part of the population of France is known to have been still illiterate.[1]

A LITTLE SAVOIR-VIVRE

Table manners have changed very little over the past two hundred years. For official dinners, banquets, and entertainments, the code of behavior has remained the same. Among the numerous prohibitions of French etiquette at table are speaking with one's mouth full, fiddling with one's bread or with objects on the table,[2] sniffing what is on the plate, spitting fruit pits onto the plate, blowing on food to cool it. In France, one's hands should be placed on the table to either side of the plate. Etiquette books at the beginning of the nineteenth century sanction holding bones in the fingers—but not gnawing them too clean or throwing them under the table. Shoes are not to be taken off, nor feet shuffled. Even today it is not considered the thing to turn over one's plate in order to examine the maker's mark or to tip it to polish off the last drops of gravy or soup. By the end of the eighteenth century, napkins played their own role at table, cunningly folded to play their part in the decorative staging at the beginning of the meal. From the early nineteenth century, napkins were not to be completely unfolded and spread out, or—in spite of considerations of cleanliness and convenience—tied around the neck. The spoon was to be brought to the mouth by its tip; fruit with pits was eaten with knife and fork, oranges with the fingers. Once the food was eaten, dirty flatware was not to be placed beside the plate or on the knife rest, but aranged side by side on the plate.

Table manners have evolved since the beginning of the nineteenth century as a result of new kinds of food and the new implements developed to deal with them. Until the mid-nineteenth century, for example, the cheese course was reserved for men, women being offered instead biscuits and preserves.

THE ORIGINS OF THE DINING ROOM AND THE DINING TABLE

In most homes the dining room and table became a standard feature at the beginning of the nineteenth century. This room had been slow to materialize. For several centuries, French kings and noblemen had taken their meals in the study or antechamber; the middle and working classes for their part had eaten in the bedchamber or in the kitchen. One of the first references to a *salle à manger*—literally, a room for eating—dates from 1694 in an inventory of Marshal d'Humières. In the eighteenth century, rooms for dining are mentioned; Louis XV created two dining rooms in the *petits appartements* at Versailles. In this period, the rooms had special furnishings: one or two stoves, a water fountain, marble-topped furniture, plain chairs, side tables, and screens. The dining table itself is not mentioned, but it can be assumed that these were collapsible affairs. The earliest recognizable cabinet-made tables, permanently installed in the dining room, did not become common until the last thirty years of the eighteenth century, a development from the drop-leaf table known as *à l'anglaise*.

After the Revolution, collapsible trestle tables disappeared and the dinner table became an integral part of the dining room. By 1808, Jacob-Desmalter made mahogany dining-room chairs, consoles, sideboards, and tables.[3]

The decoration of the table in the Empire is also worth noting. With the exception of architectural and sculptural *surtouts*, such as the fountains and temples made for the visit of King Charles IV of Spain (preserved in part at Malmaison), or the "Olympic service," from Sèvres, these decorative items consisted of ornamental sculptures, jardinieres and baskets for cut flowers and fruit, as well as candlesticks, whose function and place on the table became a permanent feature; they ranged from simple candlesticks to gigantic candelabra with multiple branches. Goblets, bowls, and metal or glass stands and dishes rounded off this collection, together with saltcellars and pepperboxes, condiment holders, and other

accessories. The symmetry that ruled the table after 1810 — with all these items arranged so that the tallest and most important were in the middle and the rest disposed in diminishing order of size — reflects the style of Carême. Even if he persisted in using the *service à la française*, he instilled some order with his symmetrical, rhythmic organization of elements and by limiting the number of dishes laid on the table at each course. Small round and oval dishes in a variety of shapes were used by Carême, thus allowing more space for each person. By doing this Carême enhanced the ambience of

234
Menu from the Tuileries Palace, 1860
Chromolithograph, pen and ink
Bibliothèque Nationale, Paris

235
Grand Buffet de la Cuisine moderne, **early 19th century**
Antonin Carême
(1784-1833)
Engraving
Inventaire Général,
Paris

236
Table centerpiece, about 1815
Pierre-Philippe Thomire
(1751-1843)
Gilt bronze, glass
Musée Marmottan, Paris

149

237
Design for a tripod jardiniere, about 1810
Jean-Baptiste-Claude Odiot (1763-1850)
Watercolor
Collection Odiot
Orfèvre, Paris

238
Design for a tureen and stand for the Empress Josephine, 1812
Charles Percier (1764-1838) and Pierre-François-Léonard Fontaine (1762-1853)
Plate 46 from *Recueil de décorations intérieures* (detail), Paris, 1812
Engraving
Cooper-Hewitt Museum, New York, Gift of the Council, 1921-6-377

239
Tureen from the service of Prince Camillo and Pauline (Bonaparte) Borghese, 1794-1814
Martin-Guillaume Biennais (1764-1843)
Silver gilt
The Metropolitan Museum of Art, New York, Joseph Pulitzer Bequest, 1934

such receptions. As he put it: "Numerous recipes are not enough to make a new cuisine; it must also have order."

Silver or gilded plate and crystal were particularly favored in this takeover of the banqueting table during the nineteenth century. A complete service could run to an incredible number of pieces. The great silver-plate set ordered by Napoleon III for Emperor Maximilian of Mexico—which was delivered in 1863 and displayed to Parisians in a stockroom of the famous silversmiths Christofle on the rue de Bondy, before it was shipped—comprised 4,938 pieces, more than 200 of them comprising the *surtout*.

Thematic subjects proliferated in the decoration of upper-class tables—industry, geography, and the arts were extremely common. Artists such as Carrier-Belleuse were called upon for designs to be produced by such leading firms as Christofle. Lighting, too, rapidly assumed a dominant role in table decoration, a position that it has kept for nearly two hundred years. On humble tables of a later date it was not unusual to use a simple oil lamp placed directly on the table to light the whole room. Two candlesticks may still form the only decoration of many tables today, and they are routinely included among the gifts and purchases made for the elegant table.

One object that reappeared with the pomp and circumstance of the Empire style before disappearing forever should be mentioned: the *nef*, which goes back to the Middle Ages. A symbol of royal or princely power and importance, the *nef* was a silver vessel in the form of a ship that was placed before a person of rank to hold his napkin, knife and fork, and spices. It made a magnificent debut once again at the wedding banquet of Napoleon I and Marie-Louise of Austria. The emperor and empress each had a *nef* in silver gilt, the work of the goldsmith Henri Auguste. The two pieces, however, were not placed before their imperial majesties. No doubt over time and with the trauma of Revolution the role and function of *nefs* had been forgotten; they were relegated to two little tables at the ends of the horseshoe banquet table.

The *service à la russe* fostered a whole collection of ornamental *surtouts*, bowls, jardinieres, and candelabra on the long dining table. This was a way to display one's fortune and status to one's guests. The opportunity was too good to be missed, and paintings of dining tables during the forty years at mid-century show the extremely limited space that was left for plates,

catch their breath. It was not simply a question of innumerable dishes, exceptional quality, and exotic elegance of presentation, but above all of the majesty and artistry with which the meal was served.[4]

In his own way, Carême transformed the dining table into a political weapon. Indeed, at the Congress of Vienna, under Talleyrand's aegis, the grandeur of the princely table so impressed lesser participants that it did France a service. Carême organized, rethought, and codified what had previously been the result of whim. He made gastronomy into an art of its own. Every great house in the nineteenth century wanted to have one of his pupils as its chef. With the triumph of the bourgeoisie after the Restoration, culinary arts changed: the extravagant display and etiquette created by Carême were quickly discarded. But the

240
Two designs for the "Service Olympique," 1806
Théodore Brongniart (1739-1813), designer
Manufacture Impériale de Sèvres
Watercolor
Manufacture Nationale de Sèvres, Archives

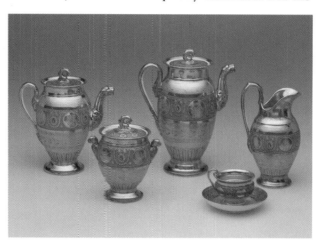

241
Coffee service, about 1820
Marc Schoelcher (1766-1832)
Porcelain
Division of Ceramics and Glass, National Museum of American History, Smithsonian Institution, Washington, D.C., Alfred Duane Pell Collection

knives, forks, spoons, and glasses, all arranged in a tight circle.

THE ROLE OF CARÊME IN THE NEW GOLDEN AGE

The famous chef Carême, as we have seen, brought more order and comfort to the dinner table. Indeed, it was he who prescribed that there should be a certain distance—about two feet—between each guest. Apparently, the mass of objects in the middle of the table, which prevented those seated on either side from seeing each other, was criticized by contemporaries and gastronomes, and distinguished guests were relieved to see that dining tables became more open toward the end of the nineteenth century.

Carême, "the chef of princes and the prince of chefs," was an extraordinary individual. In 1805 he entered into the service of the famous Talleyrand, and later on he was chef in the house of James Rothschild. The arrangements he devised must have astounded guests or at least caused them to

essence of Carême's art as it related to a new cuisine and a philosophy of gastronomy was retained intact, and has survived to the present day. The great virtuoso masterpieces he created, magnificent sculptural pieces, were abandoned, and his theatrical ideas never penetrated the houses and apartments of the nineteenth-century middle classes; but Carême's culinary inventions became a quintessential part of the French national inheritance.

The dining table conquered political as well as daily life. Henceforth—whether under Louis-Philippe, the Empire, or the Third Republic—it was at table that ambitions were declared, marriages arranged, business discussed. The pride, illusions, and aspirations of the middle class—both high and low—found a home there.[5]

THE RURAL TABLE

There has been very little study of rural dining habits. Although the distinction becomes less obvious as we get closer to our own times, the

151

objects in museums of popular history and art, as well as those in settings maintained in their original condition, show that until World War I the rural table had changed hardly at all since the Middle Ages. The occasional seventeenth- or eighteenth-century paintings that show peasants at table—or rather, in the process of eating without ceremony in the course of their everyday lives—are very similar to mid-nineteenth-century representations of farmhouse interiors. Plates, faïence or pewter dishes, jars for fat, and earthenware pans are the only dishware in these houses. There is little or no linen on the table, and no glasses, only a communal goblet in metal or wood, a dish or soup tureen, one ecuelle (small covered bowl) shared by several people, spoons and knives, but few forks as yet. The fork appeared quite late; it was not in use in the Cantal, for instance, at the turn of the century; and in another region, the Mâconnais, "There is no mention of flatware, that is, matching spoons and forks, in a precious metal among those of modest means until the very end of the nineteenth century or until the twentieth."[6] Matching table knives did not appear before the end of the nineteenth century, and even after World War II it was not unusual for men to prefer to use their own pocket knives.

At the beginning of this century, industrialization and domestic modernization led to greater comfort for all, with improved means of cooking, the availability of flatware, and the purchase at every level of society of matching tableware: a set for

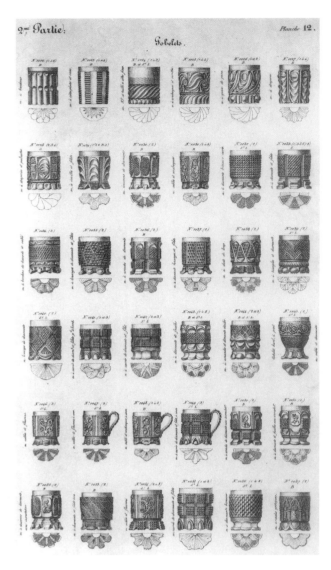

every day, of course, but also one to be brought out on special occasions. The difference between peasant and bourgeois homes disappeared, and thanks to the department stores, hardware stores, and mail-order catalogues, a certain uniformity became apparent.

THE TABLE IN ART

Although most of the many objects on the dining table are not visible in paintings and engravings,

the artists who created pictures, watercolors, drawings, and prints throughout the nineteenth century were often attracted in their choice of subject matter by domestic scenes, especially of light meals and little groups at table. Previous centuries had favored representations of parties, feasts, and banquets that set the stage for people of importance. Under Napoleon, and later under the Second Empire, great banquets were depicted. One such lavish occasion was Napoleon's wedding to the daughter of the Emperor of Austria, painted by Casanova. Later, under King Louis-Philippe, the Ladies' banquet in 1835 was recorded by Viollet-le-Duc, as was the dining room of Napoleon III's cousin, Princess Mathilde, in her *hôtel particulier* on the rue de Courcelles; all show the splendor of a wealthy Parisian household.

The princess's receptions were much sought after: Flaubert, Théophile Gautier, Prosper Mérimée, and Sainte-Beuve were all to be found there. The paintings show the new fashion for green plants in standing jardinieres. Interior decoration was standardized according to the eclecticism of the period. For bedrooms, the

Louis XV style was preferred; for salons that of Louis XVI. Dining rooms, curiously enough, took a turn back to even earlier styles, giving rise to generations of dining-room suites in the manner of Henri II. In 1859, in the Salle des Etats in the new quarters of Napoleon III in the Louvre, a painting of a banquet given by the emperor in honor of the heads of the armies of Italy provides a perfect glimpse of a formal meal in comfortable, stylish circumstances such as must have taken place among the bourgeoisie of the period on many official or family occasions.

In 1867, Baron Haussmann, the celebrated Paris prefect who transformed the city in the 1860s by, among other things, his creation of the *grands boulevards*, commissioned from Christofle for the Hôtel de Ville a large *surtout* designed by Victor Baltard, architect of Les Halles and of the church

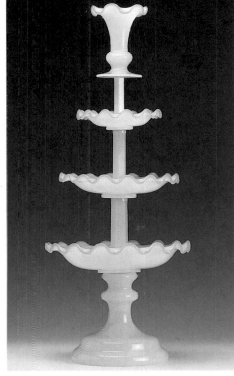

244
Footed bowl, 1845
Cristalleries de
Saint-Louis
Pressed glass
Collection Cristalleries
de Saint-Louis, Paris

245
**Tiered dessert tray,
1858**
Cristalleries de
Saint-Louis
Opaline glass
Collection Cristalleries
de Saint-Louis, Paris

246
**Maison d'Or
restaurant, boulevard
des Italiens, Paris,
about 1839**
Engraving
Bibliothèque des Arts
Décoratifs, Paris

247
Tea service, 1838
Manufacture Nationale
de Sèvres
Porcelain
Division of Ceramics
and Glass, National
Museum of American
History, Smithsonian
Institution, Washington,
D.C., Alfred Duane Pell
Collection

248
**Design for a
candelabrum, about
1840-50**
Cristalleries de Baccarat
Watercolor
Baccarat Archives, Paris

249
**Ewer presented to
King Charles X, 1828**
Cristalleries de Baccarat
Cut, engraved, and
enameled glass
Musée Baccarat, Paris

154

of Saint-Augustin in Paris. An engraving of the great hall of the Hôtel de Ville before the fire of 1871 shows all the tables laid. On the principal one is a gigantic centerpiece representing the city itself, a work of sculpture on a grand scale, surrounded by plants. The other tables, with smaller *surtouts* in the form of ships, are similarly laden with cut flowers, footed bowls, and guéridons with flowers and fruit. The hundreds of objects have been arranged with due regard to symmetry: before each guest is a set of five glasses (one for water, two for wine, one each for port and champagne); and on either side of the plate, an equally generous assortment of knives, spoons, and forks, including fish knives and forks. Another banquet under Charles Garnier, architect of the Paris Opéra, shows the imperial service in vermeil, the famous "modern" service made by Christofle; with the pieces of the *surtout* in gilt bronze and the flatware in silver gilt, this replaced the magnificent Empire silver created by Biennais and Auguste, which had been melted down for 16,638 francs under the discreet official heading of "conversion of old materials."[7] Dishes prepared in the kitchen were now brought in by the waiters, presented, and served to each guest. The sexes were seated alternately around the table, a custom that seems to have developed only during the nineteenth century. A hundred years earlier, for instance, at the banquet in honor of the prince of Asturias, women were the sole guests, with the exception of a few men seated side by side at the two ends of the table. Later, in 1810, at the wedding banquet for Napoleon and Marie-Louise in the Salle de Spectacle of the Tuileries, the women were seated on one side, the men on the other.

Depictions of more modest meals, in bourgeois interiors, show that from this time on there existed a dining room proper, with its dresser or sideboard (sometimes both), its fireplace, clock, vases, and candelabra. In the center was the dining table—round, oval, or square—often surmounted by a chandelier burning oil or candles, a combination of the two, or later on gas. There were matching chairs, with the Henri II style often in evidence. The less formal setting included numerous decanters but very rarely a bottle of wine, and a restrained centerpiece consisting of a jardiniere, a monumental bowl, or a covered chafing dish.

TABLE SERVICES

The idea of a "service"—the name given to a set of matching tableware—first appeared in the eighteenth century, although the royal factory at

250
Tureen with Napoleonic scenes, about 1829-36
Lebeuf et Thibaut, Montereau, manufacturer
Earthenware, transfer-printed decoration
Virginia Museum of Fine Arts, Richmond, Virginia, Gift of Mrs. Morton G. Thalhimer, 1985

Sèvres had already used the expression for the *grands services* it produced in some notable examples. At that time, however, the term *service* was also used to describe one of the many courses of a meal served *à la française*, and it is not unusual to see the expression *services de dessert* in price lists as well as in descriptions of meals. The notion of matching pieces used together on the table spread during the nineteenth century, while form and function were endlessly multiplied to keep up with the many culinary novelties.

Although ices or sorbets, strawberries, and chestnuts already had their own holders in the eighteenth century, the increase in containers was particularly spectacular in the nineteenth. The introduction of crystal for claret or sherry, glasses for Alsatian wine, for brandied fruit, and so on, led to the development of a variety of shapes and sizes appropriate to each drink—water, red wine, white

251
Sugar bowl, 1834
Alluaud, Limoges, manufacturer
Porcelain
Collection R. Haviland et C. Parlon, Limoges

252
**Dining Room of
Princess Mathilde,
Paris, 1859**
Charles Giraud
(1819-1892)
Oil on canvas
Musée national du
Château de Compiègne

253
**Banquet to the
Chiefs of the Army
of Italy in the Salles
des Etats, at the New
Louvre (detail), 1859**
Vivant Beaucé
(1818-1876) and Félix
Thorigny (1824-1870)
Engraving
Musée
Bouilhet-Christofle, Paris

254
**Supper at the
Tuileries Palace
(detail), 1867**
Henri Baron
(1816-1885)
Oil on canvas
Musée national du
Château de Compiègne

concerned, there was even more variety. The practice of eating grapes at table led to the creation of special scissors and grape stands, presented by Christofle to its clientele in its 1893 catalogue. Knife rests prevented dirty blades from touching the tablecloth; menu holders and napkin stands went along with *chariots à vin*, which conveyed the precious bottle and gently eased it

wine, champagne. Carafes, too, were designed specially for water, liqueurs, different wines, port, and iced orangeade. Plates and serving dishes for artichokes, asparagus, shellfish, and salad appeared, as did special receptacles for melons and for roasted chestnuts. The taste for these is attributed to Napoleon, who is said to have liked eating the fruits of his native Corsica during meals.

Where accessories and implements were

into the correct position for pouring. Expanding dish stands, coasters, and hot plates further embellished the table top. To help the nineteenth-century gastronome enjoy the most varied dishes elegantly, there were also egg cutters; fruit and dessert knives; knives and forks for fish and for cheese; specialized servers for salad, sardines, strawberries, and petits fours; forks for oysters and for mangoes; spoons—with and without a strainer—for sauce; serving spoons for compotes; spoons and knives for ice cream; carving knives, handles for legs of lamb, handles for cutlets; serving tongs for asparagus and holders for eating asparagus one piece at a time without touching it with the fingers, and servers for lobster or snails. The spread of plated silver, its acceptance on princely tables, and its "ennoblement" as a result of the imperial commissions in the years 1850-60 were to bring this entire battery within the reach of most of the bourgeoisie.

It is interesting to note how consistent the numbers and kinds of pieces of services have been from the nineteenth century to the present day. Allowing for six, twelve, twenty-four, and forty-eight places or more, each service could be adapted for a large number of people, and orders generally were for the greatest number, whether in earthenware or porcelain: several sizes of soup plate, sauceboats, vegetable dishes; series of round or oval dishes or fish dishes; eggcups, custard

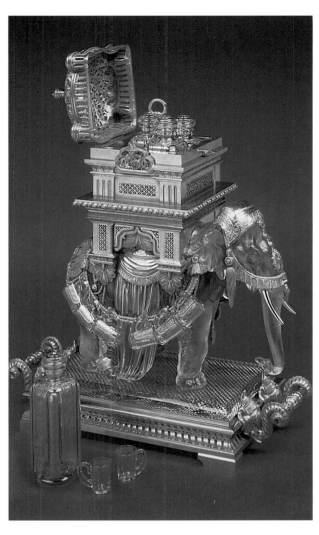

255
Liqueur service of the Maharajah of Baroda, 1878
Cristalleries de Baccarat
Glass, gilt bronze
Collection Cristalleries de Baccarat

cups, compote dishes, *guéridons* saltcellars, and mustard pots.

Although often matching the rest, dessert sets are always listed separately in catalogues, with their own little plates, cake plates, low and footed compote dishes, dessert stands, and sugar bowls, not to mention cream pitchers and tea and coffee services. Services for luncheon, ices, strawberries, and shellfish, together with menu holders, often completed the ensemble. For glassware, whether in glass or crystal, there was the same numerical

256
Liqueur service, 1867
Cristalleries de Baccarat
Engraved glass
Musée Baccarat, Paris

257
Liqueur service, 1880
Christofle et Cie
Silver plate
Musée Bouilhet-Christofle, Paris

258
**Table centerpiece
made for the
Emperor of Mexico
by Christofle et Cie,
about 1863**
Engraving
Musée
Bouilhet-Christofle, Paris

259
**Three armorial plates,
1888-89**
Faïencerie de Gien
Earthenware
Musée de la Faïencerie
de Gien

260
**Design for a dining
room in the
Renaissance style,
about 1885**
Alexandre Carrière
(1822-1909)
Pen and ink, watercolor,
gouache
Musée des Arts
Décoratifs, Paris

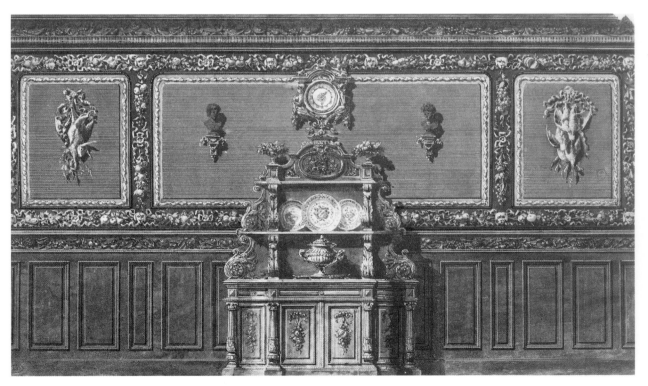

261
Coffee and tea service, about 1885
Pantographie Voltaïque, manufacturer
Silver gilt, enamel
Collection Orfèvrerie d'Ercuis, Paris

262
Chestnut dish in the form of a napkin, 1873
Christofle et Cie
Silver plate
Musée Bouilhet-Christofle, Paris

263
Sugar spoons, from a Christofle et Cie silverware catalogue, about 1900
Engraving
Musée Bouilhet-Christofle, Paris

264
Mechanical wine decanting cradle, mid-19th century
Christofle et Cie
Silver plate
Musée Bouilhet-Christofle, Paris

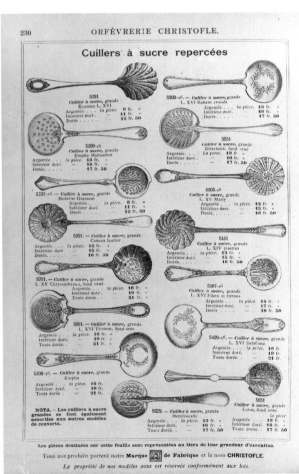

ORFÈVRERIE CHRISTOFLE.

230

Cuillers à sucre repercées

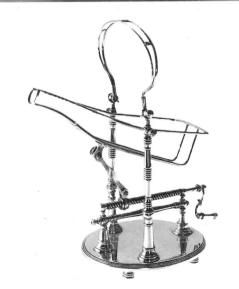

choice, always made up in the same way, with sets for beer and for fine wines, liqueur pitchers, glasses (or small cups) for port and madeira, sets for fruit and for ices. If there is one area in which tradition has remained inviolate, it is certainly that of glassware. Not until the 1920s did new forms make an appearance.

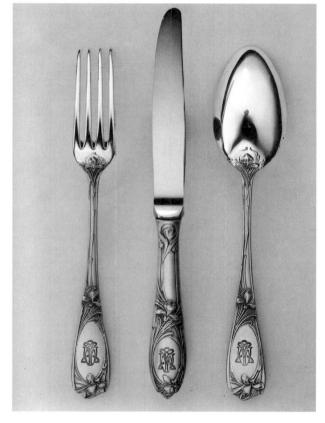

THE GRAND DÉPÔT AND THE ESCALIER DE CRISTAL

Around 1863, a new idea won the hearts of the public—Parisian, provincial, and foreign alike. This was the creation of an establishment dedicated to bringing together the best of contemporary ceramics: the Grand Dépôt, at 21 rue Drouot, which was then the only store of its kind. There, one could choose on sight, as in a department store, from more than two thousand dinner services, two thousand glassware services, English pottery or majolica, the French faïence then called *terre de fer*, porcelain, and table accessories for every day use as well as for grand receptions. The rich and wellborn, foreign as well as Parisian, were received in a special salon where the top of the line, that is, the porcelain services, were exhibited. Taste, impeccable selection, and commercial integrity contributed to the reputation of the products sold at the Grand Dépôt by Emile Bourgeois, the innovator whose brilliant idea predated today's boutiques specializing in wedding presents and tableware. Bourgeois profited from trade agreements that allowed him to import at a time when the triumph of free-trade ideas was giving industry and commerce an enormous boost.

International exhibitions had enabled people to appreciate the work of most of the great European factories, in Milan, Vienna, Denmark, Saxony, Switzerland, Spain, and Portugal. During this period, English ceramics almost ousted the native product so dear to the French. Fortunately, more than eighty makes sold under the Grand Dépôt trademark supplied tableware from a variety of French sources; designed for daily use and frequently repeated, these could be assembled at will and restocked.

The Escalier de Cristal was another specialty store. This celebrated firm published illustrated catalogues showing an immense variety of products arranged in sophisticated settings as in a store

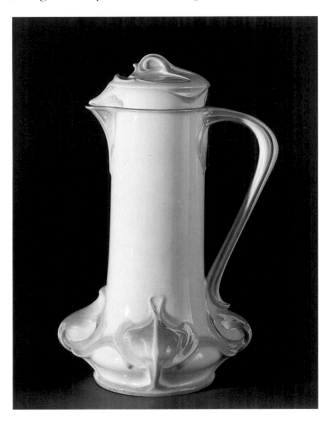

window. Founded in 1802, at 162 Galerie de Valois in the Palais-Royal, and one of the best-known shops of its kind, it took its name from its famous crystal staircase. Specializing in luxury gifts in crystal and porcelain, the firm supplied table services and *surtouts* for aristocratic clients and foreign courts. The owner, Madame Desarnaud, sold the store to Boin in 1833, who in turn sold it to Lahoche in 1854. Lahoche moved the business to the rue Scribe and the rue Auber.

In the twentieth century, it became increasingly easy to stock up on all kinds of tableware and linens at department stores, whose studios sold and distributed what the manufacturers had produced as a result of shows by artist-designers, the Compagnie des Arts Français founded by Süe and Mare, and international exhibitions like that of

1925, famous not only for its success but also for its enormous influence on popular taste and consumption. Was the "domestication of talents" so dreaded by Gabriel Mourey really something to be feared?

The creative studios of the department stores proved otherwise: at Au Printemps, the Primavera line, which goes back to 1912, was developed chiefly after 1919; Paul Follot produced the Pomone brand for Bon Marché; Trois Quartiers had Athelia, and the Louvre, Studium. In 1925, with the new Art Deco movement, the sale of sets decorated in old patterns or period designs fell by 75 percent. Shapes and decoration were freer, especially in ceramics and glassware. Motifs were scattered, no longer conforming rigidly to the structure of the object. In silver and flatware, shapes were simple, devoid of ornament. It was a question of a new aesthetic rather than a new form.

THE TWENTIETH-CENTURY DINING ROOM

In a process that began in modest households and spread gradually among the middle classes, the dining room, a separate space throughout the nineteenth century, would first open into the drawing room, and then, several years later, into the kitchen by means of a serving hatch or a movable partition. Today, it has developed into a single room combining dining room and kitchen.

For reasons of economy and above all space, the kitchen-dining-room system was applied first in workers' homes and in housing developments built before World War I. A distinction that would last until the 1950s and sometimes even later was that in bourgeois households the dining room remained separate, just as dictated by custom in the nineteenth century. In humbler houses, the dining table and its accessories—chairs, sideboard, dresser—were installed in the drawing room, or living room, but this was used only on Sundays and holidays. The practice still continues today in a number of homes, and particularly among the rural population.

After World War I, drawing room and dining room were sometimes combined, even in quality housing; an interesting example of this occurs in Le Corbusier's villa at Garches, built in 1927.

Thereafter, the large living- cum-dining-room area opened onto different parts of the house and often had direct access to a large kitchen. The space for, and furnishing of, an eating area was still an important part of the grand ensemble that formed the living room, even in well-to-do households. Certain films made in the 1930s show that it was fashionable not to shut off the dining room behind closed doors; despite the presence of the dining-room furniture, it was possible to move freely to the seating area nearby.

The English expression *living room* adopted in French, was applied from around 1922 to the large room containing the dining area and a large adjacent space. In Paris and the provinces the middle-class dining room still continued, until quite recently, to be distinct from the drawing room. Among those less well off, the dining room might be the main, single room of the household, replacing the living room and drawing room, and recalling the principal room in rural dwellings

where the occupants worked, ate, and gathered.

Special issues of magazines like *Architecture française* and *L'Art ménager français* make it possible to assess house plans and arrangements in the 1950s. In the sixties and after, these plans show no change. The "living room," part reception area and part dining room, may end up being no more than a drawing room; in certain modern residences of standing, the luxury kitchen may even serve as the locus for daily meals. The dining room and its permanent furnishings may have completely disappeared or been incorporated into the fixtures and the sometimes highly sophisticated design of the kitchen.

But this applies only to new apartments and houses. The ways in which people live and adapt old buildings dating from the eighteenth and nineteenth centuries must not be forgotten. Have they carried on the customs of the past, or have they made alterations in light of contemporary life-styles? Of necessity, the answers to these questions must go both ways.

271
Interior of dining room on the oceanliner *Normandie*, **about 1935**
Lalique Archives, Paris

272
Design for a kitchen, Plate 12 from Léon Deshairs, *Intérieurs en Couleurs*, **Paris, 1926**
André Groult (1884-1967), designer
Cooper-Hewitt Museum Library, New York

273
Table setting, about 1925
"Juliette" faïence tableware and "Margot" glass service decorated by Marcel Goupy (born 1886)
Thérèse Bonney (1897-1978), photographer
Cooper-Hewitt Museum, New York, Bonney Collection

The international exhibitions—principally those of 1900, 1925, and 1937, all key dates—were a means of publicizing the latest French goods. Indeed, every region or province, such as Sèvres, whose leading manufacturers of course had always exhibited, displayed its important products. At the same time, these exhibitions served to underline the importance that industry was assuming in every related field. The titles of surveys and catalogues are explicit: *Les Industries d'art*, for example, and *Les Arts décoratifs et industriels modernes*. The objects displayed were sometimes unique collectors' items, but a great many of them were

industrially produced. After World War I, reconstruction was rapid, and an exhibition in Amiens, in October 1919, entitled *Exposition nationale de l'ameublement et de tout ce qui est nécessaire à la renaissance des foyers dévastés* (National Exhibition of Furniture and Everything Needed for the Restoration of War-damaged Homes), showed many new objects.

The fashion for interior design shows and decorative arts exhibitions has also been a source

of information from 1904 to the present day. Demonstrating this important movement is the Salon des Arts Ménagers, which opened in 1923 and has contributed to the renewal of domestic life. An official survey entitled *L'Art ménager* of 1927 was its spokesman and representative.

The press and the daily papers published reports on the names of the leading manufacturers and on new products, while an increasing number of catalogues offered goods in every range. Special

274
Design for a silver table centerpiece, about 1925
Christofle et cie
Watercolor
Musée
Bouilhet-Christofle, Paris

magazines devoted to the home, the table, and the kitchen appeared, showing the new, popular interest in these fields.

Encyclopedias of the household arts flourished in the twenties. *L'Art ménager français*, published under the direction of J. L. Breton in 1952, is a guide on how to prepare, serve, and purchase food, and generally transform life in the kitchen and dining room. Practical guides and manuals such as *La Science et les travaux de la ménagère*, published as early as 1901, and the increasing number of women working outside the home, contributed on the one hand to simplifying and reducing the number of objects in use, and on the other to changing the materials used for kitchen equipment and tableware. Stainless steel and aluminum, available since 1929, became common in the fifties; and it was then that catalogues began publishing illustrations of tableware in plastic—nonbreakable, light, and easily cleaned. Instead of pottery for general use and porcelain for special occasions, the general public preferred these new materials.

Finally, department stores continued to operate in the twentieth century, as they had earlier, expanding their role as distributors and intermediaries between the craftsman or manufacturer and the public.

Formal tables, which during the Belle Epoque sported *surtouts* of water and flowers tucked into jardinieres in the shape of women stretched out like trailing plants, were, as early as the 1920s, relaid with simple forms. New objects in the modern manner were created by designers such as Marcel Goupy and Jean Luce. Gone were the miter-folded, starched napkins and the inevitable ice sculpture, leftovers of the ephemeral aquatic decorations of yesteryear. With Lalique, glass triumphed on the tabletop, and the silversmith Jean Puiforcat created works combining his artistic

temperament with supreme knowledge of his craft. This goldsmith became the undisputed master of table silver, causing even his colleagues to follow in his footsteps and to rethink their work.

Although the wave of modernism that followed the years 1920 to 1925 continued to have an effect, classical trends also returned with a rush; indeed, the catalogues dating from before and especially just after World War II show a marked return to traditional and regional styles. The geometric shapes created twenty years earlier developed curves again; a general process of simplification led to the gradual disappearance of stands for soup tureens, sugar bowls, and sauceboats. Materials current since the twenties include aluminum, nickel, steel, iron, pewter, chromium-plated nickel silver—all "reinforced," "very strong," "unbreakable." In flatware, apart from the "Plain"

275
Table service from the oceanliner *Normandie*, about 1935
Luc Lanel (1894-1966), designer
Christofle et Cie, manufacturer
Silver plate
Musée
Bouilhet-Christofle, Paris

style still in use, names like Empire, Louis XV, and Louis XVI speak for themselves.

Stainless steel did not count for much in the overall production of so-called silver until the thirties, when oven-to-table dishes, sauceboats, and soup tureens made their appearance. Ovenproof glass also migrated to the dining table. Pyrex, which was introduced in 1936, permitted one to keep an eye on whatever was being cooked inside. Stackable dishes were approved for their practicality. And unbreakable plates and glasses were introduced in 1958 by Arcopal and in 1959 by Duralex.

What of the dining table in the sixties? A simplified life-style, synthetic materials, functional forms, and an industrial aesthetic all left their mark. Fortunately, great creative talents like Roger Tallon were on hand to make French design competitive in the world market. Synthetic materials were modified and improved, with more attractive colors and a palette in line with table fashion as well as with interior decoration generally. Flatware was no longer necessarily in silver, glasses no longer necessarily transparent. Everything had to be adapted for a youthful clientele. Durability was no longer obligatory; purchases in every price range were made on the spur of the moment, and there was less compunction about discarding them. The appeal of the "Made in the U.S.A." label was undeniable, but other foreign goods were also the rage—Scandinavian, German, and later Italian. Adapting these designs to meet the functions and habits of daily life in France was accomplished without difficulty; great simplicity was the result. It was thus possible to see sparely decorated dining tables—devoid of superfluous ornament and decorated only with the forms of the flatware, glasses, and ceramics—side by side with traditional tables, on which fine linen, napkins, crystal, flowers, *surtouts*, lighting, silver, and porcelain continued the great French heritage.

THE POPULARITY OF RESTAURANTS IN PARIS IN THE EARLY NINETEENTH CENTURY

The end of the Ancien Régime corresponded with the advent of restaurants in Paris. One of the first, Boulanger, opened in 1765 in what is now the rue du Louvre. In 1766, Roze and Pontaillé were also among the first to open, according to the *Almanach Dauphin* of 1777. Brillat-Savarin (1755-1826), the celebrated gastronome, later gave a definition of the role of the *restaurateur*: "To offer the public a banquet ready at all times...at a fixed price...on the customers' demand." Catering establishments already existed and had paved the way for restaurant keepers by welcoming members of society escaping the taverns. The bill of fare immediately made its appearance in the form of a framed sheet of paper carried by the waiter, which showed what was available, with the price opposite.

In 1789, by Alexandre-Balthasar Grimod's count, there were already more than a hundred restaurants in Paris. Prices for meals rose very rapidly, in line with an establishment's quality and luxury status. The Palais-Royal was a sought-after locale for this style of eating. On the eve of the Revolution, the fashionable district was in the center of Paris. The famous Beauvilliers opened in 1782 at 156 Galerie de Valois. According to Brillat-Savarin, this was "the first restaurant of quality to have an elegant hall, waiters properly turned out, a well-tended cellar, and a superior cuisine. Its reputation was faithfully maintained for fifteen years."[8]

"The heart of Paris after the Revolution has become a belly. The Revolution has changed the stomachs of France."[9] Which were the restaurants that purveyed this good living? The Frères Provençaux (1786-1877), Very (1790-1859), Robert, the Bœuf à la Mode in the Palais-Royal. Luxury and

276
Placemat and napkin created for Aristotle Onassis's yacht *Christina*, 1956
D. Porthault
Embroidered linen
Collection D. Porthault, S.A., Paris

277
"Veronese" glassware service, 1987
Daum Cristal
Glass
Collection Daum Cristal,
France

comfort settled in; there were paneled interiors, little tables, paintings under glass, frescoes in imitation of those in English clubs—all to welcome the new, wealthy middle classes, who were not yet bold enough to adopt too lavish a style of dining at home. The newly elect at the beginning of the nineteenth century made the reputation of manufacturers by choosing restaurants and spending without counting the cost, thereby creating a market for products destined both for the table at home and the restaurant table. Indeed, the first manufacturers' catalogues for the dining table included all these products. Dr. Véron, in his *Mémoires d'un bourgeois de Paris*, published in 1850, listed nine hundred restaurants. The République district was the site of some famous names: the Rocher de Cancale in the rue Montorgueil (1804-45); several cafés, one of which became the Grand Véfour; the Café Hardy, which was to become the Maison Doré in 1841; the Café Riche (1791-1900), of which it was said, "Il fallait être hardi pour aller chez Riche et riche pour aller chez Hardy," which translates roughly as "You must be hardy [i.e., brave] to go to Riche's and rich to go to Hardy's"; the Café Anglais (1902-13); and the Cadran Bleu at the Châtelet. Later, establishments like the Tour d'Argent or Drouant were joined by a whole range of popular restaurants, where the regulars each had a table, napkin, and napkin ring, the last two items kept in a special set of pigeonholes.

In the mid-nineteenth century, the reign of the boulevards began. Several new restaurants opened in the Chaussée d'Antin, the events of 1848 and after having had a disastrous effect on certain establishments. "The dandies and the women of fashion, plump of purse, circulated in the calm digestion of their orgies," said Edmond Texier in his *Tableau de Paris* (1852). Sumptuous interiors, carpets, gilded salons, Oriental piles of cushions, intimate lighting, and small salons—one of the best known was the Grand Seize in the Café Anglais—reappeared. After 1855, international exhibitions gave the Champs-Elysées an opportunity to welcome new restaurants like Ledoyen.

The tableware and linen were personalized. Silver plate, porcelain, and table accessories multiplied. There were jardinieres and ice buckets on legs. Carving tables and tables with spirit lamps accompanied, among other things, the famous duck press that crushes the entire bird in front of the guest in order to extract its delicious juices. The objects on the restaurant table followed a code fairly similar to that of the private dining table. In keeping with the eclecticism of the period, decors ran from Louis XV paneling to somber Henri II interiors in Germanic style. But a new formula, bringing with it new decors, was to be the rage in Paris—brasseries.

Extending over the sidewalk under an elegant roof of cathedral glass, Mollard's establishment opened on the rue Saint-Lazare in 1895, with

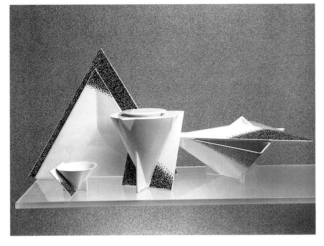

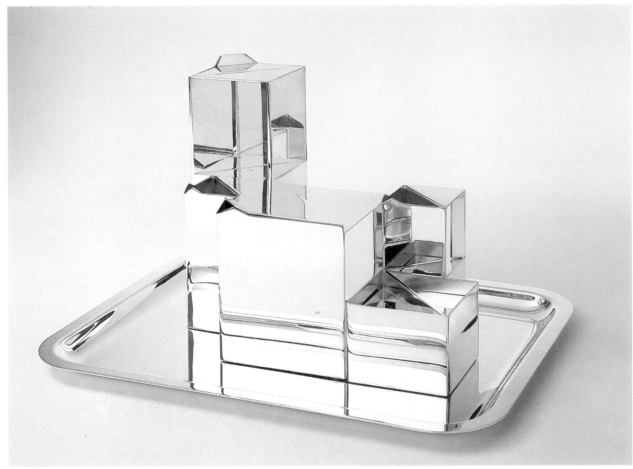

served every kind of food down to the present day, led in the 1980s to the granting of protected status to a number of restaurants and brasseries including the Fermette Marbœuf, decorated in 1898 by the architect Hurté; the Train Bleu, that famous and magnificently decorated stopover in the Gare de Lyon; Lucas Carton; and Chez Julien, decorated in 1900 by a follower of Mucha.

The evolution of the past two centuries leads one to conclude that today the dinner table has retained a certain value but is no longer the single symbol of success, social rank, or personal glory. Restaurants, fast-food chains, meals of every kind, lunches, brunches, exotic customs, and caterers all

brilliantly colored faïence tiles on the walls, and wrought-iron tulips serving as lighting fixtures. Eloquent descriptions of the ambience and decor of these rooms can be found in the press of the period. Other brasseries, symbolically decorated with everything on the menu, displayed Sarreguemines tile panels designed by Simas that reproduced game, fowl, exotic fruit, allegories of regional products, and absinth or hop leaves. Regional food was to become very fashionable. The press seems to have chosen to dwell less on the gastronomic side of restaurants than on the decor of brasseries. The general interest in these establishments, which developed in every style and

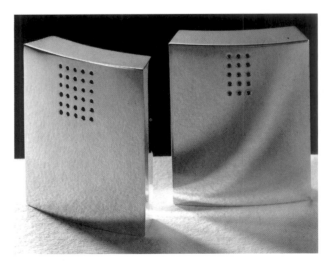

281
"Ruines d'Egypte" table centerpiece, 1979
Anne Poirier (born 1947) and Patrick Poirier (born 1942), designers
Manufacture Nationale de Sèvres
Porcelain
Musée National de Céramique, Sèvres

furnish very diverse occasions for practicing the art of eating.

The aspects of celebration and communication conferred on meals in the past have slipped in favor of a certain individualization of attitudes. Neither food nor dishes are now under the control of the master and mistress of the house, or of the servants. Guests are allowed greater liberty. Children are often present, and adults who were not permitted to smoke cigars or cigarettes now find ashtrays on the table.

Important centerpieces have vanished, to be replaced by something simple—a decorative vase,

perhaps, or a jardiniere, or candles. The use of a great many different objects, each with a specific function, is tending to disappear. The lining up of numerous pieces of flatware, the changing of plates after every course—all that has gradually been abandoned. Table linen, too, has beaten a retreat: paper napkins, often in quite sophisticated designs, are popular, and tablecloths are turning up in colorful designs while the traditional white cloth is slowly disappearing.

Symbolic of the idea of stability and still vigorous at the beginning of this century, tableware styles repeated those of the end of the nineteenth century until World War I. Only Art Nouveau

produced a temporary new wave, although not to the same extent as the Arts and Crafts movement in Britain or Jugendstil in the German-speaking countries.

In *A table*, the catalogue of the Centre de Création Industrielle, Françoise Jollant puts it clearly: "People today are buying heavily what is traditional and upscale, beautiful and expensive, from Baccarat, Saint-Louis, Christofle, and Daum, stores that are in favor with the public; only 15 percent of purchases are made in the contemporary department. Behind the history of styles, the major manufacturers for the dining table have bolted the market door and excluded collaboration with the creative artist outside."

Few porcelain or earthenware factories have so far been attracted by the difficulty of producing a contemporary collection. This is curious at a time when French cuisine has never been so well received in every part of the world, when there are festivals dedicated to the art of the table, and when even the most insignificant fifty-year-old dinner service with a mark beneath it costs a small fortune.

282
Table service for the "Concorde" airliner, about 1976
Raymond Loewy (1893-1984), designer
Porcelain: Raynaud Limoges, manufacturer
Cutlery: Bouillet Bourdelle
Glassware: Cristallerie de Souvigny
Cooper-Hewitt Museum, New York,
Gift of Air France, 1988

1. *Antoine Carême*, exhibition catalogue, Paris, Bagatelle, 1984. Peddlers likewise distributed texts in the provinces, for culinary literature has always been associated more or less closely with questions of health and has been sought after on both scores. The historiography of French gastronomic writing has been classified in a standard work by Georges Vicaire; it lists more than four thousand titles from antiquity to the end of the nineteenth century.

2. Françoise Burgaud, "Qu'en est-il aujourd'hui des convenances de table?" in *La Table et le partage*, (Paris, Documentation française, 1986).

3. Alcouffe, "La Naissance de la table à manger au XVIIIe siècle," in *La Table et le partage*, pp. 57-65, and D. Ledoux-Lebard, *Les Ébénistes du XIXe siècle...*, 2nd ed., (Paris, 1984), p. 293.

4. *Antoine Carême*.

5. J. P. Aron, *Le Mangeur du XIXe siècle* (Paris: Laffont, 1973) p. 33.

6. S. Tardieu, *La Vie domestique dans le Mâconnais rural pré-industriel* Paris, 1964.

7. See *Christofle* (Paris: Le Chêne/Hachette, 1981), p. 103.

8. See Valérie Ortoli, "La Gastronomie," *Revue des monuments historiques*, no. 131, March 1984, pp. 50-56.

9. See Grimod de la Reynière, *L'Almanach de 1804*.

FRANCE GRAND

FRENCH TASTE IN FASHION :
MYTH AND REALITY

Reflection on the cultural heritage that describes and defines any nation is always in order. Indeed, as Barthes has written, this should be a continuing process of reevaluation. The "French style" in fashion and dress has been a paradigm for well over two centuries, having served as inspiration for an extended elite in the seventeenth and eighteenth centuries. Throughout the world, French fashion has set standards of creativity and craftsmanship. But probably nowhere today are questions of past and present more lively and provocative than in the field of fashion, which has always been an immediate barometer of culture and of the preoccupations and interests that mark an epoch or period.

To appreciate the complex threads of history that are so closely interwoven into the history of *la mode* in Paris in the two centuries since the Revolution of 1789, a comparison might be made with language. Fashion, like language, changes rapidly, replacing outmoded usage with "modern" vocabulary. Yet in both language and fashion the lingering influences of tradition can be detected.

Since the time of Louis XIV, *le Roi Soleil*, French has remained the preferred language of the educated and the cultured, and especially of diplomats. Alongside this striking international recognition of the value of the French language, an even more tangible fascination with the arts of France has endured; in sophisticated social circles

in far-flung urban centers throughout
eighteenth-century Europe, French taste
predominated. Food was prepared and enjoyed,
houses were furnished, and love was made *à la
française*. Fashion reflected this phenomenon; the
mark of success and taste was made publicly
visible through dress, and, as in other matters of
elegance, Paris remained the focal point of creation
and dissemination of style

In eighteenth-century France, the court
established the canons of taste in the arts,
including fashion. From this elite, styles and trends
filtered downward, but the court remained the
source of life. As Balzac said: "Once upon a time,
under the Monarchy, the least important point on
the circumference was bound to the center, and
took life from it."[1] With the Revolution, this
complex but orderly world changed, and this
system of dissemination was replaced by others
that emerged from the rapidly growing and
increasingly powerful bourgeoisie. The beaming
splendor of the royal body was succeeded by a
centralizing principle.

Parisian families have a burning need to emulate
the luxury that surrounds them on all sides, and
few possess the good sense to suit their outward
display to their internal means. But perhaps this
sort of extravagance is a kind of peculiarly French
patriotism, designed to assure France a continued
supremacy in matters of dress. In dress, France is
the master of Europe, and every Frenchman is

173

288
A Dance, about 1828
Anonymous
Hand-colored engraving
Musée Carnavalet, Paris

289
Fashion plate from
Le Petit Courrier des
Dames, **November,**
1835
Hand-colored engraving
Cooper-Hewitt Museum,
New York, Gift of
Vyvyan Holland,
1980-36-5291

290
Fashion plate from
Le Follet Courrier
des Salons, **June,**
1834
Hand-colored engraving
Cooper-Hewitt Museum,
New York, Gift of
Vyvyan Holland,
1980-36-1679

291
Hall of the Imperial
Academy of Music
(Grand Opera), about
1857
Gustave Janet (born
1829)
Engraving
Cooper-Hewitt Museum,
New York, Kubler
Collection

292
Dressing Room of
Hortense Schneider
at the Théâtre des
Variétés, 1873
Edmond Morin
(1824-1882)
Watercolor
Musée national du
Château de Compiègne

174

eager to preserve this commercial preeminence, which makes Fashion, to the French, something of what their Navy is to the British.[2]

Nationalism and protectionism sought to turn French production into an accepted norm, and, just as in "*pompier* painting," in which the nobler the subject, the nobler the work, in dress, French taste was threatened with becoming the willing, efficient handmaid of both morality and aesthetics.

As the bourgeoisie expanded its position of power in French society, the fashion industry,

impressive "Expositions Universelles." At these spectacles, which were forerunners of the mass media in purveying images, the industries of France proudly presented their wares for public edification and for commercial seduction; the "crowd" of eighteenth-century entertainments had become the "public," and fashion took its place alongside the other decorative arts. Industrial products were transformed into the various *specialités* and then into *réclame* (advertisement)—a word now heard for the first time. The advertising onslaught with which we are

293
The Casino, Monte Carlo, about 1880
Christian Ludwig
Bokelmann (1844-1894)
Oil on canvas
Private Collection

along with others in the decorative arts, was tellingly influenced by the economics of the marketplace. Uniformity of taste could be noted among the bourgeoisie, as noted by Balzac: "...in France, as in all countries with but one metropolis, centralization cannot but bring about a dull uniformity of custom."[3] What this change also meant was that Paris, the only metropolitan center, served an audience with an appetite for fashion.

The relationship between economics and taste so well documented in middle-class Paris of the nineteenth century was suggested as early as 1798, at the first National Industrial Exposition. This effort to remedy the economic health of the nation through its industries, a favorite theme of Napoleon himself, eventually led to a series of

so familiar today had begun. This period also saw the birth of photography; the introduction of technology for reproducing illustrations in popular magazines and newspapers; the appearance of the *passages* (arcades) and the *grands magasins*, with their printed advertising and mail-order catalogues, bringing Paris's "finest" within reach of the provincial; and the mass manufacture of ready-to-wear and accessories.

And the ready garments were there, in this place of worship dedicated to the cult of female beauty.... The rounded bosoms of the dummies swelled out the fabric, their sturdy hips exaggerated the constriction of the waist; they had no heads, but wore instead great price tags pinned directly to their felt necks. The looking glasses

294
The Salon of 1874
Jean Béraud
(1849-1936)
Oil on canvas
Private Collection

176

flanking the display window by deliberate design reflected and multiplied them to *infinity*, filled the whole street with these lovely women for sale, wearing their prices in bold figures where their heads should be.[4]

What suffered most severely at the hands of such commercial expansion were traditional forms of dress—local, professional, or occupational—on the altar of ready-to-wear fashion. Leopardi lamented, "Fashion—our lady Death! our lady Death."[5] Paris, the city that had served so well the needs of the eighteenth-century aristocracy, now lured provincials and foreigners to its *grands magasins*. Fashion, in its unswerving passion for the present, had eradicated part of the cultural patrimony of the nation.

Paradoxically, along with the coming of mass production, a new relationship arose between the

"public" and the creative artist. By the middle of the nineteenth century, this new relationship had influenced language, literature, and the graphic arts. Fashion followed in the footsteps of the other arts as they moved from the protective shadow of royalty, as Ingres and Delacroix had with painting, or Baudelaire and Flaubert with literature, half a century earlier.

The success story of Worth is a matter of record; he was perhaps the first to offer a *collection* of dresses of his own conception and design, rather than the customer's. It is truly with Worth that public acknowledgment of the artistic role of the couturier can be seen to emerge. Economics and aesthetics, often held to be bitter enemies, have actually shown themselves to be amicable partners in the world of fashion, neither denying the validity or necessity of the other. Worth the couturier was not simply a purveyor; he arrogated to himself the autonomy of the creative artist. There was now a sovereign at court and another in town. He is described by Zola (under the transparent alias of "Worms") in an unsympathetic passage:

But his most important duty was to go with Renée to the illustrious Worms, the dressmaker of genius who had all the queens of the Second Empire at his feet. The great man's salon was a huge, square room furnished with big divans, to be entered with reverence. Dressmaking undoubtedly has its own characteristic fragrance.... After some minutes, the Master, as if seized and shaken by inspiration, would sketch in great, sweeping, staccato lines the masterpiece he had just imagined, jerking out such phrases as "A Montespan dress in ash gray faille, the train falling from skirts rounded at the front. . .big knots of gray satin gathering it above the hips. . .then a ruffled apron of pearl gray tulle with bands of gray satin between the ruffles." He drew back, seeming to plumb his own genius to its very depths, and with a grimace of triumph like that of a Sibyl on her tripod, uttered: "On the hair, above that smiling face, we will put Psyche's dreaming butterfly with wings of iridescent blue."[6]

Here we encounter a double dose of irony. Doubt is being cast on the artistic pretensions of

the couturier and on his relationship to society. At his "salons," a parody of a social occasion, society women rub shoulders with actresses and ladies of the night, all literally "soliciting" from him an especially brilliant illumination from the depths of his clairvoyance.

Public and aristocratic taste became more and more divergent in their routes during the nineteenth century, and this difference encouraged the "snobbism" of the fashionable aristocrat. Madame de Cambremer, in Proust's *Remembrance of Things Past*, epitomizes the attitude: ". . . 'It's just like *Pelleas*,' I said to her, to gratify her taste for

297
Poster: Folies-Bergère, about 1900
Adrien Barrère
(1877-1931)
Color lithograph

the modern, 'that scent of roses wafted up to the terraces. It's so strong in the score that, as I suffer from hay-fever and rose-fever, it sets me sneezing every time I listen to that scene.'"[7]

The "timelessness" of taste is called into question in this evocation; aesthetic judgment is presented in a manner not unlike an allergic reaction or the volatility of the stock market.

Once there was no longer a code arising from social distinctions, fashion soon ceased to be a prerogative; rather, it became a question of means. Aware of its own artificiality, it was now woven into complex technical and sensory layers. Consider the dress of Odette as described by Proust:

Save at these moments of involuntary relaxation in which Swann sought to recapture the melancholy Botticellian droop, Odette's body seemed now to be cut out in a single silhouette wholly confined within a 'line," which, following the contours of the woman, had abandoned the ups and down, the ins and outs, the reticulations, the elaborate dispersions of the fashions of former days, but also, where it was her anatomy that went wrong by making unnecessary digressions within or without the ideal form traced for it, was able to rectify, by a bold stroke, the errors of nature, to make good, along a whole section of its course, the lapses of the flesh as well as of the material. The pads, the preposterous "bustle" had disappeared, as well as those tailed bodices which, overlapping the skirt and stiffened by rods of whalebone, had so long amplified Odette with an artificial stomach and had given her the appearance of being composed of several disparate pieces which there was no individuality to bind together.... As in a fine literary style which superimposes different forms but is strengthened by a tradition that lies concealed behind them, so in Mme Swann's attire those half-tinted memories of waistcoats or of ringlets, sometimes a tendency, at once repressed, toward the "all aboard," or even a distant and vague allusion to the "follow-me-lad," kept alive beneath the concrete form the

298
The Countess Greffulhe in a gown by Worth, about 1900
Nadar (Gaspard-Félix Tournachon)
(1820-1910),
photographer
Caisse Nationale des monuments Historiques et des Sites, Paris

179

her cousin, of whom, it was rumoured, she was inclined to make fun for what she called her "exaggerations" (a noun which, from her point of view, so wittily French and restrained, was instantly applicable to the poetry and enthusiasm of the Teuton), would be wearing this evening one of those costumes in which the Duchess considered her "dressed up," and that she had decided to give her a lesson in good taste. Instead of the wonderful downy plumage which descended from

unfinished likeness of other, older forms which one would not have been able to find effectively reproduced by the milliner or the dressmaker, but about which one's thoughts incessantly hovered, and enveloped Mme Swann in a sort of nobility.... One felt that she did not dress simply for the comfort or the adornment of her body: she was surrounded by her garments as by the delicate and spiritualized machinery of a whole civilization.... And if I were to draw her attention to this: "I don't play golf," she would answer, "like so many of my friends. So I should have no excuse for going about in sweaters as they do."[8]

The passage is at once the likeness of a woman and the epitaph of an era, at once a literary metaphor and an immediate prediction. The delicate, disembodied machinery of a civilization, in what Benjamin called "Paris, capital of the nineteenth century,"[9] contrasts with the sweaters of the golf-playing women.

Here is adumbrated a whole hierarchic culture of fashion, with Odette as its fine flower. At the same time, tastes and styles are being fragmented, and the other senses, particularly the sense of smell, are yielding to the imperious tyranny of an overcharged visual world. We are to understand that clothes, like words, leave behind them an echo that at once begins to resonate.

To watch Odette dressing, Proust tells us, was like being allowed to look at a Renaissance painting; to catch sight of the Guermantes women at the opera was to visit goddesses each unique of her kind, both inspiration and model for the portrait:

It was as though the Duchess had guessed that

299
Cover of *Les Modes*, depicting gowns by Paul Poiret (1879-1944), April, 1912
Georges Barbier (1882-1932)
Color lithograph
Cooper-Hewitt Museum, New York, Picture Collection

300
Fan (detail), 1925
Georges Bastard (1881-1939)
Mother-of-pearl
The Metropolitan Museum of Art, New York, Edward C. Moore, Jr., Gift Fund, 1925

301
Poster: Tunmer Bros. sporting goods, about 1895
J.E. Gluck
Color lithograph
Musée de la Publicité, Paris

302
"Le Coin des Sports," for Jean Patou's boutique, 1925
Bernard Boutet de Monvel (1884-1968)
Collection Jean de Moüy, Jean Patou, Paris

the crown of the Princess's head to her throat, instead of her net of shells and pearls, the Duchess wore in her hair only a simple aigrette which, surmounting her arched nose and prominent eyes, reminded one of the crest on the head of a bird. Her neck and shoulders emerged from a drift on snow-white chiffon, against which fluttered a swansdown fan, but below this her gown, the bodice of which had for its sole ornament innumerable spangles (either little sticks and beads of metal, or brilliants), moulded her figure with a precision that was positively British. But different as their two costumes were, after the Princess had given her cousin the chair in which she herself had previously been sitting, they could be seen turning to gaze at one another in mutual appreciation.

Perhaps Mme de Guermantes would smile next day when she referred to the headdress, a little too complicated, which the Princess had worn, but certainly she would declare that the latter had been nonetheless quite lovely and marvellously got up; and the Princess, whose own tastes found something a little cold, a little austere, a little "tailor-made" in her cousin's way of dressing, would discover in this strict sobriety an extreme refinement. Moreover, the harmony that existed between them, the universal and pre-established gravitational pull of their upbringing, neutralised the contrasts not only in their apparel but in their attitude.[10]

The world of fashion in the nineteenth century merged into that of the twentieth with several important changes. Industrialization of the fashion industry, including the introduction of mechanical

sewing machines, die-cutting appliances, and easily available "patterns" used by manufacturers and by women in their homes, democratized fashion to an unprecedented extent. At the same time, homogeneity followed in the wake of popular consumption, as did a conservative attitude toward dress: it was economically viable for industrialists to produce only those designs that would appeal to a broad cross section of society. The rule of profit

303
Poster: Chemises Lacoste
Collection La Chemise Lacoste, Paris

304
Chart of sales by color for Lacoste shirts, 1978 to 1987
Collection La Chemise Lacoste, Paris

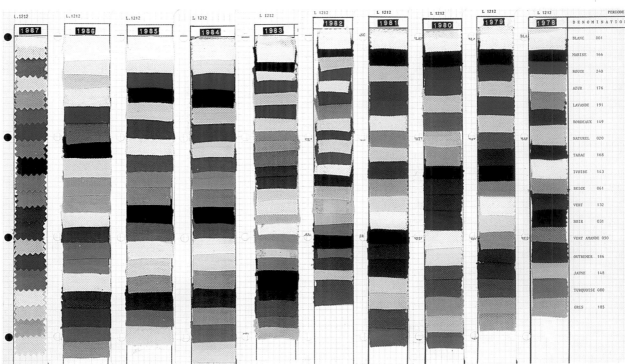

held sway within the industry, setting haute couture above the mainstream and emphasizing its artistic uniqueness and dictatorship.

Worth and Doucet still cast a long shadow among the elite, but by the second decade of the twentieth century, other couturiers had also created their own special audiences—one need only remember that Callot Sœurs, Paquin, and Poiret flourished during this exceptional period of

expansion. Fashion had to reckon with this new woman of the twentieth century.

Two couturiers reflected the changing role of women in our century. The importance of Paul Poiret has most frequently been described within the context of the Ballets Russes, which took Paris by storm in 1911. Brilliant and uninhibited color, orientalism, shocking patterns, and a rich sensuality were hallmarks of the memorable costumes created by Léon Bakst for the Ballets Russes, and certainly Poiret shared his fascination with the unexpected, the discordant, and the exotic. Poiret's dresses, however, are remembered for liberating women's bodies, and for their absence of structures to support and buttress women's forms. Poiret captured the spirit of the times in his dresses, but not without an undeniable and equally significant backward glance toward the Empire. Poiret's dresses reflected the new woman but paid homage to the *élégante* of the Napoleonic era.

The new woman, according to Virginia Woolf,

had gone "...from a nondescript influence, fluctuating and vague, to a voter, a wage-earner, a responsible citizen... Her relations now are not only emotional; they are intellectual, they are political. The old system which condemned her to squint askance at things through the eyes or through the interests of husband or brother, has given place to the direct and practical interests of one who must act for herself, and not merely influence the acts of others." She acted on her own account and was drawn increasingly to an impersonal fashion. This was Chanel's woman, an emancipated woman, who "[had] leisure, and money, and a room of [her own]."[11]

More has been written about Chanel than about most other twentieth-century couturiers. The echoes of Chanel even today resound throughout the world of fashion. Chanel's woman presented a truly objective being who participated fully in a broad spectrum of activities while remaining elegant. Chanel was the first to tap anonymous sources for her designs; one need only think of her uniformlike suits, her loose masculine sweaters, and her unabashedly fake jewelry to recognize that fashion had reached a new plateau. On no theme have so many variations been played, from status symbol to self-mockery, from the rue Cambon to the boutiques for juniors. Models were bedizened with fake jewelry, which, no matter how costly, could never be perceived as a woman's dowry or an expression of her husband's fortune or even the reward she allowed herself. Chanel recognized that a woman is not a reliquary for displaying the collection of one's ancestors. Costume jewelry, whether real "couture" or simply "fashion accessory," has only an imputed, not an intrinsic, value; it is a symbol of taste rather than a sign of wealth.

Chanel did not even give titles to her creations. Her suits and her perfumes bore numbers, not names. Her designs, as those of a confident woman should, bear unashamed witness to the passage of time and make no attempt to cheat it. Ready-made clothing, it was said, is killing fashion. "Ah," replied Chanel, "but fashion wants to die!... .A dress is not a tragedy."[12]

With a variation or two, notably Saint Laurent's pants suit, the impersonal architecture of the *tailleur* or woman's suit (as its name suggests, the feminine equivalent of a man's suit) remains to this day the garment of choice for the woman who needs something to wear at work and then straight out to dinner at a restaurant. To categorize clothes according to time of day or purpose, as in day wear, evening wear, cruise wear, is just a vestigial memory of court etiquette, gently recalled by couture.

305
Sports ensemble designed by Nina Ricci (1883-1970)
Published in *Vogue*, Winter 1937/38
Collection Nina Ricci, Paris

309
**Richard Hudnut
perfume shop, Paris,
about 1925**
Mural decoration by
Georges Barbier
(1882-1932)
Thérèse Bonney
(1897-1978),
photographer
Cooper-Hewitt Museum,
New York, Bonney
Collection

310
**Jeanne Lanvin
(1867-1946), about
1920**
Jeanne Lanvin Archives,
Paris

311
**"Liu" bottle,
Guerlain, first
produced 1929**
Cristalleries de Baccarat
manufacturer
Glass
Collection Guerlain,
Paris

312
**"L'Air du Temps"
bottle, Nina Ricci,
first produced 1948**
Lalique, manufacturer
Glass
Collection Nina Ricci,
Paris

313
**Store display of
Lanvin perfumes,
Paris, about 1925-30**
Limited edition
porcelain bottles
manufactured by Sèvres
Thérèse Bonney
(1897-1978),
photographer
Cooper-Hewitt Museum,
New York, Bonney
Collection

314
**"Normandie" bottle,
Jean Patou, first
produced 1935**
Glass, metal
Collection Jean de
Moüy, Jean Patou, Paris

315
"Mouchoir de Monsieur" bottle, Guerlain, first produced 1904
Raymond Guerlain, designer,/Cristalleries de Baccarat, manufacturer
Glass
Collection Guerlain, Paris

316
Advertisement: "Shalimar" Guerlain, about 1925
Guerlain Archives, Paris

317
Advertisement: "Chanel No. 5," 1921
SEM, illustrator
Chanel Archives, Paris

318
"Alpona" bottle, Caron, first produced 1939
Glass
Collection Caron, Paris

319
"Cantilène" bottle, Revillon, first produced 1948
Fernand Léger (1881-1955), designer
Lalique, manufacturer
Glass
Collection Revillon, Paris

rupture in French society, and the "New Look" of Dior is emblematic of this change: the restrained sensuality of couture opposed its allure to the devastating glamour of American movies, its stars, and their gowns. The luxurious intimacy of the 1930s shifted into the confidence of the post-1945 woman, as defined by Balmain, Balenciaga, Fath, Givenchy, Cardin, and Courrèges. After 1945, and

Another fundamental change in our perception of French fashion in the twentieth century can also be traced from the 1920s to the period after World War II. The great "seamstresses" of the 1920s and 1930s—Vionnet, Lanvin, Grès, Schiaparelli—created an almost autobiographical image in their dresses, whether subdued or eccentric. In the height of the Surrealist revolution, "Paris, dressed up in poufs and aigrettes, danced on a roaring volcano," said Dior later. The fascination of couturiers for modern painters was openly declared and was going to last—Cocteau at Schiaparelli, Mondrian and Matisse dresses at Saint Laurent, along with Braque and Van Gogh embroidery.

World War II, like the Revolution of 1789, was a

320
Evening gown designed by Madeleine Vionnet (1876-1975)
Published in *Harper's Bazaar*, 1936
George Hoyningen-Huene (1900-1968), photographer

321
"Bird Dress" designed by Marcel Rochas (1902-1955)
Published in *Harper's Bazaar*, April, 1934
Harry Meerson (born 1910), photographer

322
Evening gowns designed by Elsa Schiaparelli (1890-1973)
Published in *Vogue*, October, 1938
Christian Bérard, illustrator

323
"Bar" tailored suit, 1947, designed by Christian Dior (1905-1957)
Collection Christian Dior, Paris

324
***Time* cover, March 4, 1957**
Robert Vickery, illustrator

continuing to the present day, an international audience played an important role in the making of "French style." Communication and travel improved dramatically after the war. It was no longer necessary to come to Paris to purchase fashion: fashion came to the buyer not only through press and publicity, but also through the boutiques opened in cities ranging from Texas to Tokyo.

How did all of these technological, social, and economic conditions alter the course of French fashion, as well as our perception about the mythology of fashion in the twentieth century? Today it is at the *défilés*, or showings, that fashion is developed. The discerning taste of true lovers of fashion at these events is to be contrasted with the gluttonous hunger of those who are not aware of the interrelationships of aesthetics or who can see only through the eyes of others.

From one year's collections to the next, today's designers strive to assert individuality, consistency in time and place, and the influence of their own success on their image. Can these witnesses of time still understand one another? Or is each, in today's world, wholly isolated and distant?

All "inhabit the same country—the deep virgin forest of reality."[13] But what if the paths diverge, if fashion is no longer a pyramid from whose summit commands bounce down (more ineffectually carried out as they approach the base), but rather a landscape where every individual has his own plot of ground, does the spadework on it, discovers how to move freely around the temporal plane by means of juxtapositions, omissions, and rejections of forms from the past? Then it appears that fashion has now engendered its own culture, its own memories, its own body of styles.

In the sixties and seventies, the resurgence of the feminist movement, among other forces, fragmented the fashion world into various schools of ready-to-wear clothing, reflecting a diversity of ways of life. The media, which continued to photograph all these divergent tastes on one stereotyped body, finally began in the eighties to acknowledge the fact that each woman has her own body and that each designer favors one aspect of that body or one particular type of woman. Individuality is now conceded to designer and model alike, in showings where every creative artist has to reassert his qualifications, reexamine his values, deepen his vocabulary—in short, distinguish his own specificity from the banalities lurking in ambush ready to drag him down with the weight of success until he is no more than the label on his own work.

The flow of information has speeded up, become fragmented and diffused; pictures circulate more widely than clothes, and can rob them of their freshness before they are worn. The designer must therefore reaffirm his style by a coherent modification of fashion history, as well as of his own work. At the same time that he is making over the past into news, he must ensure that the future is imminent in the present.

To develop his own approach or those shapes current in the vocabulary of fashion, the designer must take account of received wisdom. During the week of showings, there must be a compelling effervescence and an aesthetic rapture for the

325

Evening gown designed by Jacques Fath (1912-1954)
Published in *Vogue*, September 1950
Irving Penn (born 1917), photographer

326

Audrey Hepburn in an ensemble by Hubert de Givenchy (born 1927), 1961
Publicity photograph for the film *Breakfast at Tiffany's*
Givenchy Archives, Paris

twenty or thirty minutes that the models are on view. The original piece, as soon as it leaves our presence to disappear into the changing room, will become an article of commerce, not a unique *chef d'œuvre* as in couture. "Beauty," Breton told us, "will be the magic of circumstance."

There is a burst of language that accompanies the debut of coherent fashion. The show will immediately evoke commentary, passwords, conversations. Nowadays in France the daily papers take notice of fashion at the time of the shows rather than when it reaches the market, and sometimes the language used, in particular in *Libération*, is crypto-Parisian; fashion magazines

327
**Evening dress
designed by Pierre
Balmain (1914-1982)**
Published in *Harper's
Bazaar*, March, 1960
Derujinsky,
photographer

328
**Evening dress, 1974
Guy Laroche
(1921-1989)**
Collection Guy Laroche,
Paris

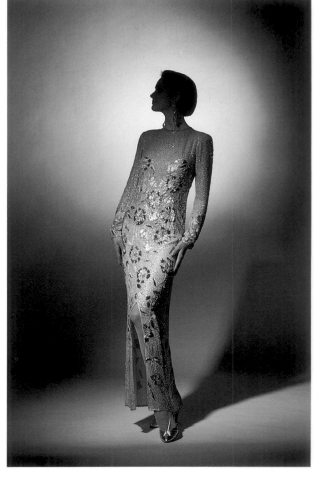

329
**Suit designed by
Coco Chanel
(1883-1971)**
Published in *Harper's
Bazaar*, March, 1960
Derujinsky,
photographer

330
**Evening gown
designed by Cristóbal
Balenciaga
(1895-1972)**
Published in *Vogue*,
September, 1950
Irving Penn (born
1917), photographer

seem to follow their own conventions and their own markets, selling as they do, magazines rather than dresses.

The designer knows that the attention paid him by press or public, no matter how ironic or critical, no matter how crudely or clumsily distortive of his dreams, is his indispensable link with reality. Description, approval, rejection—all engender immediate aftershocks of consensus, of puns, of free associations. At his show, or his fête, and in his ads and video clips, the designer states a theme, and so touches off a continuing dialogue between word and image. Jean-Paul Gaultier, for example, in his play on popular titles and phrases for his collections, has come up with such themes as Douce France [Sweet France], Le Charme coincé de la bourgeoisie, [The Uptight Charm of the Middle Class], and La Concierge est dans l'escalier [The Concierge Is on the Stairs].

The scheduled showings bring together the producers of fashion and those whose approval keeps them in business—an international gathering of professionals, curious spectators, indispensable worldlings, and groupies. Each time these passionate days come around they remind us how essential it is that the champions be retested, and the aspirants reacclaimed, by a group of connoisseurs that flocks and regenerates

331
Metallic skirts and tops designed by André Courrèges (born 1923)
Published in *Vogue*, March, 1969
Bert Stern, photographer

itself in twice-yearly migration.

And what of "French taste"? Is it a historical fact or a commercial reality? Is it visible or merely a figment of the imagination? Taste, it now becomes clear, is an exercise—not a happening, or a transaction, or a bloodless narrative. And it is not Frenchness or Italianness or Japaneseness that is on display, but a self-consistent individuality. It is not the national component that is proclaimed, but a capacity to question and integrate fashion. There is a kind of pseudo-French taste that is of the same order as fake Louis XIII, Louis XIV, or Louis XVI furniture; it meets commercial demand, but does not call on creativity, and the public cannot but be

disappointed, just as they are with today's fan magazines, which are filled with over-emphatic praise for designers and rock stars and present their lives as the equivalent of "the golden legend of saints and heroes." Whatever our desires, no designer can persist in the attempt, ill-fated in the contemporary world, to achieve a totality.

In *Six Memos for the Next Millennium*, Italo Calvino recalls a myth of the harmonious whole:

Mercury with his winged feet, light airborne, astute, agile, adaptable, free and easy, established the relationships of the gods among themselves and those between the gods and men, between

332
Evening gowns designed by Yves Saint Laurent (born 1936)
Published in *Vogue*, November, 1969
Irving Penn (born 1917), photographer

universal laws and individual destinies, between the forces of nature and the forms of culture, between the objects of the world and all thinking subjects.

There is, however, another god with family ties to Saturn for whom I feel much affection... I am speaking of Vulcan—Hephaestus, a god who does not roam the heavens but lurks at the bottom of craters, shut up in his smithy, where he tirelessly forges objects that are the last word in refinement: jewels and ornaments for the gods and goddesses, weapons, shields, nets, traps. To Mercury's aerial flight, Vulcan replies with his limping gait and the rhythmic beat of his hammer. In the end, in the

well-balanced, luminous realm of Jupiter, both Mercury and Vulcan carry with them the memory of some dark primordial realm, changing what had been a destructive malady into something positive: syntony and focalization.[14]

At a time when Mars and Venus are sundered, Vulcan threatened, and Mercury unleashed on the shadowy, image-strewn surface of our planet, Paris is still the place where, for historical reasons and because of the continual cultivation of professional competence, the taste and culture of fashion are most fully practiced. The final dimension—that of the bodies, the street—must come to enlarge and

333
**Pantsuit designed by
Yves Saint Laurent
(born 1936)**
Published in *Vogue*,
September, 1966
Irving Penn (born
1917), photographer

confirm these acts of belief. Witness the fact that
while Paris may be the capital of fashion, she must
so far defer to other cities in such fields as music
or architecture.

On this fertile soil, this mulch of words and
images, of events and intervals, designer and
connoisseur of fashion alike enter with open
minds, not ignorant but as yet uninformed. Each
seeks to test and exercise his taste, to come face to
face with the best, to bear witness to norms, to
illustrate the changing rules of the game, in a
word, to free his imagination, but in a setting that

334
**"Chasuble" ensemble
designed by Pierre
Cardin (born 1922)**
Published in *Harper's
Bazaar*, September,
1969
Cooper-Hewitt Museum,
New York, Picture
Library

is committed to the contemporary.

Taste is not a sleeper seeking a cooler spot on
the pillow. In this context, it is the active link
between desired form and admired form, or, to
quote Breton, "a wonderful precipitate of desire."

1. Honoré de Balzac, "Les Employés," *La Comédie humaine,* vol. 7. (Paris: La Pléiade Gallimard, 1977), p. 906.

2. Ibid, p. 1046

3. Balzac, "La muse du département," *La Comédie humaine,* vol. 4 (Paris: La Pléiade Gallimard, 1981), p. 671.

4. Emile Zola, *Au Bonheur des dames* (Paris: Folio Gallimard, 1980), p. 33.

5. Giacomo Leopardi, quoted by Walter Benjamin in "Paris, capitale du xixᵉ siècle," *Essais II, 1935-40* (Paris: Médiations Denoël-Gonthier, 1971, 1983), p. 44.

6. Emile Zola, *La Curée* (Paris: Livre de Poche, 1966), p. 147.

7. Marcel Proust, *Remembrance of Things Past,* translated by C. K. Scott Moncrieff, revised by Terence Kilmartin, vol. 2 (New York: Random House: 1981 p. 842; © 1981, by Random House Inc. and Chatto and Windus.

8. Proust, translated by Moncrieff, vol. 1, pp. 665-68.

9. Walter Benjamin, op. cit.

10. Proust, translated by Moncrieff, vol. 2, pp. 49-50.

11. Virginia Woolf, "Women and Fiction," in *Granite and Rainbow* (London: The Hogarth Press, 1958), pp. 83-84.

12. Coco Chanel, as reported by Paul Morand in *L'Allure de Chanel* (Paris: Hermann, 1977), pp. 107-08.

13. Juan José Saer, as quoted in "La forêt épaisse du Réel," in *Magazine littéraire,* September, 1979, translated by Gérard de Cortanze, pp. 151-52.

14. Italo Calvino, *Six Memos for the Next Millennium* (Cambridge: Harvard University Press. 1988); reprinted by permission of Harvard University Press, © 1988, by the Estate of Italo Calvino.

335
"Astarte" evening gown designed by Christian Lacroix (born 1951), from the autumn haute couture collection, 1988-89

EVELYNE POSSÉMÉ

BIJOUTERIE AND JOAILLERIE

It is no light task to attempt an overview of the development of design and technique in French jewelry in the nineteenth and twentieth centuries. Henri Vever, both *bijoutier* and *joaillier*, brought a master hand to the task early in the present century; his account, *La Bijouterie française au XIXe siècle*, is fascinating, full of life, and abounding in valuable, previously undisclosed insights into his craft and his circle.[1] In design, the wide range of sources from which inspiration could be drawn, as well as constant changes in fashion, lent themselves readily to a high level of creativity and a constantly improving armory of techniques. It was during these same two centuries that such families of *bijoutiers-joailliers* as Fouquet, Falize, Froment-Meurice, Sandoz, Boucheron, and

Templier first made their appearance, sometimes passing their craft along over as many as three generations. Justice cannot be done in a few pages to this richly creative branch of the useful arts, to which other historians have devoted several volumes. Our objective here is a limited one: to summarize the story as clearly as possible, highlighting the broad lines along which jewelry evolved in a period of changing aesthetic doctrines, drawing attention to the artists who applied these doctrines to jewelry, and setting the whole in historical perspective against its contemporary background of policies and fashions in clothing.

First of all, some definitions are required. The English language makes use of the single term *jewelry*, which is ambiguous, and takes no account of the technical diversity prevailing in France from the seventeenth century onward and particularly marked during the whole of the nineteenth century, as indicated by the successive reports from a series of international exhibitions. Fossin, who wrote the official account of *bijouterie-joaillerie* exhibited at the Universal Exposition of 1867 in Paris, and himself one of the city's leading *joailliers*, reminds us that "*bijouterie* is the art of metalworking, enriched by all the resources of the craft and by the rich hues of enamel and precious stones; *joaillerie* is the art of presenting diamonds and precious stones in the most favorable light and in the fullness of their luster, with settings which, while dependably solid, do not annoy the eye with any extraneous material."[2] If *bijouterie* may be understood as a generic term embracing all the techniques of the craft, it follows that *joaillerie* is no more than one branch of *bijouterie*, which, responding to the demands of fashion, has since the eighteenth century evolved independently, to the detriment of the craft as a whole. Throughout the nineteenth century this evolution accelerated, until many artists rebelled against the ever-greater vogue for *joaillerie*. There were many who maintained that the two techniques are complementary. Eugène Fontenay, for instance, has this to say: "There is no reason why gold jewelry and fine *joaillerie* should not flourish side by side, for they serve different needs. Diamonds can be seen at their best only by artificial light, whereas the beauty of gold and enamel is set off by the light of day."[3] This rivalry, and the ever-increasing preference accorded to *joaillerie* over *bijouterie*, is one of the salient features of the development of jewelry in the nineteenth and even in the twentieth century.

Joaillerie and fine *bijouterie* are the industry's two flagship sectors, through which France acquired an international reputation in the field; because of them, French jewelry was in worldwide demand from the early nineteenth century onward. From them evolved other sectors that, although not innovative in design, made use of different materials and techniques. Rolled-gold jewelry involves application of a thin layer of gold on a sheet of copper (or, toward the end of the nineteenth century, of silver). Other jewelry included pieces in stamped and gilded copper; in cut steel, a technique developed in England in the eighteenth century; in *fonte de Berlin* (supple, delicate cast-iron jewelry made in Germany and France); in jet and black enamel, two materials whose principal use was for mourning *parures*

(matched sets of jewelry to be worn as an ensemble). Throughout the nineteenth century there were special trades, such as the production of cameos from coral, hardstones or shells, the making of little pictures in glass mosaic, and even the working of hair, all subsidiary branches of the jewelry industry important nonetheless to the overall trade. In the twentieth century, novelty or costume jewelry (*bijoux de fantaisie*) has made use principally of plastics, glass, rubber, lacquer, and base metals.

During the violent years of the Revolution, women gave up wearing the *parure*; indeed, they scarcely dared wear any jewelry, considered as it

was an outward symbol of wealth. A shortage of both materials and craftsmen endangered the very survival of the industry. But, as always, the desire to be well turned out triumphed over all obstacles; alongside medallions bearing such patriotic emblems as the cap of liberty, the lictor's fasces, and even, improbable as it may seem, the guillotine itself, there appeared gold crosses worn around the neck, as well as more medals adorned with motifs in fashion under Louis XVI: quivers of arrows, doves, and baskets of flowers.

The Consulate, Directory, and Empire witnessed a return to Greek and Roman models of antiquity. Women appeared lightly shod in lawn tunics belted under the bosom; these simple, airy garments did not encourage the wearing of much jewelry.

Simple earrings, a comb or tiara on the head; a necklace or chain, often worn across the bosom; and a bracelet on each wrist—these were all the *parure* a woman needed. Favored materials were coral, cut steel, and woven or braided hair. Necklaces and bracelets were made up of several strands of gold chain, linking medallions with cameos in shell, or with plaques of such stones as carnelian, moss agate, amethyst, aquamarine, or topaz mounted in gold filigree stamped with tiny leaves and roses. This particular style of filigree, developed under the Empire and popular throughout the first half of the nineteenth century

337
Necklace, about 1950
Madame Gripoix, designer, for Chanel
Glass, simulated pearls, metal
Primavera Gallery, New York

338
Brooch with pendant flowers, about 1860
Unknown maker
Diamonds, silvered gold
Collection Mellerio dits Meller, Paris

339
Necklace of Empress Marie-Louise, 1811
Nitot et fils
Diamonds, white gold, silver
Department of Mineral Sciences, National Museum of Natural History, Smithsonian Institution, Washington, D.C.

340
Designs for earrings, about 1860-70
Chaumet
Pen and ink, watercolor
Musée Société Nouvelle
Chaumet, S.A., Paris

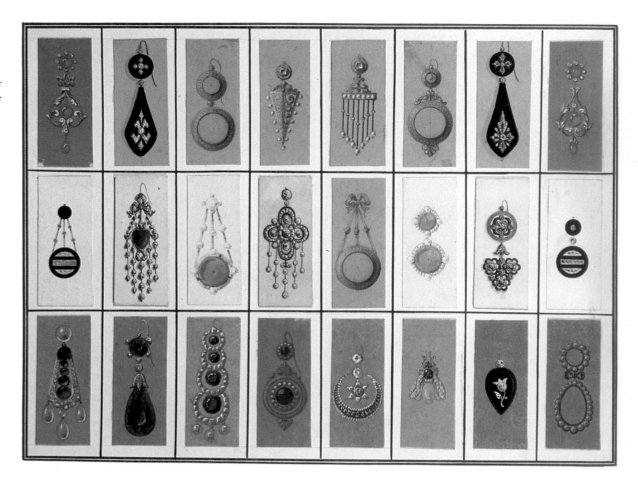

341
Interior of a jewelry shop (detail) on a plate from the "Industrial Arts Service", 1823
Jean-Charles Develly
(1785-1849), painter
Manufacture Nationale
de Sèvres
Porcelain
Museum of Fine Arts,
Boston, Bequest of
Forsyth Wickes, Forsyth
Wickes Collection

342
"Sloe Berries and Wasps" Brooch, 1904
René Lalique
(1860-1945)
Gold, glass, enamel
Musée des Arts
Décoratifs, Paris

and especially during the Restoration, involves the application of tightly coiled metal wire to a gold or silver ground; it was often used in conjunction with the so-called *graineti* (granulation) technique, in which tiny gold beads are sweated onto a gold surface.

The coming of the Empire, and particularly the coronation of Napoleon I and Josephine in 1804, rekindled the luxury of the court. Official receptions and court soirées ousted Revolutionary simplicity; imperial power was evoked through the display of wealth. Thus *joaillerie*, in hiding since the fall of the Ancien Régime, reappeared with the birth of the Empire, its favored manifestations being diamonds mounted in silver, and pearls. The many official portraits of the Empress Josephine and of Napoleon's sisters have preserved for posterity their magnificent *parures*, usually comprising a tiara or forehead band, a comb worn in the front of the hair (along with an empress's coronet when appropriate), earrings, a necklace, a jeweled belt worn under the breast, and a pair of bracelets. Etienne Nitot and his son, *joailliers* by appointment to the emperor and empress, were given charge of the former crown jewels and, along with Foncier and his son-in-law Marguerite, were commissioned to make the coronation regalia and to remount the diamonds and other precious stones from the old crown. Nitot made Napoleon's gold crown, with incised gems and cameos mounted on eight stems that met at the top to support an orb and cross. Josephine's favorite *joaillier* was Edmé Foncier, but after his retirement she turned to Nitot or his son François-Regnault, who succeeded him in 1809.

In 1807 Napoleon commissioned from Nitot a ruby tiara with diamond laurel leaves—a design that, more than fifty years later, the Empress

Eugénie was to copy. In 1810, on the occasion of his marriage to Marie-Louise, Napoleon sent Marshal Berthier to Vienna bearing as a gift a diamond *parure*. It comprised a tiara, a comb, a coronet, a pair of earrings, a necklace, a belt, and the traditional pair of bracelets. In 1812, the younger Nitot made for Marie-Louise a jewel of a more personal nature—a bracelet of woven hair whose clasp bore in its center an ornament containing the hair of her son, the king of Rome, along with a large flat diamond surrounded by colored stones arranged according to their variety

343
Earrings in the form of guillotines, 19th century
Unknown maker
Silver
Musée Carnavalet, Paris

**Marriage parure of
Empress Marie-Louise
(jeweler's document
version), 1810**
Nitot et fils
Garnets, white
sapphires, gold
Musée Société Nouvelle
Chaumet, S.A., Paris

345
**Empress
Marie-Louise, 1812**
Robert-Jacques-François-
Faust Lefèvre
(1755-1830)
Oil on canvas
Musée Société Nouvelle
Chaumet, S.A., Paris

so that the first letters of the stone types spelled out the name of the Emperor.

In 1814 the Bourbons were restored to the French throne, and except for the interlude of the Hundred Days in 1815, they remained in power until July, 1830. Characterized by some historians as a period of reaction, the Restoration was not a distinguished epoch for the decorative arts. The men who set its tone came out of the Ancien Régime, which they attempted to resurrect unscathed by the intervening Revolution and Empire. Although a tentative return to the style of Louis XVI can be noted, the Restoration essentially continued the Empire style, but with a heavier hand. Around 1820 women's dresses began to emphasize a slender waist, often necessitating recourse to a corset. At the same time, shoulders and upper sleeves were padded. Colored gold, popular under Louis XVI, reappeared: used with filigree and *graineti* work so admired at this time, it often enriched floral *parures* enlivened by colored enamels, amethysts, and topazes. These *parures* generally included a necklace, earrings, a pair of bracelets, and a belt buckle—this last an item now made indispensable by the fashionable new waistline, and destined to remain so through the reign of Louis-Philippe. The enterprising jeweler Simon Petiteau was highly regarded at this time for the exquisite finish of his *bijouterie* in filigree and *graineti*. He also enjoyed a well-earned reputation for the quality of simpler *parures*, of stamped gold, often chased with leaf patterns and adorned with flourishes of foliage; typical are a

parure of gold, black enamel, and half-pearls, or another with turquoise beads surrounded by rose-cut diamonds, set on gold plaques linked by a finely braided gold chain.

This was a sentimental period that cherished mementoes of the dear departed; mourning became an institution with precise rules, which

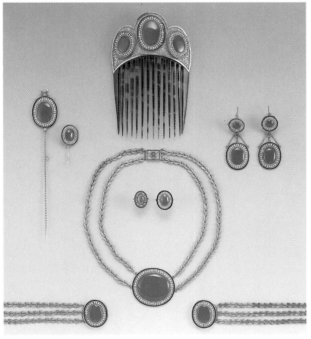

every well-brought-up person was assumed to know, and its own jewelry, whether the jet, black glass, or *fonte de Berlin* of full mourning, or the cut steel, less resplendent than precious stones, of half-mourning. Sentimentality was also served by a fashionable revival of hair jewelry. Braided-hair bracelets had clasps on which, against a ground of hair, the initials of the departed stood out in gold or silver—or even hair of a different color!

Jetworking still flourished in the Ariège region, though the original deposits were exhausted and the raw material now came from Spain. Cut and polished steel, of British origin but long-naturalized in France, appeared in the form of bunches of artificial flowers, or scarves as light and airy as gauze; steel beads and steel mesh were used in such accessories as handbags and purses, as well as for appliqué on dress fabrics. Cast-iron jewelry, still a novelty in France, soon came to rival the long-established Prussian product. Forms were often inspired by classical antiquity, and *parures* included a necklace or bracelets of cast-iron medallions bearing busts in the manner of classical cameos, linked together by wide bands of woven

349
Chatelaine in the Gothic or "troubadour" style, about 1845
Morel et Cie
Silver, gold, enamel
Musée des Arts Décoratifs, Paris

steel wire, although arabesques, foliage or even stylized flowers were also popular.[4]

Under Louis XVIII and Charles X, the Bapst family replaced Nitot and Fossin as court jewelers, and in 1814 Louis XVIII entrusted to them the resetting of some of the *parures* of Napoleon, including one of diamonds from 1810, and one of emeralds. Other pieces followed in 1815, most of them reset by Bapst before 1820. The royal *parures* were made under the supervision of Ebrard Bapst, many of them designed by Seiffert, the establishment's official designer. Their manufacture was entrusted to Charles-Frédéric Bapst, who ran the family workshops for more than fifty years. The

350
Title page from *Picturesque Journeys in Ancient France; Dauphiné*, 1838
Eugène-Emmanuel Viollet-le-Duc (1814-1879)
Graphite, watercolor
Centre de Recherches sur les Monuments Historiques, Paris

firm made the crown, sword, and a hat-ornament for the coronation regalia of Charles X.

The house of Bapst also made several *parures* for the royal family, including an emerald and diamond tiara, a turquoise and diamond *parure*, and another in sapphires and diamonds fashioned into scrollwork, continuous motifs of foliage, and husks — pieces that reappear in the catalogue of the sale of the crown jewels in 1887.[5] Other pieces were commissioned for the duchesse de Berry, particularly a set of jewelry presented to her on the occasion of the birth of the duc de Bordeaux in 1820 (also sold in 1887). In January 1829, on the night of the famous "Mary Stuart Quadrille" at the Tuileries, the duchesse de Berry wore a parure composed of stones from the crown jewels, specially set by Bapst for the occasion and valued then at more than three million francs. Fashion rediscovered the diamond and white feather aigrette and the multi-strand pearl necklace. Also popular were jeweled wheatheads, worn in the hair or scattered across the top of a dress.

In 1830 the *Trois Glorieuses*, the three days of rebellion on July 28, 29, and 30, induced Charles X to abdicate in favor of Henri V, the duc de Bordeaux. The duc d'Orléans was named regent before Charles X's exile to England. But on August 7, the Parliament offered the crown to Louis-Philippe, the duc d'Orléans, requiring him to subscribe to the "Constitutional Charter." His accession brought to power the *haute bourgeoisie* of finance and industry, a group that admired and appreciated the quiet, unpretentious family life of which the "Citizen King" was himself the leading exponent — a style not likely to give rise to luxurious display. Queen Marie-Amélie herself had little fondness for jewelry, seeking a tranquil, comfortable existence surrounded by her numerous children and grandchildren. Fashion, however, rejected such simplicity: emphasized increasingly was a waist that seemed ever more slender by contrast with the conical skirt and exaggerated leg-of-mutton sleeves. The reign of Louis-Philippe witnessed both the birth and the flowering of a new and important aesthetic, "Romanticism", which has been defined as "the triumph of imagination and sensibility over observation and understanding."[6]

The dawn of the movement can be seen as early as the Restoration, when recently published

351
Princess de Broglie, 1853
Jean-Auguste-Dominique Ingres (1780-1867)
Oil on canvas
The Metropolitan Museum of Art, New York, Robert Lehman Collection, 1975

masterpieces by Chateaubriand in France and Goethe and Schiller in Germany stimulated an interest in the life and art of the Middle Ages. Although literary in origin, the movement eventually affected all the arts and, particularly, the decorative arts. After 1830, the success of Victor Hugo's novel *Notre-Dame de Paris* and of Dumas's play *La Tour de Nesle* confirmed the modishness of the medieval. In jewelry, the first fruits of Romanticism made their appearance at the 1834 Exhibition of French industrial products, where the

352
"Diane" bracelet, 1883
Alphonse Fouquet (1828-1911)
Model by Albert-Ernest Carrier-Belleuse (1824-1887), enamels by Paul Grandhomme
Gold, enamel, diamonds
Musée des Arts Décoratifs, Paris

353
Design for a pendant brooch, about 1855
Alexis Falize
(1811-1898)
Graphite, gouache, varnish
Cooper-Hewitt Museum, New York, Purchased in memory of Mrs. Gustave E. Kissel, 1950-6-1

354
Chatelaine with watch, 1878
Boucheron
Gold, enamel
Collection Boucheron, Paris

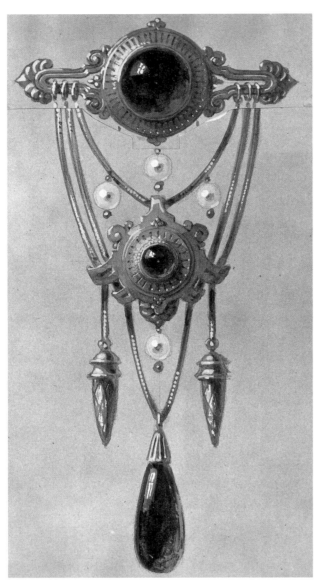

355
Covered cup in the Renaissance style, about 1860
Morel et Cie
Rock crystal, gold, enamel
Musée Société Nouvelle Chaumet, S.A., Paris

208

goldsmiths and *bijoutiers* Mention and Wagner were the first to display goldwork adorned with niello — designs traced in black on a silver or gold background, a technique developed by German master-craftsmen. Baron Charles Dupin, the official reporter, was alert to the importance of this novelty: "Here we have a new source of inspiration for the artist and of revenue for the manufacturer — the art of niello, which, passing from the Orient to Italy, burned brightly there during the fifteenth century."[7]

All observers agreed that the French jewelry

displayed at the 1839 Exposition had struck a new course, reminiscent of the masterpieces of the thirteenth, fourteenth, and fifteenth centuries. Wagner and Mention displayed niello jewels, pieces of "Byzantine" goldwork, vessels carved from hardstones and others decorated with enamels. The exhibit of Benoît Marel included objects in the style of the fifteenth century: ewers, cups, and pitchers set with semi-precious stones (*pierres fines*), niello work, and enameled or chased arabesques. François-Désiré Froment-Meurice was awarded a silver medal for goldsmith's work and another for *bijouterie*. At this same exposition, the *joaillier* Maret exhibited "a magnificent diadem or garland of flowers set with brilliants, serving to hold the hair in place," which could be separated into individual stems, while Dafrique had a "magnificent necklace in gold and enamel" made for Queen Marie-Amélie.[8]

More and more, designers sought "to uncover

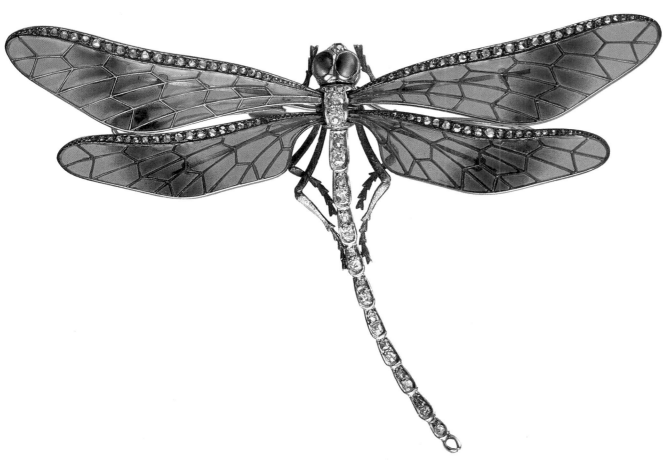

359
Parure in the Egyptian style, 1878
Emile Philippe (active after 1866)
Silver gilt, enamel, hardstones, semi-precious stones
Musée des Arts Décoratifs, Paris

360
Design for a buckle, about 1900
Eugène-Samuel Grasset (1841-1917)
Graphite, gouache, watercolor
Cooper-Hewitt Museum, New York, Purchased in memory of Mrs. Gustave E. Kissel, 1950-6-7

361
Brooch or belt buckle, late 19th century
Chaumet
Gold, opal, rubies, emeralds, diamonds, agates
Musée Société Nouvelle Chaumet, S.A., Paris

362
Brooch in the form of a dragonfly, about 1900-05
Boucheron
Gold, enamel, diamonds
Collection Boucheron, Paris

211

novelty in the records of the past, much more concerned to find therein the components for some new conception of their own, than to determine how things were really done in those days." Thus the public was offered "bracelets of linked ogives, each containing an armored warrior, lance in hand, standing watch."[9] The first exponents of the renascent Romantic tradition were goldsmiths who also worked in *bijouterie*, such as Charles Wagner, François-Désiré Froment-Meurice, Rudolphi, Morel, and Duponchel. Since the human figure served as an important motif in the period, goldsmiths and jewelers often called upon sculptors like Pradier, Feuchères, Klagmann, Geoffroy de Chaumes, Caïn, and Cavelier. Romanticism also created a link between the nineteenth century and the Renaissance; the jewel became once more an independent work of art, relying on both the skill and the intelligence of the artist. Other echoes of the past can also be noted: at the 1844 Exposition, Froment-Meurice offered parures of *joaillerie* in the style of Louis XIV, as well as such objects as flasks and bonbonnières in the style of Louis XV. The majority of his display, however, was neo-Gothic in spirit, with a fine collection of bracelets, brooches, and chatelaines ornamented with figurines and open strapwork, a lily bracelet, a Joan-of-Arc bracelet, François I and Medici brooches, and a group of pins bearing figurines of such personalities as Esmeralda (the

heroine of Victor Hugo's novel *Notre-Dame de Paris*), Truth, Joan of Arc, and St. Michael. His rings included the naiads designed by the sculptor Pradier, a guardian angel, a tortoise, and a "Mettray" ring, on which a child from the Mettray penal settlement is shown giving thanks to Heaven under the protection of an angel. A beautifully designed bracelet by Morel showed courtiers of Charles VII revering Joan of Arc. Also noteworthy were the highly decorative designs of Rudolphi, successor to Mention and Wagner, of which the official reporter, the vicomte Héricart de Thury, said "their style is so clearly defined that they could be taken for replicas of the masterpieces of the German, Saxon or Swedish jewelers of old."[10] It was Rudolphi who first exploited oxidized or blackened silver in his jewels, a technique imitated by many others.

Jewelers also continued to produce objects that, white admittedly less eye-catching than *bijouterie* inspired by the Middle Ages, were no less delightful. Thus during the 1840s, Marchand, drawing his inspiration from the Renaissance, revived strapwork designs for medallions, brooches, and chased bracelets. From the eighteenth century he borrowed the ribbon knot for gold brooches set with pearls or gems, and others enameled with foliage and fruit. The conquest and colonization of North Africa under the July Monarchy popularized the "Algerian knot." During the 1860s Crouzet hung chains, tassels, and coral, onyx, or lapis medallions from bracelets composed of Algerian knots; some pins and bracelets survive, with the Algerian knot twined

around spheres of lapis lazuli. Jean-Paul Robin introduced the coiled-gold bracelet with clasped ends shaped like the heads of eagles, serpents, or chimeras. In the 1840s, Petiteau designed brooches and pendants in which birds frolic and peck at ruby berries within a garland of diamond leaves.

In 1848 all Europe was in the grip of crisis. In France, shortages following several poor harvests resulted in widespread strikes; not even the bankers were unscathed, and the railroad workshops lay idle for lack of credit. With the Revolution of February 1848, Louis-Philippe was compelled to abdicate in favor of his grandson, the comte de Paris, but a republic was proclaimed under a provisional government including such

large flounced skirt draped over a wire frame. The tight corsage had a deeply plunging neckline that exposed the upper bosom, shoulders, and arms. The slenderness of the tightly cinched waist was emphasized by the bouffant skirt.

The new plunging neckline aptly set off the splendor of the *parure* in *joaillerie*, which regained its popularity at court, particularly after the marriage of Napoleon III and Eugénie de Montijo in 1853. The house of Bapst, now under the direction of Charles Bapst and his nephew Alfred, designed most of the *parures* for the empress. At the 1855 Universal Exposition in Paris, where the crown jewels were on display, visitors took note of "a dress ornament, in the shape of a

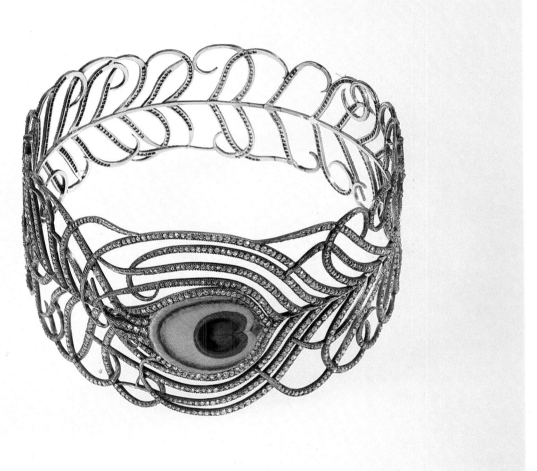

365
Neck ornament, about 1895
Mellerio dits Meller
Gold, diamonds, enamel
National Museum of American Art, Smithsonian Institution, Washington, D.C., Gift of Laura Dreyfus Barney in Memory of her mother Alice Pike Barney

luminaries as Lamartine, Ledru-Rollin, the socialist Louis Blanc, and the worker Albert. On December 10, 1848, Prince Louis-Napoléon Bonaparte was elected President of the Second Republic. A coup d'etat on December 2, 1851, followed by a plebiscite on December 20 of the same year, vested him with plenary powers to modify the Constitution; the Second Republic was history, and the Second Empire succeeded it.

Under the Second Empire fashion rediscovered the crinoline (the word is derived from the French *crin*, hair, and *lin*, flax or linen), used to stiffen a

bertha (an ornament lying over the shoulders like a lace collar), made of red-currant leaves, in the midst of which glittered a magnificent breast ornament in the same style, made by Bapst."[11] The state crowns of the emperor and empress were made by Lemonnier to designs by Gilbert. The emperor's crown was a circlet set with great diamonds and emeralds surmounted by a diamond cross, with the regent diamond at its base. That of the empress was also of gold and featured eagles surrounded by a wreath of palms. Also evoking the admiration of the Parisians were a pearl *parure* by

213

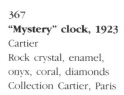

Lemonnier, a belt by Kramer, and a spray of brilliants by Fester. As a result of this show five gold medals were awarded, the first to the house of Bapst for its brooch of the kind called "Sévigné" (a large ribbon bow derived from eighteenth-century jewelry) in pearls and diamonds, made for the empress; another to the house of Marret and Baugrand for a wreath of cornflowers and a necklace of black pearls and ribands; to Mellerio for his daring floral designs and his happy use of flexible settings lending lightness to his flower compositions; to Marret and Jarry Frères for a breast ornament in rubies and diamonds with Renaissance motifs; and to Rouvenat for a diamond dress trimming, representing wildflowers, that could be taken apart and reassembled to form a *parure* of *rivière*, tiara, bracelet, and brooch. This artist also exhibited a brooch in diamonds on gold, representing an eagle on its nest defending its eggs against a snake. As these descriptions indicate, the main theme of *joaillerie* in 1855 was floral; the elder Fossin used it to create bouquets of flowers set with brilliants.

Bijouterie, too, had its place at the Fair. Jules Wièse, exhibiting for the first time, showed a silver hand mirror with a repoussé design by Lienard

(originally intended for a wood carving) depicting a trellis of vine tendrils with little birds poised for flight. Although 1855 was the year of François-Désiré Froment-Meurice's death, he was represented at the exposition by a cameo pendant showing "Venus at Her Toilette," as well as by bracelets with jeweled flowers on a naturalistic background of green enamel foliage.

Fossin and Baugrand, official reporters on *bijouterie-joaillerie* at the 1867 Universal Exposition in Paris, noted that the general trend was "to study the great periods of art, and at the same time avoid eclecticism.... Some are admirers of the Greek, Tuscan, or Roman—in a word, of classical antiquity; others of the Byzantine; yet others of the Romanesque and Gothic. Many affect the Renaissance; the eighteenth century has its impassioned partisans. In short, everyone does

research; our knowledge is broadened and extended; our taste is being educated and cannot fail to improve—though, in the present period of transition, the co-existence of so many different periods may perhaps result in some apparent aesthetic confusion."[12]

The principal exponents of the classical style, popularized by the exhibition of the Campana Collection, which the emperor had purchased in 1861, were Eugène Fontenay and the Italian Castellani; the former drew on the patterns and techniques of antiquity as the inspiration for new

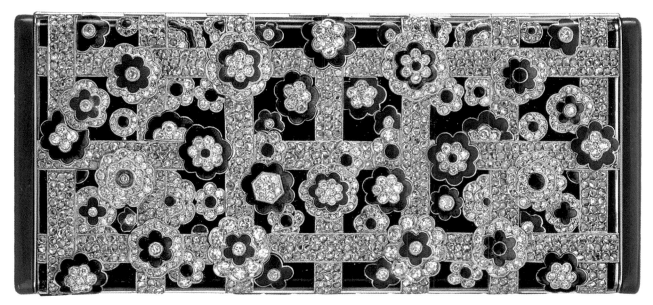

368
Vanity, or
Nécessaire, 1925
Van Cleef & Arpels
Gold, jasper, lacquer,
diamonds
Collection Van Cleef &
Arpels, Paris

designs, while the latter recreated antique jewelry modeled on fragments uncovered in his archeological research. Fontenay took a gold medal for two necklaces, one representing grains of oats and the other grains of wheat, which "so clearly bear the stamp of classical simplicity that they might have come from some Apulian tomb."[13] Fontenay also showed a range of nature-inspired works depicting grasshoppers and beetles. Emile, the younger Froment-Meurice, exhibited a brooch in the Renaissance manner consisting of a crystal scallop shell with an aluminum (then a rare and unusual metal) statuette of Venus rising from the sea, surrounded by enameled leaves and pearls, as well as a necklace simulating _guipure_, a decorative kind of lace.

The Workers' Commission report of 1867 on _joaillerie_ records that, whereas for twenty years _joailliers_ had been employing heavy gold settings to disguise mediocre stones, silver settings now reappeared.[14] The _joaillier_ Oscar Massin was awarded a gold medal for his delicate naturalistic designs. He showed an emerald cameo between two laurel branches; a breast ornament in the form of a branch of dog rose; a bandeau with a central shell surrounded by two laurel branches; a feather; and a spray of daisies. The displays of Mellerio and Frédéric Boucheron (who participated for the first time) included pieces by Massin: in Mellerio's group, a headband, its center set with pearls and mobile briolettes, a marabou plume, and a peacock's feather; in Boucheron's, a magnificent parure in the style of Louis XVI after a design by Jules Debut, foreman of the Boucheron workshop,

ornamented with cameos by Bissinger and comprising necklace, brooch, earrings, and rings.

The house of Bapst exhibited a shell surmounted with fern fronds disposed in an aigrette and a laurel crown with onyx beads, while Baugrand's entry included a _parure_ of brooch and ribbon necklace, and a peacock in colored stones with movable feathers. A much-praised piece by Rouvenat, later purchased by the Empress, was a remarkably flexible life-size spray of lilac set with brilliant-cut and rose-cut diamonds.[15] While the 1867 Exposition indubitably witnessed the rebirth of _joaillerie_, thanks to creative artists like Massin, _bijouterie_ retained an important place, and many _joailliers_ also worked as _bijoutiers_, further blurring distinctions between the two.

The reign of Napoleon III came to an end in September 1870. With the defeat of the French Army at Sedan by the king of Prussia, the Third Republic was proclaimed. It was able to survive the war, the annexation of Alsace and Lorraine, and the uprising of the Paris Commune in 1871. In spite of these problems and a major economic crisis, the internal affairs of France made a speedy recovery, and its industries, along with those of other nations, participated brilliantly in the Vienna Universal Exposition of 1873. The discovery of the diamond deposits of Cape Province in South Africa improved the fortunes of _joaillerie_; the Universal Expositions in Vienna (1873) and Paris (1878) confirmed what the Paris Fair of 1867 had already suggested: _joaillerie_ was now the strongest and most fashionable sector of the jewelry trade. Since 1867 it had continued to derive most of its

369
Bracelet in the
Egyptian style, 1924
Van Cleef & Arpels
Rubies, emeralds,
sapphires, onyx,
diamonds, platinum
Collection Van Cleef &
Arpels, Paris

inspiration from nature, and particularly from flowers, as E. Bergerat explains: "A resistless current is sweeping modern art toward naturalism . . . Today's goldsmiths and *joailliers* recognize (perhaps as a consequence of Europe's obsession with Japanese art) that their most various and attractive subjects are, as they have always been, furnished by Nature herself."[16] Lucien Falize attributes the revival to the great *joaillier* Massin: "He is the originator of a new school. To the depiction of living flowers he brings all the precision and imagination of the finest silk flower maker; he has invented new flowers of his own, their leaves and petals brilliant with all the fire of the diamond; he has set his gems in filigrees that faithfully render the delicate substance of the plant itself."[17] Massin and Frédéric Boucheron each won a prize for *joaillerie*. The former exhibited an azalea spray, a rose modeled in the round, and a pansy in amethyst, all reflecting a close observation of nature. Boucheron exhibited an astonishingly lifelike spray of thistle, with two leaves and a flower. Other exhibitors confined their themes to a more traditional ornamentation. The house of Bapst displayed classic *joaillerie*; Alphonse Fouquet reverted to the Greek and the Egyptian, using figures and animals in the ornament of his "chimera" tiaras; Ernest Vever drew attention with a technically perfect Greek bandeau edged with brilliants and pearls.

Bijouterie appeared to be in a state of crisis. Nonetheless, it was given impetus by such creative artists as Alexis Falize, who won one of the three prizes (along with Massin and Boucheron), Eugène Fontenay, Alphonse Fouquet, Téterger, and Frédéric Boucheron, who exhibited damascened steel jewelry with ornaments by Tissot. Alexis Falize revived the popularity of enamel, using both painted and cloisonné techniques in his *bijouterie*. His display in 1869 at the exhibition of the Union Centrale des Beaux-Arts, comprising cloisonné enamel jewels in the Japanese taste, attracted much

attention. In 1878 Martial Bernard stressed the originality of Falize's work: "He has been inspired to employ the magical effects of clear Renaissance enamels in Limoges settings, enhanced by a felicitous contrast of raised and lowered areas provided by cloisonné enamels in unusually deep cloisons, so that the background colors deepen in the recessed parts. He has thus been enabled to design into his bracelets names, dates or mottos of charming appearance."[18]

The Renaissance was still an important source of inspiration, as could be seen in Hippolyte Téterger's chatelaine of gold, diamonds, and enamel chased with female figures, in an enameled griffin mask (now in New York's Metropolitan Museum of Art), or an enameled pendant imitating the sixteenth-century designer of ornament, Stephanus. Alphonse Fouquet was also faithful to the Renaissance in his gold and enamel chatelaine portraying Diana the huntress, his sphinx chatelaine, and his Renaissance brooch bearing an enamel portrait of Elisabeth of Austria by Grandhomme.

At the Paris Universal Exposition of 1889 the considerable advance achieved by *joaillerie* in 1878 was sustained. E. Marret, the official reporter, explained this in terms of the supply of diamonds:

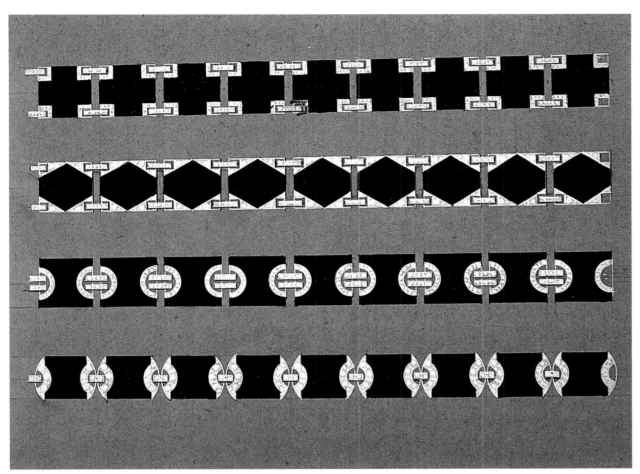

372
Designs for bracelets and boxes, about 1925-30
Chaumet
Gouache
Musée Société Nouvelle
Chaumet, S.A., Paris

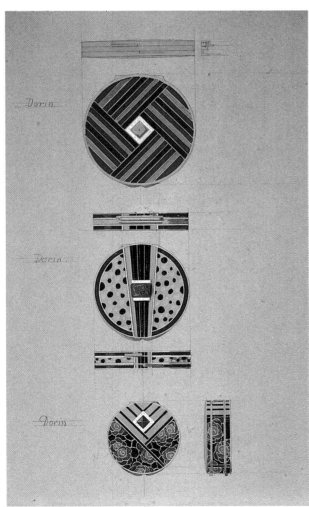

373
Designs for bracelets and brooches, about 1925-30
Mauboussin
Gouache
Collection Mauboussin, Paris

374
Mauboussin shopfront, Casablanca, Morocco, about 1925
Mauboussin Archives, Paris

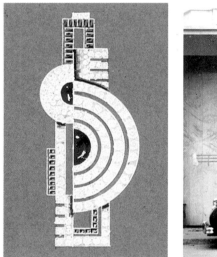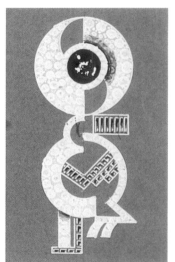

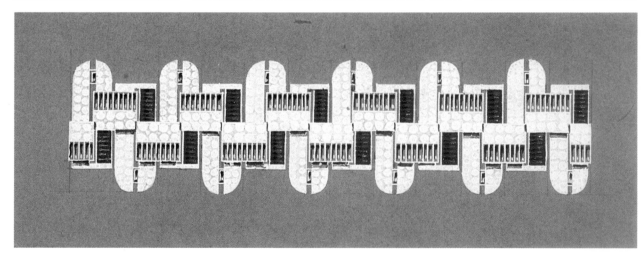

375
Brooch, about 1925-30
Raymond Templier (1891-1969)
White gold, lacquer, diamonds
Primavera Gallery, New York

376
Watch with louvered case, 1931
Van Cleef & Arpels
Yellow and white gold, lacquer
Collection Van Cleef & Arpels, Paris

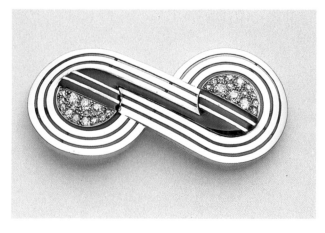

"The diamond *parure*, now more affordable, is no longer the exclusive domain of the rich, and the taste for these stones is spreading through the middle classes; hence the competition among *joailliers*."[19] As in 1878, leaf and flower motifs were all the rage, especially for hair and breast ornaments. Boucheron, one of the grand prix winners, exhibited a cluster of cyclamen with jeweled flowers, a spray of mimosa, and a vine leaf with a bunch of grapes in brilliants. In another vein, the same house produced a riband coronet in diamonds intertwined with pearls, another with trilobe foliage, a very elegant coiled necklace with a fall of brilliants and pearls, and another in which pearls were interspersed with little faceted diamond beads. The Vever brothers, who took the other grand prix, exhibited a spray of almond blossom, its buds set in gold; a sun tiara; and a neoclassical knot set with a black pearl. Others stayed with tried-and-true classic shapes: the house of Sandoz displayed a small breast ornament in Louis XVI style after a drawing of the period; Bapst and Falize, who had joined forces in 1879, presented a breast-knot in the manner of Gilles Légaré.

"The gold jewel properly so-called, though largely ousted by everyday jewelry, still boasts some loyal exponents, few in number but wedded to the great tradition."[20] They still favored the Renaissance, as with Emile Froment-Meurice's pendants in gold, enamel, and pearls. The Vever brothers chose the style of Louis XV for silver mirrors, fans, bracelets, or comfit dishes, adorned by the engraver Jules Brateau with repoussé putti in the manner of Watteau. In a period of eclecticism, the enameled bracelets, and others inset with antique medallions exhibited by Bapst and Falize displayed outstanding originality of style and technique.

377
Bracelet and ring, about 1930
Jean Fouquet
(1899-1984)
Rock crystal, amethysts, moonstones, platinum
Primavera Gallery, New York

The 1900 Universal Exposition in Paris witnessed the appearance of Art Nouveau, literally, a "new art," purged of the historic nostalgia that had characterized jewelry in the second half of the nineteenth century. This change in *bijouterie* was summed up by the critic Léonce Bénédite: "But if there is one art which offers us, perhaps more than any other, an occasion of unreserved

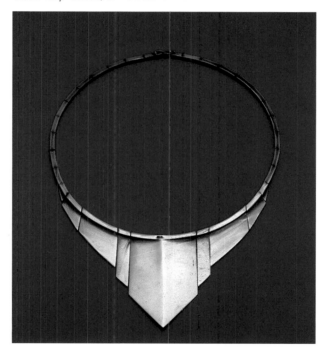

378
Necklace, about 1925
Jean Desprès
(1889-1980)
Silver
Primavera Gallery, New York

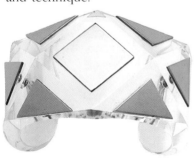

379
Bracelet and clips, about 1935
Suzanne Belperron
(active 1930s to 1960s)
Rock crystal, gold
Primavera Gallery, New York

rejoicing, it is the art of the *bijoutier*. Here we are confronted not merely with progress but with a transformation amounting to a revolution. The nature and appearance of contemporary *bijouterie* have been so radically changed that what used to be no more than a brilliant industry is acquiring before our very eyes the weight and dignity of an art, characterized by a wealth of vitality, variety and individuality."[21]

A new generation of *bijoutiers* was at work. It did not reject the lessons of earlier periods, but assimilated them. If its favorite themes — women and flowers — were scarcely original, they were now revitalized by a return, following the Japanese

380
"Ludo-Hexagone"
bracelet, about 1938
Van Cleef & Arpels
Platinum, diamonds,
sapphire
Collection Van Cleef &
Arpels, Paris

example, to nature as a direct source of inspiration; at the same time, the conventional order of precedence of the *bijoutier's* materials was drastically revised. René Lalique, Paul and Henri Vever, and Georges Fouquet were the principal exponents of this Art Nouveau, with Lalique universally acknowledged as the father of the movement and its most important creative force. The official reporter, Paul Soufflot, recognized his preeminence, saying that:

Lalique had exhibited works that have more to do with art than with traditional *bijouterie* or *joaillerie*. It goes without saying that their craftsmanship is perfect, but it is their strongly individual design that stamps them as the work of this artist and no other. Employing precious metals with stones both costly and common, chosen for their distinctive colors, using the widest possible range of enamels both translucent and opaque, demanding that the metalwork enhance these elements to create a surprising unity, Mr. Lalique may be said to possess a magical palette, which permits him to address any subject and all forms.[22]

The spirit of the Renaissance was still present in some of his pieces: a dragonfly with a woman's head and wings of transparent enamel, or intertwined serpents with a fall of pearls. Others drew directly on nature, such as a rooster's-head headband or a "hazelnut" necklace in enameled gold, opals, cabochon sapphires, and brilliants.

The Vever brothers, in a more traditional vein, exhibited the "Sylvia" pendant, a butterfly-woman whose carved-agate body was clad in yellow

enamel spotted with black, and whose wings were of green enamel rimmed with diamonds. Vever and Fouquet commissioned from such painters as Eugène Grasset and Alphonse Mucha designs for highly individual jewels.

At the Universal Exposition *joaillerie* cut a splendid figure in the display of the house of Vever. Forsaking gold and silver for platinum, the

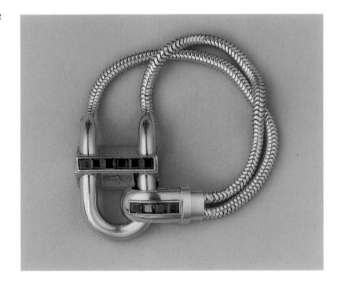

brothers enriched their flower compositions with translucent enamels and gave pride of place to opals in a number of light, openwork tiaras. Frédéric Boucheron, in line with the new trend, submitted a necklace composed of red currants in rubies with diamond-set leaves, an elegant tiara in diamonds with clusters of fruit and foliage, and several objets d'art with wood carvings by Edmond Becker. The house of Chaumet, successors to the house of Morel, had put together a group of objects outstanding for the quality of their stones: a "waterfall" breast ornament and tiara, a ribbon tiara, an amazingly flexible ruby and diamond choker. And, from now until the outbreak of World War I, the house of Cartier was to adorn a multitude of crowned heads and royal necks with its "garland" and "interlaced" tiaras and necklaces in brilliant-cut diamonds.

381
Bracelet/watch, 1936
Van Cleef & Arpels
Gold, sapphires
Collection Van Cleef &
Arpels, Paris

382
"Peony" clip, 1936
Van Cleef & Arpels
Rubies, diamonds, gold,
platinum
Collection Van Cleef &
Arpels, Paris

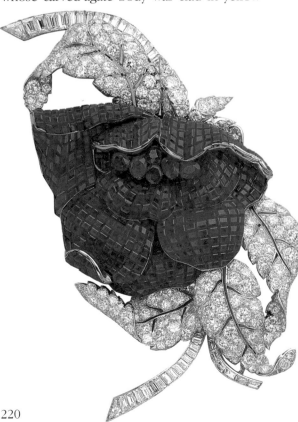

383
**"Soleil" vanity case,
or minaudiere, 1934**
Van Cleef & Arpels,
Paris
Gold, rubies
Collection Van Cleef &
Arpels, Paris

For Art Nouveau, the Universal Exposition of 1900 was both zenith and swan song. The style, already stigmatized by some as decadent, soon showed signs of flagging. In 1902, the periodical *Les Modes* summed up the general feeling in the words of a young lady of fashion: "I'm getting tired of the song. When are we to have done with peacock feathers, swans, irises, orchids, and what-have-you? Imagine what a relief it will be to return to the styles of yesteryear—the exquisite Louis XV, the delightful Louis XVI, even the glacial Empire, which was deemed repellent a decade ago and is even now passing out of fashion again."[23] In fact, at the Milan International Exhibition of 1906, the dominant note was a return to the Louis XVI and Empire idioms. Only a few *joailliers*, such as

rather than carefully cut to her measure by a couturier, the nature of the jewelry she can wear has changed. You can't pin jewels on a butterfly's wings. Gone are the scintillating breast ornaments of the MacMahon period; gone are the sumptuous tiaras, since our latter-day Eve has bobbed her hair. The only appropriate jewelry, apart from brooches and shoulder or side clips, is that worn next to the skin: drooping chains, pendants, necklaces, bracelets, rings, earrings.[24]

Combs, tiaras, belt buckles, dog collars yielded place to hair- or hat clips, necklaces, pendants, strings of pearls, cuff bracelets, and wristwatches, which first appeared in 1918. Perhaps for the first time, *bijoutiers* and *joailliers* became involved with

384
Bracelet, about 1950
Mellerio dits Meller
Gold, diamonds
Collection Mellerio dits
Meller, Paris

Georges Fouquet, displayed pieces of a new and contemporary character, while others such as Eugène Feuillâtre and Lucien Gaillard remained faithful to Art Nouveau.

World War I represented a complete break with the closing years of the nineteenth century. By 1919, economic and social conditions had changed dramatically: women's emancipation, their new lifestyles, and their participation in active sports dictated their new appearance:

Jewelry is intended to put a finishing touch to the whole look: to impart to it richness and sparkle. It must be consistent with it. Now that the Parisian lady dresses in airy, supple fabrics that look as though they had been artistically draped over her

fashion: they wanted their jewelry to harmonize with the shapes and colors their customers were wearing.

In the area of design, the decorative arts of the 1920s responded to sources of inspiration that had made their appearance earlier in the century—African art, the Russian ballet with its Oriental overtones, and Cubist painting. By creating new forms, contemporary jewelry kept pace with the new movement: "Is this a style—the critic might ask—with such disparate elements? The gems in this brooch, I concede, are simply and beautifully arranged. But is not this tiara somewhat Oriental? This necklace vaguely African? This compact Chinese? And what business has this Cubist pendant on the graceful neck of a girl? How is this style better than another? You say it's new? No, say rather that it answers the needs of present-day fashion; it is in period. Therein lies its worth."[25]

Continuing the trend of the nineteenth century, *joaillerie* enjoyed pride of place in 1925. Designers used vertical, horizontal, and broken lines; transparent stones (aquamarines, topazes, amethysts) were contrasted with massed translucent or opaque stones (unpolished rock crystal, onyx, lapis lazuli). Little by little, color reappeared— tentatively at first, in black and white jewelry around 1920, and then with the introduction of new materials such as jade and coral, following the Far Eastern example. Diamonds, thanks to such innovative cuts as the baguette, the trapezoid, and the hexagon, lent themselves to more versatile uses: they emphasized line and delineated mass.

Around 1925, the most creative names in *bijouterie-joaillerie* were Paul-Emile Brandt, Gérard Sandoz, and Raymond Templier. Fouquet commissioned designs from the architect Eric Bagge, the painter André Léveillé, and Louis Fertey for various styles of jewelry. Eric Bagge contributed some very structured pendants in onyx and unpolished rock crystal; André Léveillé translated his Cubist compositions into jewelry; Georges Fouquet designed his pendants after Chinese or African masks. Fouquet credited Raymond Templier with leadership of the Art Moderne movement: "The play of planes and shadows in his work has something of the rigor of a mathematical equation,

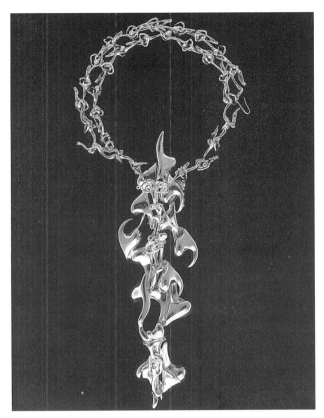

but is softened by his harmonious use of enamels."[26]

At the Exposition internationale des Arts decoratifs et industriels modernes in 1925, Templier exhibited a tiara in amber and brilliants, as well as platinum pendants and brooches making use of diamonds and green enamel in chevron patterns. The designs of Gérard Sandoz, executed in the workshop of his father Gérard-René Sandoz, featured pendants and brooches in structured shapes, decorated with geometric designs such as circles and triangles in black and white. Louis Boucheron and his designer Charles Massé favored rounded brooches in which onyx and coral were set against a background of diamonds.

Others still preferred the gentler patterns of nature. Lacloche displayed flower jewelry carved of coral, and a bracelet and pendant illustrating episodes from La Fontaine's *Fables*. The house of Van Cleef & Arpels, founded in 1898, submitted for this exposition jewels reminiscent of ancient Egypt. Mauboussin used mother-of-pearl as a background for designs in onyx, diamond, or pearl, and also showed a diadem in the form of a water fountain, carried out in diamonds. Chaumet once again paid tribute to the Far East with his necklaces of ribbed emerald balls, ruby beads, brilliants, and onyx. Following the lead offered by the *minaudière* of Van Cleef & Arpels, everyone offered what was then known as a "vanity case," a sort of lady's emergency kit in metal, shaped like a cigarette case and fitted with compartments of

385
"La Grande Voie" necklace, 1970
Jean-Petit Filhos (born 1921)
Gold
Private Collection

386
"Zip" necklace/bracelet, 1951
Van Cleef & Arpels
Gold, diamonds
Collection Van Cleef & Arpels, Paris

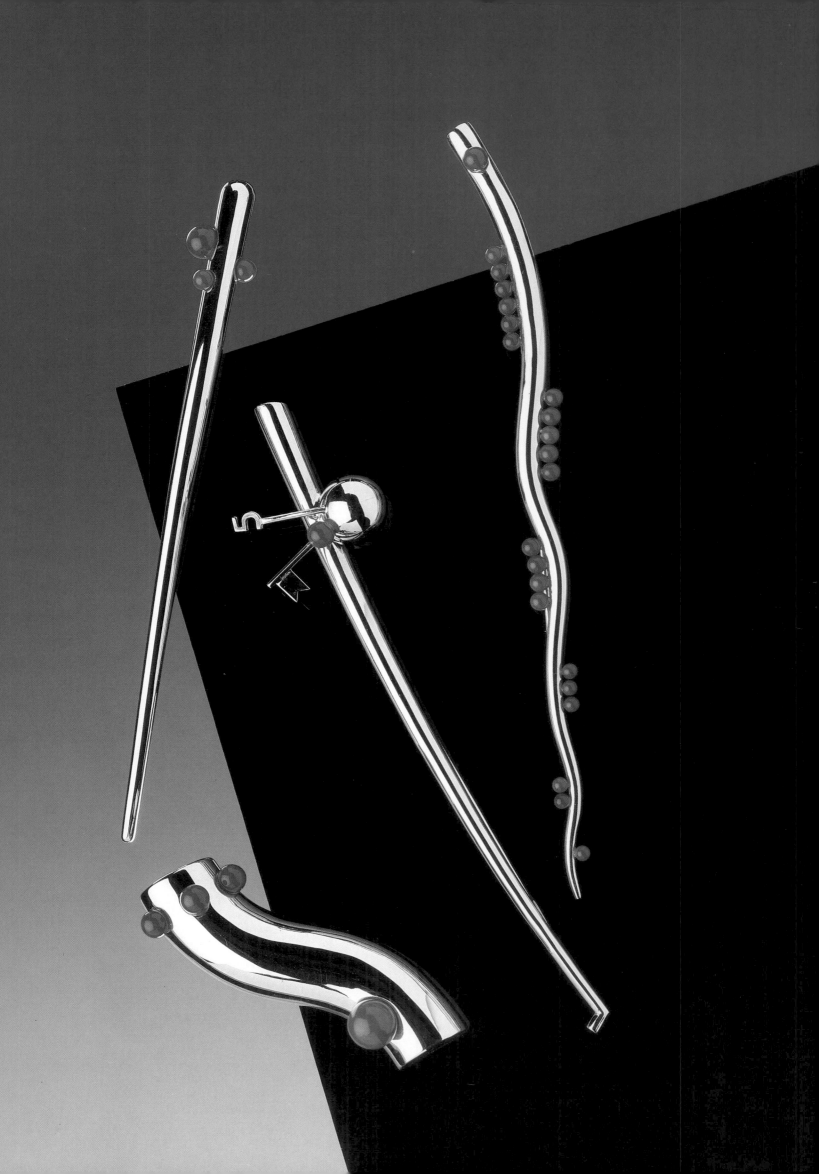

different sizes for handkerchief, small change, a lighter, cigarettes, face powder, a lipstick, and even a watch.

At the 1929 Exposition in the Musée Galliera, diamonds once again predominated. There appeared the first indications of the fad for white *joaillerie* that was to prevail throughout the 1930s, though *joailliers* also displayed daring color combinations of emeralds and sapphires or emeralds and turquoises. This latter stone was often used in its "matrix" form, with dark veins running through the blue; these picked up the color of the onyx background with which it was often associated. Platinum and white gold were used as settings for a variety of cut diamonds to emphasize their reflected light and clarity. Baguette cuts were increasingly favored for outlines and borders.

Jewelry drew inspiration from contemporary technology. The Fouquets took ideas from automobiles, aircraft, and phonographs; Dusausoy went so far as to design a brooch shaped like a gear wheel; Jean Desprès had a brooch like a center bit and a ring modeled after a coil spring; Raymond Templier adorned one cigarette case with a railroad map and another with the outline of a typewriter; Gérard Sandoz depicted, on the lacquer of his cigarette cases, boxing matches and automobile races. Raymond Templier, now in the full flush of his creativity, used reliefs of jagged geometric forms interlinked with each other. Dusausoy made cascades of pearls fall from a scroll of *pavé* diamonds. René Boivin exhibited bracelets and rings in unpolished rock crystal. There were still devotees of naturalistic jewelry: Lacloche's brooches took the form of baskets of flowers set with colored stones, while Georges Fouquet displayed a "pomegranate" brooch in cabochon rubies and brilliants.

At the 1937 International Exposition in Paris, "Few indeed were the artists and *joailliers* still faithful to the austere, semi-geometric shapes that had ushered in a revolution in jewelry in 1925. Almost all the great *joailliers* paid dutiful tribute to the rather ponderous taste for gold jewelry, adorned with volutes and with flowers set with colored gems, reminiscent of the pieces that pleased our great-grandmothers and the flower sprays so popular in 1878 and 1889."[27] The return to gold reflected the Depression of the 1930s and the shortage of other raw materials, such as platinum and osmium. The designs harked back to the Second Empire and betrayed an unbridled taste for overnaturalistic flower themes. Techniques, on the other hand, were impeccable: "The settings of these flowers, marvelously flexible, are a mechanical masterpiece."[28]

The "invisible" setting was introduced in 1935 by Van Cleef & Arpels. Motifs favored in this period are scrolls, falls of diamonds, ribbon clips, and elliptical forms, using white metals, *pavé* diamonds, moonstones, and caliber-cut amethysts and topazes.

After World War II, the German occupation, and the years of shortage, the Liberation touched off an explosion of joy and a "rage to live." The women of Paris could once again pay attention to fashion, and to jewelry. The New Look of Christian Dior successively introduced the A, H, and Y lines. Fashion was by now international, and each year's collections touched off changes around the world. In jewelry there seems to have been a ten-year cycle of creativity, so that today we can readily distinguish the *bijouterie* of the forties from that of the fifties and the sixties—while we wait for the perspective of time to show us the distinguishing

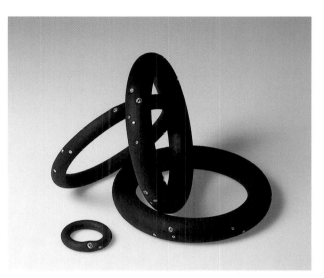

marks of the jewelry of the seventies and eighties.

World War II did not impose an abrupt break on the progress of *bijouterie-joaillerie*; conditions in 1945, like those in 1937-38, were characterized by economic crisis and shortage of materials, and were unpropitious to the creative artist. Thus, prewar trends reappeared between 1945 and 1950. Gold was still the preferred material, and this fact determined the color schemes of *bijouterie* and even of *joaillerie*—both richly chromatic, with marked color contrasts provided by, for example, the juxtaposition of sapphires, rubies, and emeralds, or of turquoises and amethysts.

The 1987 sale of the Duchess of Windsor's jewelry in Geneva provided a perfect example of the richness and creativity of the period. Her favorite *joailliers* were Cartier and Van Cleef & Arpels, along with Suzanne Belperron, who, after working for Boivin in the 1930s, was a partner with Herz. Cartier produced its finest work for her: the "flaming" brooch in 1940; two breastplate necklaces, one in 1947 of trellised gold set with

Brooches, 1988
Gilles Derain (born 1944), designer, for Gay Frères
Gold, coral

388
Bracelets and ring, 1982-88
André Ribeiro (born 1953)
Industrial rubber, diamonds
Collection ABC (Atelier de Bijoux Contemporains), Paris

turquoises, amethysts, and diamonds, and the other, in 1945, a ruff of articulated diamond-shaped plates of gold, their centers set with rubies and emeralds.[29]

Between 1945 and 1962 there was a whole series of enameled-gold "panther" pieces inspired by Jeanne Toussaint (1887-1978), Cartier's chief designer. As early as 1936, Van Cleef & Arpels made two holly-leaf pieces for the duchess, both using their "invisible" setting, one in diamonds and the other in rubies.

The most common motifs in the *bijouterie* of the period were scrolls, coils, knots, feathers, bunches of flowers with colored stone blossoms, and gold leaves. Representational themes reappeared in brooches shaped like birds of paradise, butterflies, or dancers. The flexible, closely linked necklaces known as *tubogaz*, or snake chains, became popular with women. Bracelets were made with treadlike patterns, and for this reason are sometimes called "tank" bracelets. The supple mesh belt bracelets fashionable in the nineteenth century were now transfigured into "ludo" bracelets, adorned with ruffles, or fashioned in the form of padlocks or bridges (with decorated closures), or treated like fiber: cabled, woven, twisted, or braided.

The 1950s brought no change in subject matter, and gold, although differently worked, was still the material of choice. Foliage, bunches of flowers, knots, and ellipses were outlined in slender, cabled gold wire, or in strips of gold mesh. Necklaces were made of "fishbone chains," angel's-hair chains, knitted chains, and even zip-fastener chains.

During these two decades many fine artists turned to jewelry design in the spirit of the Renaissance, and they have left us some imaginative and technically accomplished pieces. The first to take this path was the Surrealist painter Salvador Dalí; although no jeweler, he loved gems, and designed jewelry in the style of his paintings. Jean Schlumberger (1907-1987) worked in the same vein, first in Paris, where he continued to maintain a presence, and after 1945 at Tiffany's in New York. Before the war, Elsa Schiaparelli had

already been attracted by the originality of his work and had asked him to design for her. His favorite theme was nature realistically portrayed; he loved to represent flowers, birds, and marine life (starfish and jellyfish) in a fashion at once naturalistic and—because of the richness and diversity of the stones he used—wholly baroque. Pierre Sterlé, who at the end of his working life in 1972 was associated with Chaumet, was another consummate craftsman who like Lalique, Schlumberger, or the duke di Verdura understood and applied all the technical resources of his profession, as well as the limitless possibilities of the mineral kingdom.

In these same years a number of artists, painters, and sculptors followed the example set by Salvador Dalí and began to take an interest in jewelry. Thus we have the jewels of Alexander Calder in beaten silver wire, we see Max Ernst and Jean Cocteau working with the *bijoutier* and goldsmith François Hugo, and finally we have Georges Braque, whose designs were executed in collaboration with Baron Heger de Lowenfeld.

In the 1970s fine *joaillerie* reverted to more classic shapes and color schemes. Precious stones were back in favor, and *joailliers* turned out two-colored *parures* of diamonds and rubies, diamonds and sapphires, or diamonds and emeralds. A new trend became evident in *bijouterie* with the arrival of a new kind of creative artist: the craftsman-jeweler. Some of these people were more or less under the influence of Scandinavian simplicity, introduced into France by the Scandinavian Torun Bülow-Hübe. For example, Costanza "worked metal directly in large, sleek surfaces or supple strips."[30] Jean Filhos created sculptor's pieces, where tiny beings frolicked in vigorous dances. Jean Vendôme turned out

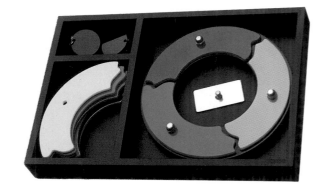

necklaces and brooches on whose mobile elements he mounted large mineral plaques—of tourmaline, for example, or even ammonites. Goudji drew from antiquity the inspiration for his hammered-gold or -silver torques, bracelets, or cups, while Claude Lalanne employed electroplating on copper to produce jewels in botanic shapes — seeds, stalks, and petals.

Contemporary *bijouterie* encompasses many different fields. Fine *joaillerie* is found in shops clustered around the Place Vendôme, but supports workshops all across Paris; then there is everyday jewelry, novelty jewelry, designer jewelry, fashion jewelry, each with its individual style. This diversity of shapes and manufacturing techniques is matched by an equal diversity of materials: precious metals and precious and semi-precious stones, of course, but also glass, plastics, rubber, ivory, concrete reinforced with gold, slate, wood, and such new metals as titanium and steel.

At the close of the eighteenth century, after the convulsions of the Revolution, it appeared that the decorative arts in France were seeking new roots. Throughout the nineteenth century, artists were groping for sources of inspiration: antiquity, the Middle Ages, the Renaissance, the seventeenth and eighteenth centuries all served as reference books from which they could draw forms and ideas, to be reassembled with great technical skill into new compositions. At the end of the century, naturalism, and Japanese art, came as revelations to these designers, allowing them to develop in Art Nouveau a truly original idiom, liberated from the dead hand of historicism. In the twentieth century, emboldened by their new independence, they began to draw their inspiration from the world around them. But even in this cursory account of two centuries of the history of French jewelry, it is clear that there are some continuing themes. There seems to be a frequent divergence between gold *bijouterie* and *joaillerie*. The latter often comes into fashion at times of political or economic uncertainty, when precious stones assume the character of an investment, or of flight capital, as in the 1930s, or again at the time of the first crude-oil crisis of the 1970s.

Divergence may also result, more simply, from the vagaries of fashion, according to whether women do or do not wear jewels in the daytime. At the end of the nineteenth century this trend caused distress among the *bijoutiers*; today it seems as though the variety of raw materials and styles would provide suitable jewelry for all hours of the day or night. And whereas taste now admits the wearing of gold *bijouterie* in the evening, wearing diamonds in the daytime is generally considered tasteless.

1. Henri Vever, *La Bijouterie française au XIXᵉ siècle*, 3 vols., Floury, 1906-8.

2. Fossin and Beaugrand, *Exposition universelle de 1867: rapports du jury international publiés sous la direction de Michel Chevalier*, Paris, imprimerie administrative de Paul Dupont, 1868, vol. IV, section IV class 36, p. 412.

3. Eugène Fontenay, *Les Bijoux anciens et modernes*, Paris, Quantin, 1887, p. 2.

4. Vicomte Héricart de Thury, *Rapport sur les produits de l'industrie française présenté, au nom du jury central, à S.E.M. le comte Corbière, ministre secrétaire d'Etat de l'intérieur, approuvé par S.S.M. le duc de Doudeauville, pair de France, ministre d'Etat, directeur général des Postes*, Paris, Imprimerie royale, 1824, chapter XXII, section III, pp 283-4.

5. *La Vente des diamants de la Couronne. Son histoire, ses préparatifs, ses résultats, avec le catalogue raisonné des joyaux par Arthur Bloche*, Paris, Quantin, 1888.

6. Quoted in Henri Vever, *op. cit.*, vol. 2, p. 148.

7. Baron Charles Dupin, *Rapport du jury central sur les produits de l'industrie française exposés en 1834*, Paris, Imprimerie royale, 1836, vol. 3, chapter 23, section 2, p. 146.

8. Viscount Héricart de Thury, *Rapport des produits de l'industrie française en 1839*, Paris, L. Bouchard-Huzard, 1839, vol. 3, section 3, p. 41.

9. Eugène Fontenay, op. cit., p. 293.

10. Viscount Héricart de Thury, *Exposition des produits de l'industrie française en 1844: rapport du jury central*, Paris, Imprimerie Fain et Thunot, 1844, vol. 3, section 4, p. 162.

11. Marie Martin, in J.J. Arnoux, *Le Travail universel. Revue complète des œuvres de l'art et de l'industrie exposées à Paris en 1855*, vol. 2, class 17, p. 194.

12. Fossin and Beaugrand, op. cit., p. 413.

13. Ibid., p. 418.

14. *Exposition universelles de 1867 à Paris: rapport des délégations ouvrières*, Paris, A. Morel, 1868, vols. 1 and 2.

15. *La Vente des diamants...*, op. cit.

16. E. Bergerat, *Les Chefs-d'œuvre d'art à l'Exposition universelle de 1878* (Paris: Ludovic Baschet, 1878), vol. 1, p. 112.

17. Lucien Falize, "Les industries d'art au Champ de Mars," *Gazette des beaux-arts*, Paris, 1879, pp. 335-6.

18. Martial Bernard, *Exposition universelle de 1878 à Paris*, Paris, Imprimerie nationale, 1880, section IV, class 39, p. 25.

19. M.E. Maret, in Alfred Picard, *Exposition universelle de 1889 à Paris: rapports du jury international*, Paris, Imprimerie nationale, 1891, class 37, p. 21.

20. Ibid., p. 27.

21. Léonce Bénédite, "Le bijou à l'Exposition universelle," *Art et Décoration*, Paris, 1900, no. 8, p. 65.

22. Paul Soufflot, *Exposition universelle de 1900: rapport du jury international*, class 95, p. 384.

23. Gabriel Mourey, "L'art décoratif aux Salons de 1902," *Les modes*, No. 17, May 1902, p. 19.

24. Henri Clouzot, "Le bijou moderne," *L'Illustration*, December 1927, no. 4422, n.p.

25. Paul Léon, *Exposition internationale des Arts décoratifs et industriels modernes, Paris, 1925: rapport général*, 1927, Part|9|, class 20-4, pp. 85-6.

26. Georges Fouquet, ed., *La Bijouterie, la joaillerie, la bijouterie fantaisie au XXᵉ siècle* (Paris, 1934), p. 191.

27. G. Guérin, *Exposition internationale des arts et techniques, Paris, 1937: la section française... rapport général*, vol. 7, p 12.

28. Ibid.

29. "The Jewels of the Duchess of Windsor," sale catalog, Sotheby's, Geneva, April 2nd and 3rd, 1987.

30. *Les Métiers d'art*, exhibition catalog, Paris, Musée des arts décoratifs, 1980, p. 320.

RAYMOND GUIDOT

FORTY YEARS OF
FRENCH DESIGN

391
**"2 CV" Citroën
automobile, 1948**
Pierre-Jules Boulanger
(concept)
Flaminio Bertoni and
the André Lefebre team
(design)
Walter Becchia (engine)

392
Chair, 1943
Jacques Dumond (born
1906), designer, for
Société Industrielle du
Rotin
Wood, rattan
Musée des Arts
Décoratifs, Paris

393
**"Gigogne" goblet,
first produced 1948**
Les Verreries de
Saint-Gobain
Molded glass

On page 228
Mirror, about 1987
Olivier Gagnère
(born 1952)
Glass, gilt bronze,
gold leaf
Collection Galerie
Adrien Maeght, Paris

Petit, wrote about the building and public-works projects of the reconstruction programs: "Everything was still dependent on manual labor; everything seemed to be aging—not just the tools, but the men themselves, their habits and their way of working."

In fact, aside from the basic sectors—energy, iron and steel, transportation—France at the end of World War II still clung to its strong agricultural traditions. (In the thirties, France was still the most agriculturally intensive country of all the Great Powers of the Western world; in 1940, Germany attempted to make of her the breadbasket of Europe.) But another tradition, that of craftsmanship, determined the country's major exports: textiles, clothing, leather goods, luxury items, and furniture.

It was largely owing to the indubitable presence of a group of highly skilled craftsmen—especially

I n 1945, although France was on the side of the "victors," the country had been cruelly ravaged by years of war. Yet the pressing need to rebuild cities, harbors, railways, factories, and other essential industries would eventually stimulate economic recovery—thanks to the Marshall Plan (in other words, the generous flow of American equipment and consumer goods). In retrospect, the recovery seems little short of miraculous.

In many ways it bore out the old adage that "à tout bonheur, malheur est bon" ("every misfortune serves a useful purpose"). Recovery, which started by putting heavy industry back on its feet, also had the positive effect of pointing up serious deficiencies in the French "system," some of them long-standing, not to say congenital. For example, there was an unbelievable shortage of decent housing, for reasons that went beyond specific problems related to reconstruction. Many factories were grossly underequipped as well as poorly managed. The Minister of Reconstruction, Claudius

the furniture makers and glassworkers—that the Art Nouveau movement developed in France at the end of the nineteenth century, notably within the framework of the School of Nancy. The excellence of these craftsmen, some decades later, enabled leading Art Deco designers to experiment skillfully with form and color combinations in precious materials for their luxurious, one-of-a-kind pieces. Finally, it permitted the purists of the Union des Artistes Modernes (UAM) to design prototypes for mass production that stressed simplicity and economy almost to the point of schematization, and through which industrial materials (preferred over traditional ones) could be shown to be appropriate to functional requirements.

It was because of the international reputation of their handcrafted objects that, after the war, designers could safely yield to the temptation of incongruity. This new look was expressed more in freedom of form than in the materials themselves (massive wood doing duty for steel). Eventually these influences led to the appearance of a style

394
**"Djinn" seating
furniture (as seen in
the Stanley Kubrick
film *2001: A Space
Odyssey*), 1967**
Olivier Mourgue (born
1939), designer
Airborne, manufacturer
Steel tube frame, foam
lining, nylon jersey
upholstery

395
**Dining room
furniture, 1948**
Jean Prouvé
(1901-1984), designer

396
Tea service, about 1951
Stéphane Faniel
(1909-1978), designer
Christofle, manufacturer
Silver, ebony
Musée
Bouilhet-Christofle, Paris

397
"Sorcy" glassware service, first produced, 1950
Michel Daum (born 1900), designer
Daum Cristal, manufacturer
Glass
Collection Daum Cristal

398
Cigarette lighter, first produced 1945
S.T. Dupont
Gold, lacquer
Collection S.T. Dupont, Paris

that was essentially a reaction against the conscious angularity made universally famous in the 1930s by the Modern movement. But even some of the prominent names from the Modern movement would be tempted into use of the free-form style; for example, Le Corbusier in his Notre-Dame-du-Haut at Ronchamp (1954). Another name that comes to mind is Charlotte Perriand, who by the late thirties was combining the structural strength of steel with the warmth of such natural materials as pine to achieve the flexibility of "organic" forms. That same affinity for natural materials reached a high point for Perriand in 1939, when she visited Japan and was able to study an industrial project for the mass production of local handicrafts. In a similar vein were Jean Prouvé's experiments with his famous "présidence" desk, whose elaborate shape eschewed the severity of right angles. His ergonometric approach to the work-study area was fundamental to functionalist thinking, and proved, if proof were needed, that utility and rigidity were not inseparable. Far more surprising is the work of Louis Sognot—one of the most rigorous of the UAM group in the

thirties—expressing a special predilection for sculptural forms. In an approach curiously paralleling that of Isamu Noguchi, Sognot applied sculptural ideas to the design of everyday objects, thereby achieving a synthesis of the arts.

The attempt to bring together all the arts into a conceptual unity, eliminating the invidious distinctions between "fine" or "applied," or "major" and "minor" arts, was to be a dominant theme of the 1950s. What proved to be a favorable circumstance for its development was a renaissance of religious arts, under the auspices of Father Couturier. Certain projects, such as the churches at the Plateau d'Assy and at Audincourt, were able to enlist the participation of great artists, such as Fernand Léger, in the architectural program. But it was perhaps when such projects came under the total control of one individual that the results were at their most exceptional: there is Matisse's masterpiece, the chapel at Vence, which seems to

have been crafted from empty space and clear colored light; then there is the chapel of Notre-Dame-du-Haut at Ronchamp, where Le Corbusier succeeds in integrating the various sides of his creative genius to create a unified work that stands as a testament to the contemporary spirit.

Taken to its furthest limits, this pursuit of the extraordinary brought together in France (as in Italy) creative artists from many fields. This permitted decorators and furniture makers like Jean Royère to come up with unique mixes of historicism, free form, and a certain predilection for the sweet, plush style of Hollywood musical comedies.

Even if some were inspired to use industrial materials (like steel tubing or perforated metal sheet), this was still far removed from the spirit of true industrial mass production. However, it was in this period that industrial design began to find a receptive audience among designers (mainly engineers and technicians), manufacturers, intellectuals, and higher officials. To be sure, much

399
Poster: Joies de l'Outil, Exposition d'Art Décoratifs Mobilier Architecture, 1950
Roger Adam, designer
Color lithograph
Musée de la Publicité, Paris

400
**Interior of the
Joseph Vallier
supermarket in
Grenoble, 1960**

of this trend could be explained as the consequence of economic resurgence. Since French industry could now compete with imports, and particularly those from America, it occurred to some industrial patriots that competition should be not only by virtue of economics, but also by technical performance, appearance, and ease of use. The famous slogan of Raymond Loewy, "Ugly does not sell," coined after the Depression of 1929, seemed to bear out a simple fact: namely, that, except for the most essential items, the only ones to weather the economic hard times were those with the best packaging and design—an idea that was to become the controlling concept behind a new crusade.

The crusade, one of the final acts of the UAM through its Formes Utiles affiliate, founded in 1949, had as its main purpose "to promote industrial design in France" and to present the best products selected from an international competition. The

Chambre syndicale des esthéthiciens industriels was formed in 1955. And in 1956 a graduate course in industrial design was offered by L'Ecole des Arts Appliqués à l'Industrie.

During these formative years, Jacques Viénot played an important role, serving as a guiding force and also heading up his own agency. In 1949, le founded the TECHNES group, which was essentially devoted to the development of industrial products. In a matter of years it would become the largest of its kind in France. Three years later, in 1952, Raymond Loewy acted on his impression that things were beginning to happen in France and founded the Compagnie d'Esthétique Industrielle (CEI), in Paris. For six years CEI was directed by

401
Travel iron, 1986
Pierre Paulin (born
1927), designer
Calor, manufacturer
Polypropylene, metal

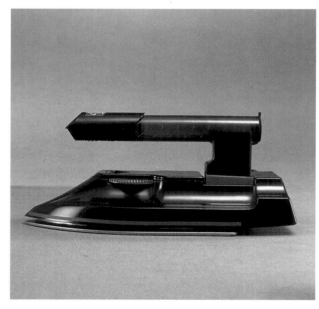

402
**"Moulinette"
foodmill, first
produced 1932**
Jean Mantelet, designer
Moulinex, manufacturer
Metal
Collection Moulinex,
Alençon

first group of selections was made in 1949, at the Musée des Arts Décoratifs, and annually thereafter at the Salon des Arts Ménagers. In 1950, Jacques Viénot led an active campaign to promote industrial design. In 1951, he founded the Institut français d'esthétique industrielle in order to "set down the basic principles and to apply the techniques of industrial design." That same year, he founded the magazine *Esthétique Industrielle*, and participated in the first World Congress of Industrial Design in London, where he proposed that the 1953 conference be held in Paris. It was in fact at this second congress that talk began of an International Council of Societies of Industrial Design (ICSID), which was to come into existence in 1956 at the Aspen Congress, in which Viénot also participated. In 1953, still under the aegis of Viénot, the "Beauté France" label was unveiled. The

Harold Barnett, and from 1958 to 1978, by Evert Endt. Jacques Viénot, showing remarkable foresight once again, called upon the services, first, of Jean Parthenay, and, in 1953, of Roger Tallon as technical and artistic director of his agency. By the end of the fifties, Tallon's creations in such specialized fields as machine tools, public works projects, transportation, photography, etc., were instrumental in helping the French *esthétique industrielle* move into the larger, international context of "industrial design."

During the fifties, it seemed that French

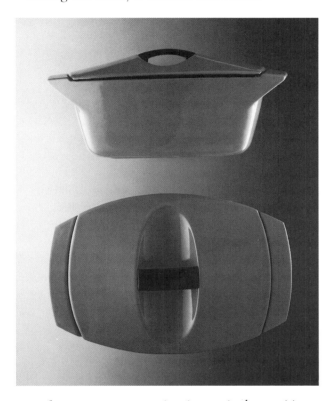

manufacturers were growing increasingly sensitive to the visual presentation of their products. That new awareness led, in turn, to the appearance of numerous independent design groups, the most notable of which were headed by Philippe Charbonneau, Maurice Delieuvin, Jacques Goudeman, Georges Patrix, and Tiarko Meunier. One could add the name of Louis Lepoix, were it not for the fact that he eventually left to work in Germany, a move that was prompted by his disappointment with what he saw as the slow mobilization of production in France.

It was about this time, though, that some of the objects most representative of the inventiveness of French industry were being produced. Those most worth noting include the "Caravelle" of Sud Aviation in 1958; the astonishing 1948 Citroën 2CV (the culmination of a 1937 project in which aesthetics were strictly defined in terms of function and low production cost); and the remarkable 1956 Citroën DS19, whose virtually perfect lines, designed by Bertoni, earned it the grand prize for

industrial design at the 1957 Triennale in Milan. But a few such beautiful swallows do not make a summer, and it would be years before the tenets of "industrial design" would attract enough skilled practitioners to constitute an organized movement.

During this period in West Germany, the doctrines of functionalism were nurtured in a school for the advanced study of design, the Hochschule für Gestaltung, at Ulm. Its basic proposition was that object and user be viewed in a new relation, one in which appearance and ease of use are tied to the aesthetics of mass production. In the late fifties, radios, tape recorders, and electrical appliances designed for the Braun company by Hans Gugelot, an instructor at the Ulm school, and later, by Dieter Rams, were the fruits of this philosophy. The appearance of these mass-produced objects supported the *esthéticiens industriels* of France. Not only were they experimenting along similar lines, but they had not given up hope that French industries would one day embrace an approach that, on an international level, had just begun to pay off.

With the fifties came the "Plastic Age," and the sixties were to ensure its perpetuation. As far as mass production was concerned, the technique of injection-molding with thermoplastic resins meant lower production costs. In fact, the cut in cost was such that when it came to lightweight lids, containers, coverings or the like, not intended for heavy-duty use, other materials such as stamped metal or cast aluminum could not really compete.

In France, the use of household electrical appliances began to spread at about the same time that new forms of credit were being introduced. According to the figures published in 1983 in *De la 4CV à la vidéo* to mark the thirtieth anniversary of Cetelem (the first European company

specializing in consumer credit and financial services), in one year, from 1953 to 1954, the number of vacuum cleaners in service in French households grew from 290,000 to 2,130,000; 3 million coffee grinders were sold in 1957, and Moulinex saw its sales of food processors and mixers increase from 20 million francs in 1958 to 800 million in 1973, and 2 billion in 1979! The boom in sales of electric coffee makers began in 1974 when models costing under 150 francs were put on the market. As for "major appliances," the most universal of them all, the refrigerator, progressively became more widely used, and the

washing machine (which appeared in France in the early fifties, and in a semi-automatic model in 1965) came into popular usage around the same time.

Developing in tandem with the market for electrical appliances were those for electric tools and audio-visual equipment (radio, television, record players, tape recorders). As prices dropped lower and lower, all of these labor saving or recreational devices became accepted as part of every household. At the same time, they called for an increased use of molded plastics, and especially of thermoplastic resins—from polystyrenes and

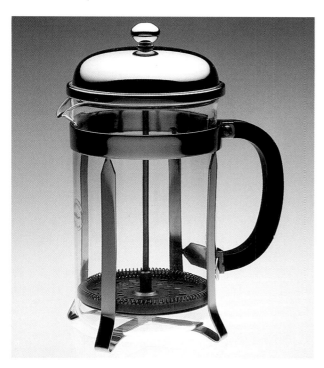

polycarbonates to ABS and polyamides. Reflecting the influence of market forces, plastics would undergo improvements in quality and appearance, making it possible to create new and unusually striking products, especially in housing. The demand for preformed plastic products was such that, by the fifties, craftsmen and small factories in the Jura region, traditionally producers of wooden toys, converted to injection-molding and blow-molding of thermoplastics. Oyonnax became the center of the plastics industry.

With the advent of new household appliances in smooth, sculpted forms and in the bright colors of molded plastic, the French *esthéticiens industriels* (called *designers* after 1965) were to discover—just like their German, English, and Italian counterparts—where best to ply their talents. Sometimes the results proved to be veritable masterpieces, as in the Téléavia television set designed by Roger Tallon in 1963.

However, it was in a different area altogether—furniture in this case—that French design of the sixties and seventies came into its own. There was a reappearance of tubular steel, a direct outgrowth of UAM in particular and of the thirties in general. But this time, it was in the bright colors that had become the trademark of a period that was to see the simultaneous triumph of Pop Art, Op Art, Minimalism, and Psychedelic art.

In addition, although the use of tubular-steel bases supporting top-slabs of wood continued, the idea that the supports be paired with fabric was introduced by Marc Berthier and by the styling

409
Bedroom, shown at the Paris Expostion of 1937
Jean Royère
(1902-1981), designer, for Gouffe
Published in Maurice Dufrène, *Ensembles Mobilier: Exposition Internationale de 1937*, vol.1, Paris
Cooper-Hewitt Museum Library, New York

410
Bedroom shown at the Salon des Arts Ménagers, Paris, 1954
Jean Royère
(1902-1981), designer

411
"Elephant" armchair, 1966
Bernard Rancillac, designer, for Lacloche
Iron, polyester
Musée des Arts Décoratifs, Paris

412
"Antony" chair, about 1950
Originally designed for the University of Strasbourg
Jean Prouvé (1901-1984), designer
Steel tubing, molded plywood
Barry Friedman Ltd., New York

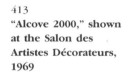

413
"Alcove 2000," shown at the Salon des Artistes Décorateurs, 1969
Christian Ragot (born 1933) and Michel Cadestin, designers

414
"Tapis siège" carpeted seating furniture, 1969
Olivier Mourgue (born 1939), designer, for Prisunic

415
Portable television set, 1964
Roger Tallon (born 1929), designer, for Thomson
Téléavia, manufacturer

office at the Prisunic department-store chain. These collapsible, foldable units were directly inspired by camping outfits and were a direct response to the public's taste for kits. But the trend also reflected a new outlook on life: young people no longer assigned so much importance to being surrounded by their own furniture. Modernism was to become a leitmotiv of contemporary culture, best expressed in the hippie movement.

Tubular metal was frequently used in conjunction with synthetic materials, such as molded polyester reinforced with fiberglass, or heat-pressed sheets of polystyrene. Such combinations of materials could be seen in the bodywork of the "Mehari" car, designed in 1968 by

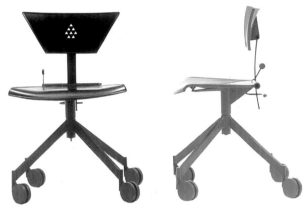

Jean-Louis Barrault and manufactured by Citroën. Steel tubes were also used in seating, as frames for stretch-knit jersey protective covers over a layer of polyurethane foam padding, to ensure maximum comfort and give the seat a flexibility that was very characteristic of the "sixties style." It was a style that the French trade papers were quick to dub "design."

The *style design*, while based mainly on simple geometric shapes, reserved its most angular forms for folding furniture, and returned to the curve when it was a question of supporting the human frame. Among the French innovators, the leader was Pierre Paulin, a prophet who as early as the fifties had developed such major pieces as the "Corolla" chair. By the end of the sixties an equal international reputation had accrued to Olivier Mourgue, designer of the "Djinn" series issued in 1964, who prefigured the future by assisting in the production of Stanley Kubrick's movie *2001: A Space Odyssey*.

The major trend of the sixties was the integration of component parts into smooth overall shapes. The headlights of the Citroën DS series, at first projecting, were in 1962 recessed into the fenders; their mountings were concealed within a "skin" that flowed smoothly over the whole car. The logical conclusion of the trend was to

dispense entirely with framework, as was done with the freestanding body in several lines of automobile, particularly the DS. The potentials of the new synthetic materials extended beyond the wildest dreams of the past: blocks of polyurethane foam imparting both flexibility and firmness, furniture cast in one piece of polyester reinforced with fiberglass, inflatable armchairs made of fused sheets of polyvinyl chloride.

In 1955, Formes Utiles held the first awards competition for plastic furniture at the Salon des Arts Ménagers, with encouraging results. In effect, it was as if an entire generation of designers had tapped into a vein of ore and were intent on mining it for all it was worth.

Polyester was very popular, to the point that some manufacturers even came up with their own designs. Among those who were to make good use of this material (which had been endowed with respectability by American designers such as

419
Furniture for the Elysée Palace, Paris, 1971-72
Pierre Paulin (born 1927), designer,
Produced by the Mobilier National
Aluminum, leather, glass
Mobilier National, Paris

Charles Eames and Eero Saarinen in the fifties), were Marc Berthier and Marc Held, who sought ways to adapt it for mass production. Pierre Paulin, although he sometimes used polyester (in 1960 for his "300" chair and ten years later for the furnishings of the Elysée Palace), seemed most fascinated by flexible polyurethane foam, because it reconciled a sufficiency of comfort with a Minimalist austerity of form. It was to have a similar appeal for Christian Ragot and Bernard Govin.

Inflatable, or "blow-up," furniture would lead Bernard Quentin, and the Quasar and Utopie groups, to offer some memorable pieces. Although Quasar in particular explored ways to adapt the inflatable theme to fit almost every aspect of the living space (including floor, walls, and ceiling), the group never really went so far as to envision a completely inflatable architecture. That would come with Bernard Quentin, the Utopie group, and Hans-Walter Muller.

The concept of treating a living space as a harmonious whole was another of the leading ideas of the sixties and seventies. The main trends in interior design aimed at integrating the furniture with all of a room's boundaries; it often seemed that the floor, ceiling, and walls all melded into one continuous surface. There was also a tendency to have the furniture spread about the floor, away from the walls, creating little multi-purpose islands rising from the floor. This was the idea behind Marc Held's beds with built-in lamps and bedside tables, Marc Berthier's stackable nursery desks, and Pierre Paulin's "Boudin" chair.

Another important theme was that of making liberal use of bold colors: reds, oranges, and greens were frequently played off against a white background. Brightly colored vinyls, available in a limitless range of shades (and even with metallic finishes), were very popular, even with important fashion designers like Courrèges, who designed a line of clothes in perfect keeping

420
"Sportes Mesh Chair,"
designed for the
private apartments of
the Elysée Palace,
Paris, 1982
Ronald Cécil Sportes
(born 1943), designer
Steel
Courtesy JG Furniture
Systems, Inc.

421
"Barbare" chair, 1981
Elizabeth Garouste
(born 1949), and Mattia
Bonetti (born 1952),
designers, for Néotù
Iron, leather
Courtesy V.I.A., Paris

with the spirit of the times.

In the plastic arts, New Realist artists like Martial Raysse infused their work with intense, fluorescent colors. Soon interior designers followed suit, always alert to the results of research and experimentation in the visual arts.

By the mid-1960s, Op Art in France had also gained an important following. Victor Vasarely became a kind of guru for designers of carpets, furniture coverings, and wallpaper. It was Yaacov Agam, however, who was entrusted with the design of a representative contemporary decor for the presidential apartments of the Elysée Palace. Even the fashion world submitted to the newest Op Art designs. Pierre Cardin printed Op Art patterns on his fabrics and heat-formed the fabrics so that he could tailor pyramidal outlines for his highly structured clothes. Courrèges, too, gave his fabrics a kinetic effect through the rhythmic placement of cut-outs or sewn-on loops of ribbon. And Paco Rabanne's unusual dresses, made of small, shimmering metal plates, echoed Julio de Parc's mobiles.

Sometimes the "psychedelic movement" from distant California made itself felt in free-flowing forms and floral colors; the hippie movement, decidedly "anti-fashion," encouraged people to

dress as they pleased, and, ironically, created a style. This was in many ways an outgrowth of the 1950s, which began with young people who lived out their fantasies by emulating the styles worn by the stars of stage and screen. The latest creations of haute couture concerned them little, and in any case had small effect on *prêt-à-porter*, or ready-to-wear; there were already *stylistes-designers* specializing in this field, *stylistes-designers* who were increasingly able to follow, or even to anticipate trends. Special tribute is due to Maïmé Arnodin, who paved the way toward an independent existence for "mass-produced" clothing. Her success helped transform the ready-to-wear *stylistes* into designers in their own right—a development particularly appropriate when it transpired that a new kind of city clothing was developing not as a conscious act of styling but as an evolution from the utilitarian plainness of work clothes. Picking up on this trend, Michel Schreber explored new

422
"Lune d'Argent" chair, 1986
Pascal Mourgue (born 1943), designer, for Fermob
Steel
Cooper-Hewitt Museum New York, Gift of Vecta, member of the Steelcase Design Partnership, 1988-99-1

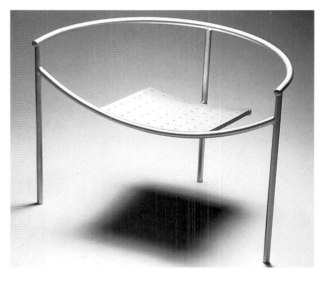

423
"Sonderbar" chair, first produced 1983
Philippe Starck (born 1949), designer, for X.O.
Steel
Courtesy V.I.A., Paris

424
"Synthèse" chair, 1985
Christian Duc (born 1949), designer, for C&M.B.
Steel, aluminum
Courtesy V.I.A., Paris

definitions of functionalism that, by the sixties, had already become the mainstream in other areas of industry.

Although the unusually lively ready-to-wear industry made it possible to popularize fashion without sacrificing quality, that was not at all the case for the furniture industry—at least not until Prisunic boldly led the way under the initiative of Denise Fayolle, director of style and promotion for the Sapac-Prisunic firm from 1953 to 1967. The department-store chain not only created a dynamic ready-to-wear line but also drew on the talents of some of the most important names in furniture design, including Marc Berthier, Olivier Mourgue, and Marc Held, and Italy's Gae Aulenti, not to mention Britain's Terence Conran, who was to open the first Habitat outlet in London in 1964. In 1966, the first Prisunic mail-order catalogue for furniture appeared.

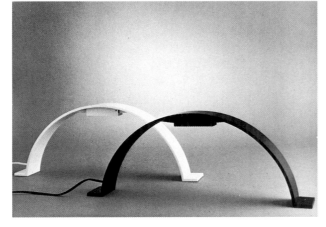

425
**"Omega" lamps, first
produced 1983**
Gilles Derain (born
1944), designer, for
Lumen Center
Aluminum
Collection Lumen
Center,
La Fare-les-Oliviers

426
**"W&0" desk lamp,
first produced 1985**
Sacha Ketoff (born
1949) and André
Lavigne, designers
Aluminor Luminaires,
manufacturer
Aluminum, steel,
makrolon polycarbonate
Cooper-Hewitt Museum,
New York, Gift of
Aluminor Luminaires
France, 1988

427
**"Electra-Blue" lamp,
1987**
Didier La Mache (born
1945), designer, for
Megalit
Metal, glass
Courtesy V.I.A., Paris

428
**"Washington" lamp,
first produced 1983**
Jean-Michel Wilmotte
(born 1948), designer,
for Lumen Center
Metal
Collection Lumen
Center,
La Fare-les-Oliviers

activities in Paris eventually set the standards for almost every aspect of magazine layout, as well as for a wide range of graphics from promotional materials to road signs for public parks. After 1970, though, the preeminence of the Swiss graphic designers was seriously challenged by the work of the American "Push Pin Studios," introduced in France by Albert Hollenstein.

The seventies lifestyle, at least as it was envisioned by French designers of the time, promised a number of innovations that were to place the French on a higher plane internationally. This change was brought about by a new concern

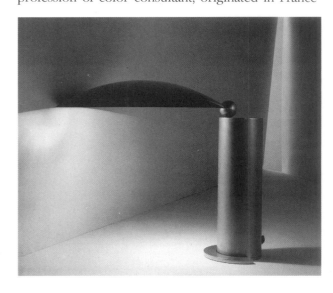

In the meantime, years of continued growth and increased private consumption led to a boom in the construction of private homes and housing complexes (dramatically overtaken in 1973 by the oil crisis, which introduced a sort of endemic state of emergency without really reducing output). With changing housing patterns and, to a large extent, *because* of them, the first shopping centers appeared. In due course they would become major centers of commerce as well as new arenas for competition between producers.

At all levels, competition was sustained by an up-to-date advertising industry that brought together the biggest names in photography, illustration, and graphic design. When Robert Delpire organized the publicity campaign for Citroën, he called on, among other celebrated experts, William Klein for photography and André François for illustrations. There was also the Swiss school of typography, with Albert Hollenstein, Peter Knapp, Adrian Frutiger, and Jean Widmer, whose

for light, used to bring out clear colors that aimed at a certain mood or psychological effect, whether in the home, in the workplace, or on the street. So important was the new role of color that the profession of color consultant, originated in France

429
"Archéologie Future" lamp, 1987
Christian Duc (born 1949), designer, with Patrick Desserme and Bernard Pictet, for Délisle Luminaires
Patinated bronze, glass
Courtesy V.I.A., Paris

by Jacques Fillacier in the late forties, assumed new importance some years later with Georges Patrix and Bernard Lassus, and attained general acceptance at the end of the sixties through Jean-Philippe Lenclos.

As for furniture, it was less rigid and no longer tended to inhibit body movement, as it had in the past. Now it was designed to conform to the body, primarily through curvilinear shapes aided by foam padding. This meant, for one thing, that it was becoming more common to relax or entertain closer to the floor. With that idea in mind Michel Cadestin and Christian Ragot produced their "Alcôve 2000" in 1962, as their version of the future. Pierre Paulin, for his part, offered his "Adjustable Plan," and Olivier Mourgue his "Chair Carpet." In another proposal, Olivier Mourgue unveiled his "Visiona 3" as a contribution to a trade show sponsored by Bayer, the German chemical company noted for its

designers, contrary to the great expectations built up in the fifties. Everyday objects were, for the most part, constant reminders that mediocre design prevailed among household items, from electrical appliances to teaspoons, bathroom fixtures, lighting, audio-visual equipment, office machines, tools, electric screwdrivers, or portable drills. Some prime exceptions: the machine tools by Mondiale, the portable Téléavia TV sets, the System T tableware designed by Roger Tallon, Poclain hydraulic shovels, dumptrucks and diggers by Jean Parthenay, the "Mobilair 50" compressors by Louis Lepoix, the Thomson CSF color television camara by François Quirin, the "Elna Lotus" sewing machine by CEI, the F39 spotlight by Etienne

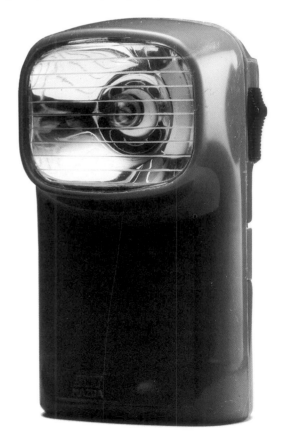

pharmaceuticals—and its polyurethane foam.

Around the same time, the objects displayed at the *Domus: Formes italiennes* exhibition, organized in 1968 by Marc Berthier at the Galeries Lafayette, where he had set up the first department-store design studio, underlined the need for French industry to become more inventive and more competitive on an international level. Some of the brilliant designers mentioned above buckled down to the task. Howewer, in the sectors that were highly dependent on automation, only limited improvements were realized through the work of

Fermigier, the "Saft B12" unbreakable pocket polypropylene flashlight by Guy Boucher. These admirable and exceptional products competed head to head, in the French domestic market, with American, German, Italian, or Japanese rivals, also from the hands of expert designers.

But there was still a great reluctance to depend on industrial designers—in-house or from outside; their role, for the most part, entailed "packaging" an object in whose conception they had not participated. Perhaps, too, many professional designers suffered from a lack of the basic knowledge that would have enabled them to deal effectively with technicians or businessmen.

These facts, seen in the context of the political, economic, psychological, and cultural aftermath of the events of May 1968, go a long way toward explaining why so many organizations, agencies, books, and magazines sprang up, centering on various aspects of design. Reassessment, reeducation, and reorganization were brought to bear on design, and on the qualifications of those who practiced it.

In 1969, the Centre de Création Industrielle (CCI) was established, followed in 1970 by the Conseil Supérieur de la Création Industrielle. The Institut de l'Environnement appeared the same year. An industrial design curriculum was created in 1962 at the Ecole Nationale Supérieure des Arts Décoratifs under the auspices of Jacques Dumond

and Roger Tallon, but the program only became truly operational once its teaching staff was increased in 1969. *CREE* magazine, which focused on trends in interior design in France and overseas, appeared from 1967 to 1977. In 1974, Jocelyn de Noblet's *Design* appeared, one of the few books offering a historical and international overview of the practice of industrial design.

With the first *Qu'est-ce que c'est que le Design?* exhibition in 1970 and another, *Le Design Français*, in 1971, the Centre de Création Industrielle undertook a long series of exhibitions dealing with architectural design and visual communication. The Center's influence would be greatly augmented in 1977 when the CCI became a department of the Centre national d'art et de culture Georges Pompidou.

For the design industry, and in some ways, for almost every area of research and development, the 1970s seemed like a long waiting (if not gestation) period. One area, however, had avoided this slowdown and experienced a string of successes: that of transportation. In car design, there was the R5, a compact model that was enormously popular. Designed by Michel Boné in a Renault "design department," it made its appearance in 1972. An interesting characteristic of this vehicle was that, for the first time, the bumpers were not chrome but synthetic resin. In the railroad sector, 1975 saw the birth of the "Corail" train, for which Roger Tallon had designed the interior spaces and exterior color scheme. In aviation, a Franco-German consortium unveiled the Airbus in 1974. November 1977 saw the Concorde put into service, after a joint Franco-British development program. In the field of avionics, privileged domain of a sophisticated technology, a major success was scored with the launching of Ariane, the first European rocket.

433
Chronometric watch, 1973
Roger Tallon (born 1929), designer
LIP, manufacturer

434
"Plack" disposable picnic set, 1979
Jean-Pierre Vitrac (born 1944), designer, for Diam
Polystyrene

435
Suitcase, 1984
Jean-Pierre Vitrac (born
1944), designer, for
Superior
PVC,
Thermo-compressed
polyethylene foam

436
"Keepall" travel bag,
first produced 1959
Louis Vuitton
PVC-treated canvas,
leather
Collection Louis Vuitton,
Paris

437
"Espace" suitcase,
1988
Hermès
Carbon fiber, metal,
leather
Collection Hermès,
Paris

By and large, though, things seemed stagnant. Yet the questioning (which seemed to have replaced action) was paving the way for profound changes in "modern" man's ways of being and seeing. The winds of discontent that blew so strongly in May 1968 had not yet subsided, at least as far as challenging tradition-bound values was concerned. For the time being, the winds of change were blowing from Italy. It was there that, by 1966, architectural groups like Archizoom Associati and Superstudio undertook a demonstration by *reducto ad absurdum* of the need to react against an intensive "production-consumption" cycle that seemed to lead only to a further dehumanization of lifestyle. The provocative attitude of these groups led to proposals for entirely new ways of envisioning living spaces, confirming, in large measure, the idea of independent thinkers like Ettore Sottsass and Gaetano Pesce.

Their work inspired talk of "anti-design" and later of "new design." By any name, it aimed its criticisms at bourgeois values and, above all, at the wasteful society born of the illusion of economic growth. At issue was the makeup of the entire industrial process. Design, the vassal of that

process, and the functionalist thinking that claimed to provide industry with an aesthetic, not to say an ethical, justification, now became a sitting target.

The cult of uniformity arising from mass production had to be ended. Everyday surroundings had to become more playful, more in keeping with earlier symbolic and spiritual values. The production process had to veer from a too straight-and-narrow path. The trend of repetitive perfection had to be discouraged and, when appropriate, manufacturing imperfections had to be transformed into virtues.

In this latest movement, which by the beginning of the 1980s was becoming international, a new type of designer appeared, one who would model himself on avant-garde artists, who were intent on shaking things up, rather than seek the kind of catastrophic discontinuity so frequent in the history of our artificial environment. In 1962 François Mathey prepared his *Antagonisme 2: l'objet* exhibition at the Musée des Arts Décoratifs, and invited all designers and creators to rethink the

everyday object; his act now seems strangely prophetic.

In view of the contentions and diverse trends that ensued, it is difficult to determine today what is destined to disappear and what will endure. And even if the objects and concepts that emerged do stand the test of time, it is too early to tell what theories will, some decades from now, be proved to have borne fruit. On the other hand, it seems clear that there has been a return to traditional pieces of furniture (chairs, tables, beds, chests of drawers, wardrobes, etc.). The criticism leveled at industrialization and mass production has once again put emphasis on the beauty of one-of-a-kind pieces and the magical virtues of craftsmanship. The Italian designer Andrea Branzi speaks of "new craftsmen." This does not imply a total abandonment of today's machine tools or a return to manual labor; rather, it means that "artists'" studios must become laboratories of sorts, where

438
"Calandre" bottle, Paco Rabanne, first produced 1969
Pierre-François Dinand (born 1931), designer
Glass, plastic

439
"Opium" bottle, Yves Saint Laurent, first produced 1977
Pierre-François Dinand (born 1931), designer
Plastic, glass

440
"Poison" bottle, Christian Dior, first produced 1985
Veronique Monod (born 1954), designer
Glass

441
"Parfum de peau" bottle, Montana, first produced 1986
Serge Mansau (born 1930), designer
Glass

442
"Lacoste" bottle, first produced 1983
Alain Carré (born 1945), designer
Glass, plastic
Collection La Chemise Lacoste, Paris

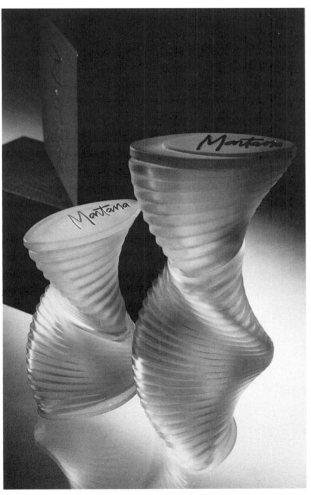

249

443
Teapot, 1986
Olivier Gagnère (born
1952)
Silver plate, wood
Collection Galerie
Adrien Maeght, Paris

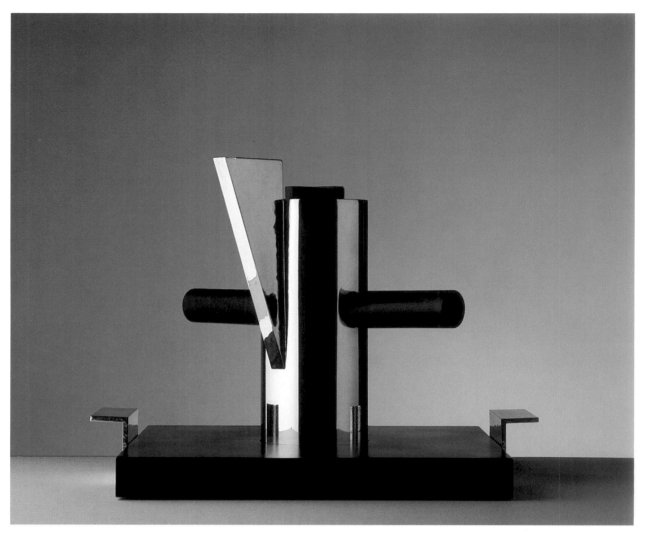

diversification is the rule, and where the most sophisticated production methods, particularly computer-aided laser-cutting, are used in a way that makes it economical to design new objects for limited production.

By the beginning of the eighties, many of the central ideas behind "new design" had taken hold and were being reinterpreted by some of the young French designers (who now have their own followings), as well as by some of the "old guard" like Pascal Mourgue or Marc Berthier, whose earlier works predisposed them to this new approach.

When the Memphis group began under Ettore Sottsass, the names of two young French designers seemed to be mentioned most often: Martine Bedin and Nathalie du Pasquier, both of whose works had already appeared in the first Memphis collection of 1981. At that time, the Totem group came out with furniture whose function was precisely defined, though each piece seemed strangely assembled. Some of its rigidity and preciseness recalled the radicalism of De Stijl, while also evoking a symbolic perception of African art through a gamut of outrageously vivid colors. At the same time, the Nemo group drew on

comic-book images, borrowing the forms and materials of the fifties in a witty pastiche of furniture from the period. Martin Szekely created disturbing furniture in which a metallic frame was covered with canvas slipcovers to give each piece a rather eerie, phantomlike appearance.

By 1980, Pucci di Rossi had introduced his three-dimensional collages of components from old furniture he had assembled into wholly non-functional objects. The result was a veritable anthology of past styles that was also authentic sculpture. Sylvain Dubuisson's furniture incorporated secret fairy-tale elements relying on some of the same *trompe-l'œil* effects found in his "Régie-Atelier" toolshed begun in 1980 and completed in 1982. Jean-Michel Wilmotte presented himself as a proponent of unworked materials, notably in his tables made of blue limestone slabs with notched edges or of iron (often pre-rusted). Elizabeth Garouste's and Mattia Bonetti's delvings into "neo-primitivism" suggested a very subtle juggling of the most traditional materials. Philippe Starck's international career had its start in 1980, when he showed signs of being the legitimate heir to the UAM designers. Sticking firmly to traditional formality and not anxious to follow current trends,

his 1983 designs for the Elysée Palace demonstrated his incredible aptitude for dismantling "bourgeois" taste and exposing its banality.

Did all this come about by coincidence? In 1979, at the instigation of the Union Nationale des Industries Françaises de l'Ameublement and the Ministry of Industry, a new organization, the Valorisation de l'innovation en ameublement (V.I.A.), was set up. This group would function as an important information exchange, and provide a meeting ground for manufacturers and designers.

Yet, in spite of all of the V.I.A.'s enthusiasm and dynamism, and its frequent exhibitions, French manufacturers seemed unconvinced by the efforts of the new generation, which led many young artists to devote their energies to stage settings or interior architecture and to settle for one-of-a-kind or limited edition pieces of furniture. It should be pointed out that galleries like Néotù, and later, Barbares, Perkal, Yves Gastou, to mention only those in Paris, also played an important role. These galleries enabled the public to discover foreign as well as French works; the specialized French press (*Intramuros, City Magazine, International, Architecture intérieure-CREE*, and others) took pains to comment on the latter. To understand the full weight of the cultural impact, it is also necessary to single out the exhibitions organized by the Centre de Création Industrielle and the Musée des Arts

444
V.I.A. showroom, Place Ste Opportune, Paris

445
"Carré d'As (Jour)" carpet, from the collection "L'Année du Dragon," 1988
Christian Duc (born 1949), designer
Toulemonde-Bochart, manufacturer
Wool
Collection Christian Duc

251

Décoratifs based on these new trends.

If the media gladly boosted avant-garde experiments in the appealing area of interior design, that was not at all the meaningful collaboration promised between designers and manufacturers in the eighties. To be sure, industry had shown no great interest in the new lifestyle images that were being proposed; nor did postmodernism, in any of its various forms, take readily to technological advances. In furniture, for example, it is surprising to see how little has been

France. Roger Tallon, that "blue chip" of French design, continues to assure his role as a leading force by following up his designs for the first TGV (very-high-speed) trains with the TGV Atlantique (planned completion date 1990) and the "Trans-Euro-Star" (that will pass through a tunnel under the English Channel). But the new generation has arrived, and already has its own internationally renowned stars, like Jean-Pierre Vitrac.

The idea of a designer intervening in the

446
"T.G.V. Atlantique" high-speed train, to be launched 1990
Roger Tallon (born 1929), designer
Alsthom Atlantique, manufacturer

made, in France or elsewhere, of new materials or tools. The few exceptions to this rule include Marc Berthier's "Magi's Chair," a computer-assisted design, Martin Szekely's carbon-fiber chairs, and Philippe Starck's tables assembled from a plate of glass and an aluminum base with a super-holding synthetic glue.

Now we will have to wait until the barriers separating interior design from what is more commonly referred to as industrial design fall of their own accord. The latter relies on mass production to some degree, whether mechanized, automated, or robotized. Thanks to fast, easy-to-modify computer programs that control machine tools, assembly-line production can now mean more than exact duplication.

Faced with this tempting prospect, it seems quite possible that in the course of this decade the role of the "industrial designer" has been accepted in

production process seems to have taken hold in France. To ensure that it continues to work efficiently, the government has enacted several important measures: in 1982, the Ecole Nationale Supérieure de Création Industrielle was created, and the same year saw the inauguration of the Grand Prix National du Design, followed in 1983 by the Agence pour la Promotion de la Création Industrielle.

Never have conditions been so advantageous for design, in the broadest sense of the word, to prosper in France. But if these efforts are one day to bear fruit, it is up to those responsible for the harvest to ensure that the ground is properly cultivated.

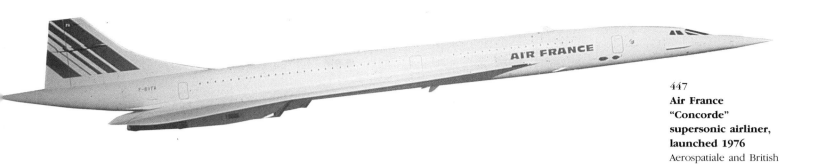

447
**Air France
"Concorde"
supersonic airliner,
launched 1976**
Aerospatiale and British
Aerospace, designers
and manufacturers

INDEX

PHOTO CREDITS